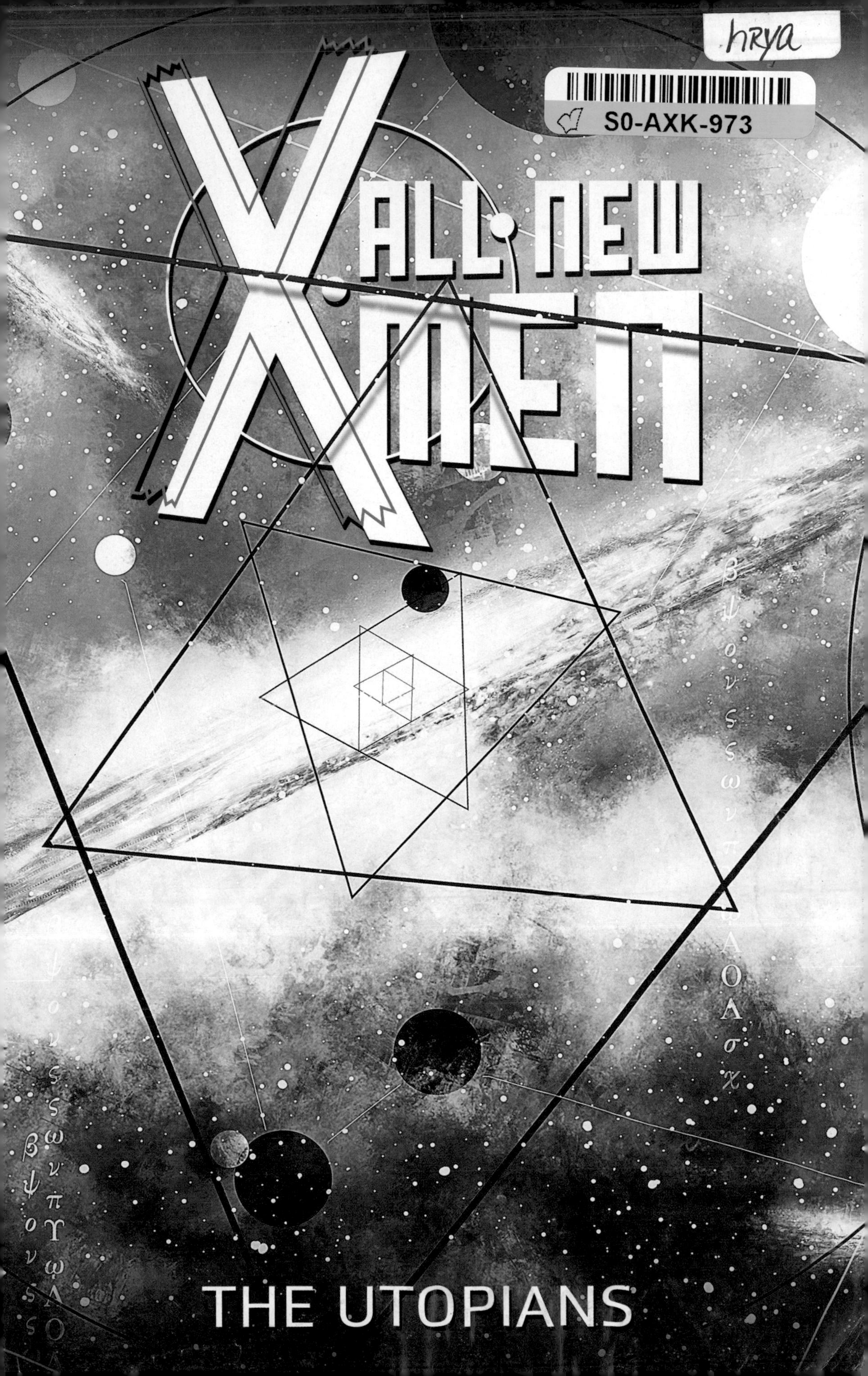
ALL-NEW X-MEN
THE UTOPIANS

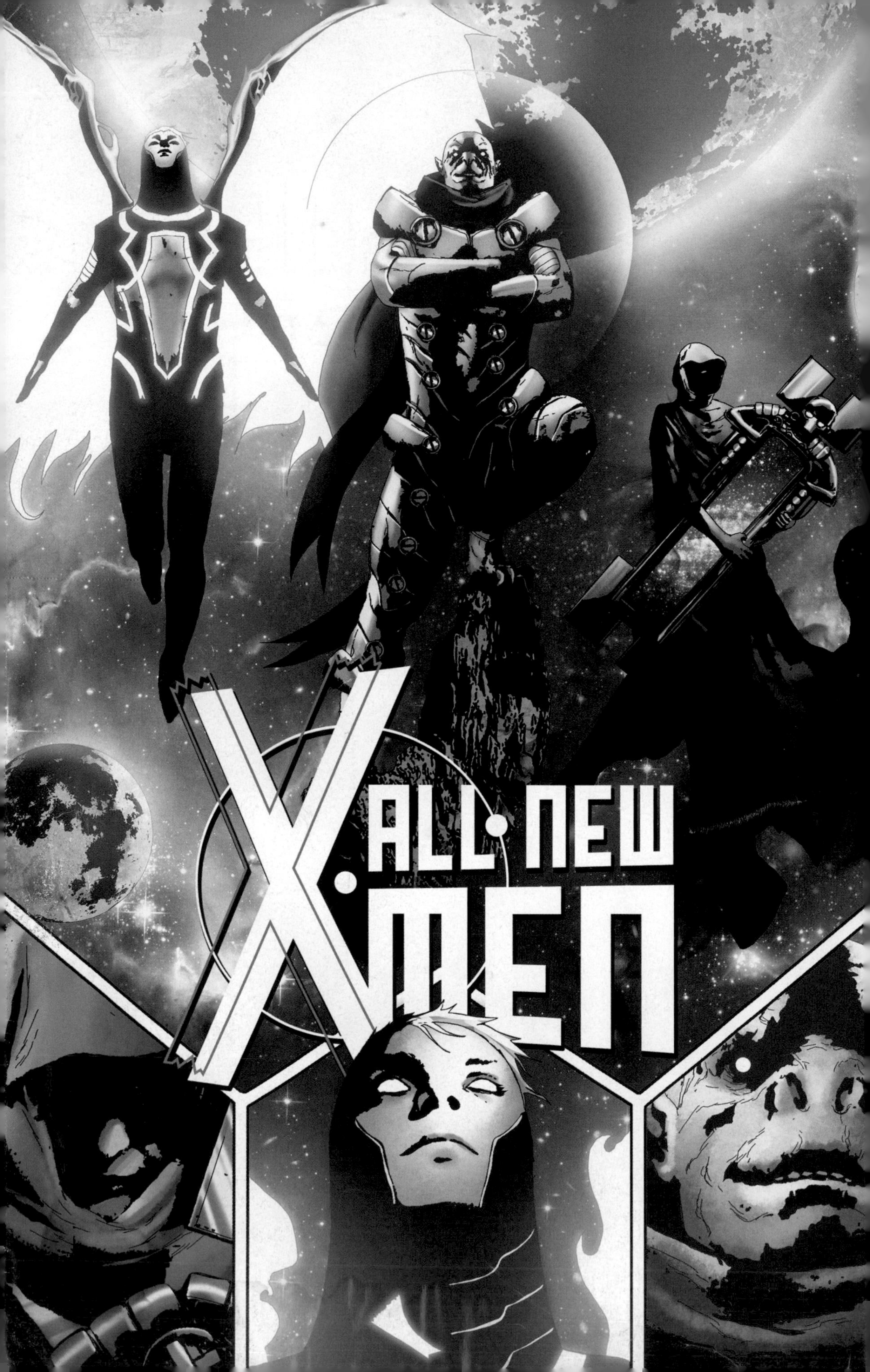
ALL-NEW X-MEN

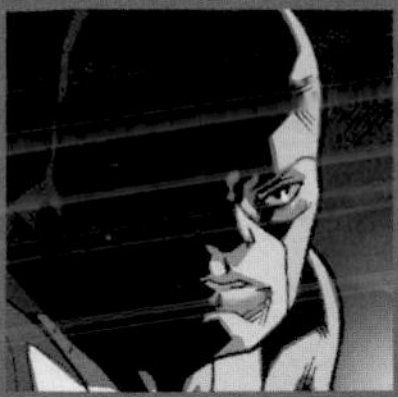

BEAST
HANK McCOY

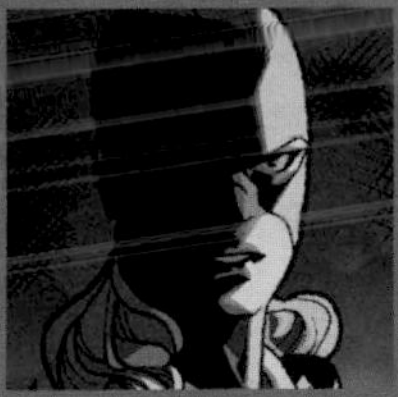

MARVEL GIRL
JEAN GREY

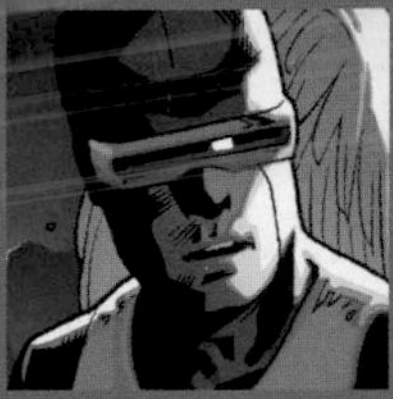

CYCLOPS
SCOTT SUMMERS

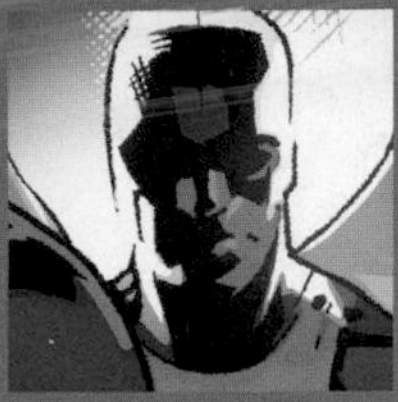

ANGEL
WARREN WORTHINGTON III

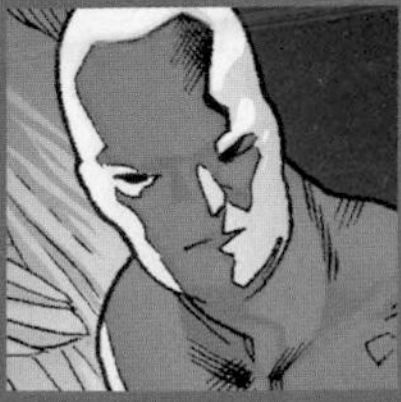

ICEMAN
BOBBY DRAKE

THE UTOPIANS

BRIAN MICHAEL
BENDIS
WRITER

ISSUE #37

MIKE
DEL MUNDO
WITH MARCO D'ALFONSO (COLORS)
ARTIST

ISSUES #38-39

ANDREA
SORRENTINO
ARTIST

MARCELO
MAIOLO
COLORIST

ISSUES #40-41

MAHMUD
ASRAR
ARTIST

RAIN
BEREDO
(#40)

MARTE
GRACIA
(#41)
COLORISTS

CORY
PETIT
LETTERER

MIKE
MARTS

XANDER
JAROWEY
EDITORS

COVER ART: **KRIS ANKA** (#37), **ANDREA SORRENTINO & MARCELO MAIOLO** (#38 & #40),
ALEXANDER LOZANO (#39) AND **MAHMUD ASRAR & MARTE GRACIA** (#41)

X-MEN CREATED BY **STAN LEE & JACK KIRBY**

COLLECTION EDITOR: **JENNIFER GRÜNWALD** ASSISTANT EDITOR: **SARAH BRUNSTAD**
ASSOCIATE MANAGING EDITOR: **ALEX STARBUCK** EDITOR, SPECIAL PROJECTS: **MARK D. BEAZLEY**
SENIOR EDITOR, SPECIAL PROJECTS: **JEFF YOUNGQUIST** SVP PRINT, SALES & MARKETING: **DAVID GABRIEL**
BOOK DESIGNER: **JAY BOWEN**

EDITOR IN CHIEF: **AXEL ALONSO** CHIEF CREATIVE OFFICER: **JOE QUESADA**
PUBLISHER: **DAN BUCKLEY** EXECUTIVE PRODUCER: **ALAN FINE**

ALL-NEW X-MEN VOL. 7: THE UTOPIANS. Contains material originally published in magazine form as ALL-NEW X-MEN #37-41. First printing 2016. ISBN# 978-0-7851-9235-0. Published by MARVEL WORLDWIDE, INC., a subsidiary of MARVEL ENTERTAINMENT, LLC. OFFICE OF PUBLICATION: 135 West 50th Street, New York, NY 10020. **Printed in the U.S.A.** ALAN FINE, President, Marvel Entertainment; DAN BUCKLEY, President, TV, Publishing and Brand Management; JOE QUESADA, Chief Creative Officer; TOM BREVOORT, SVP of Publishing; DAVID BOGART, SVP of Operations & Procurement, Publishing; C.B. CEBULSKI, VP of International Development & Brand Management; DAVID GABRIEL, SVP Print, Sales & Marketing; JIM O'KEEFE, VP of Operations & Logistics; DAN CARR, Executive Director of Publishing Technology; SUSAN CRESPI, Editorial Operations Manager; ALEX MORALES, Publishing Operations Manager; STAN LEE, Chairman Emeritus. For information regarding advertising in Marvel Comics or on Marvel.com, please contact Jonathan Rheingold, VP of Custom Solutions & Ad Sales, at jrheingold@marvel.com. For Marvel subscription inquiries, please call 800-217-9158. **Manufactured between 11/27/2015 and 1/4/2016 by R.R. DONNELLEY, INC., SALEM, VA, USA.**

10 9 8 7 6 5 4 3 2 1

Born with genetic mutations that gave them abilities beyond those of normal humans, mutants are the next stage in evolution. As such, they are feared and hated by humanity. A group of mutants known as the X-Men fight for peaceful coexistence between mutants and humankind. But not all mutants see peaceful coexistence as a reality.

The original X-Men — Jean Grey, Cyclops, Iceman, Angel and Beast — were brought forward in time in an attempt to shine a light on the errors of the present-day X-Men. Unable to return to the past, they have taken up residence at the New Xavier School along with new teammate X-23. Recently the young Scott Summers left the team to explore space with his father, Corsair.

Since arriving in the present, Jean Grey has developed a series of new psychic abilities. In the absence of Professor Xavier, Emma Frost has offered to act as Jean's new instructor. Though Emma's former bitter rivalry with Jean's future self initially caused tension with Jean, her psychic tutelage has slowly begun to heal the rift between the two X-Men.

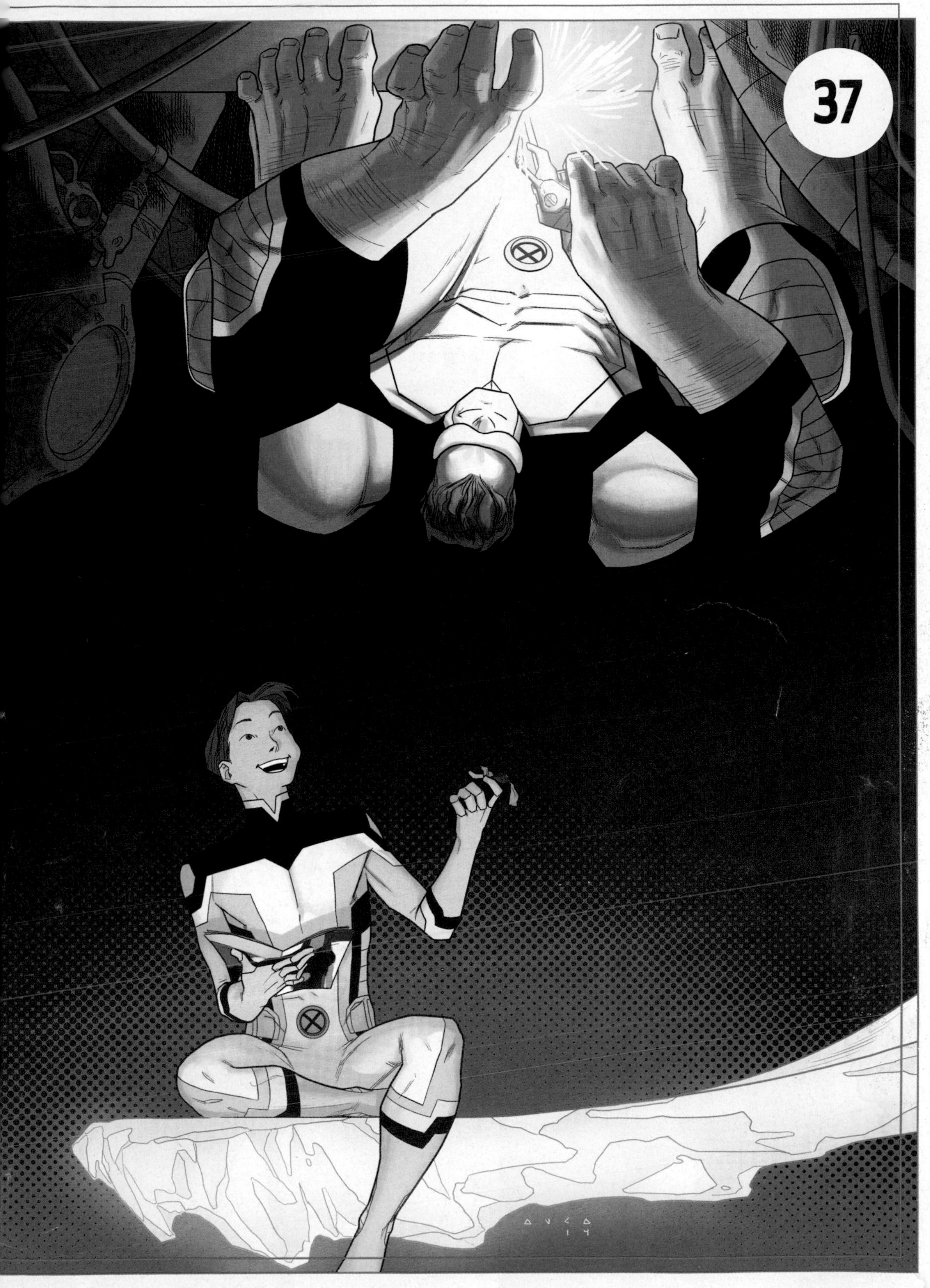
37

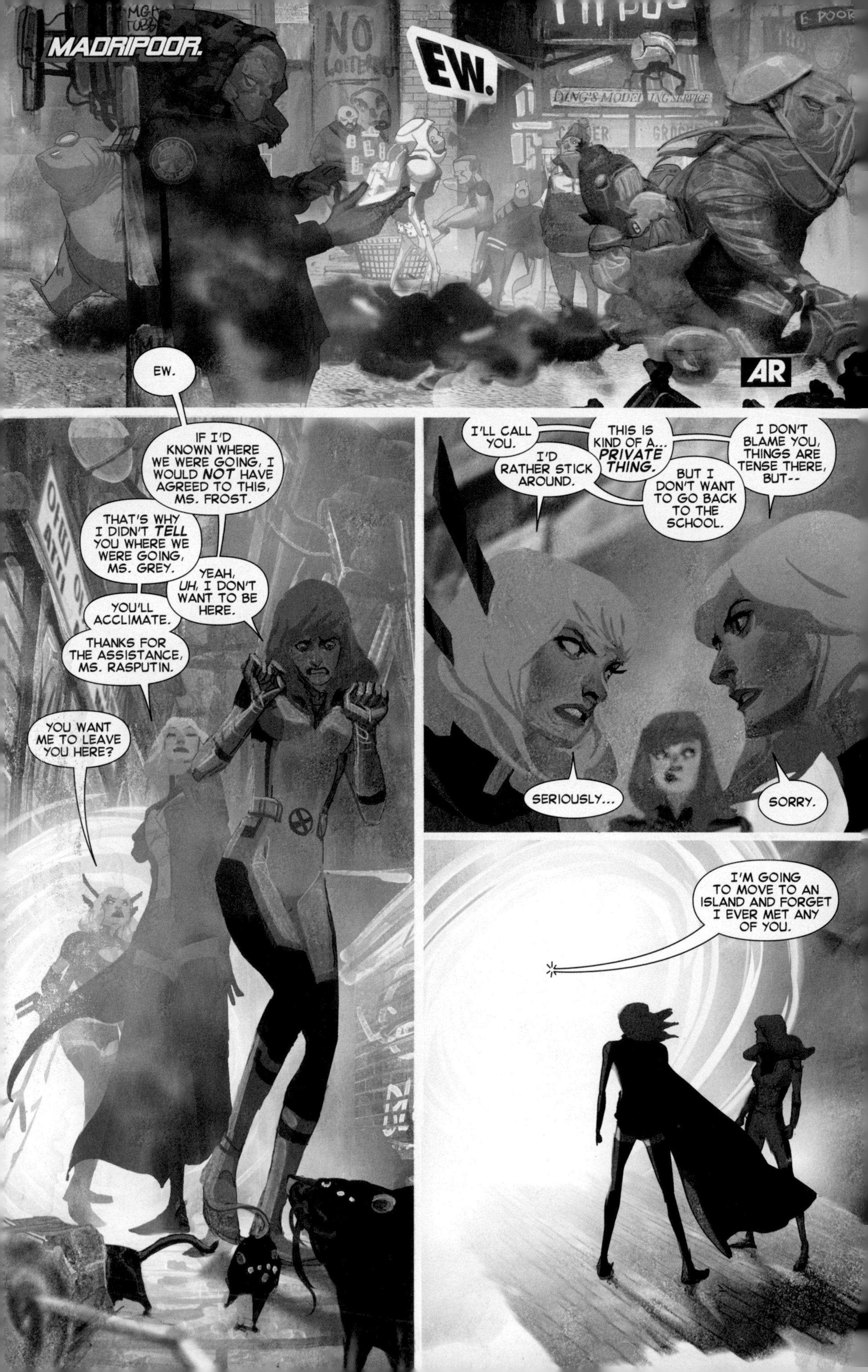

MADRIPOOR.
NO LOITERING
EW.
DING'S MODELING SERVICE
EW.
IF I'D KNOWN WHERE WE WERE GOING, I WOULD NOT HAVE AGREED TO THIS, MS. FROST.
THAT'S WHY I DIDN'T TELL YOU WHERE WE WERE GOING, MS. GREY.
YEAH, UH, I DON'T WANT TO BE HERE.
YOU'LL ACCLIMATE.
THANKS FOR THE ASSISTANCE, MS. RASPUTIN.
YOU WANT ME TO LEAVE YOU HERE?
I'LL CALL YOU.
I'D RATHER STICK AROUND.
THIS IS KIND OF A... PRIVATE THING.
BUT I DON'T WANT TO GO BACK TO THE SCHOOL.
I DON'T BLAME YOU, THINGS ARE TENSE THERE, BUT--
SERIOUSLY...
SORRY.
I'M GOING TO MOVE TO AN ISLAND AND FORGET I EVER MET ANY OF YOU.

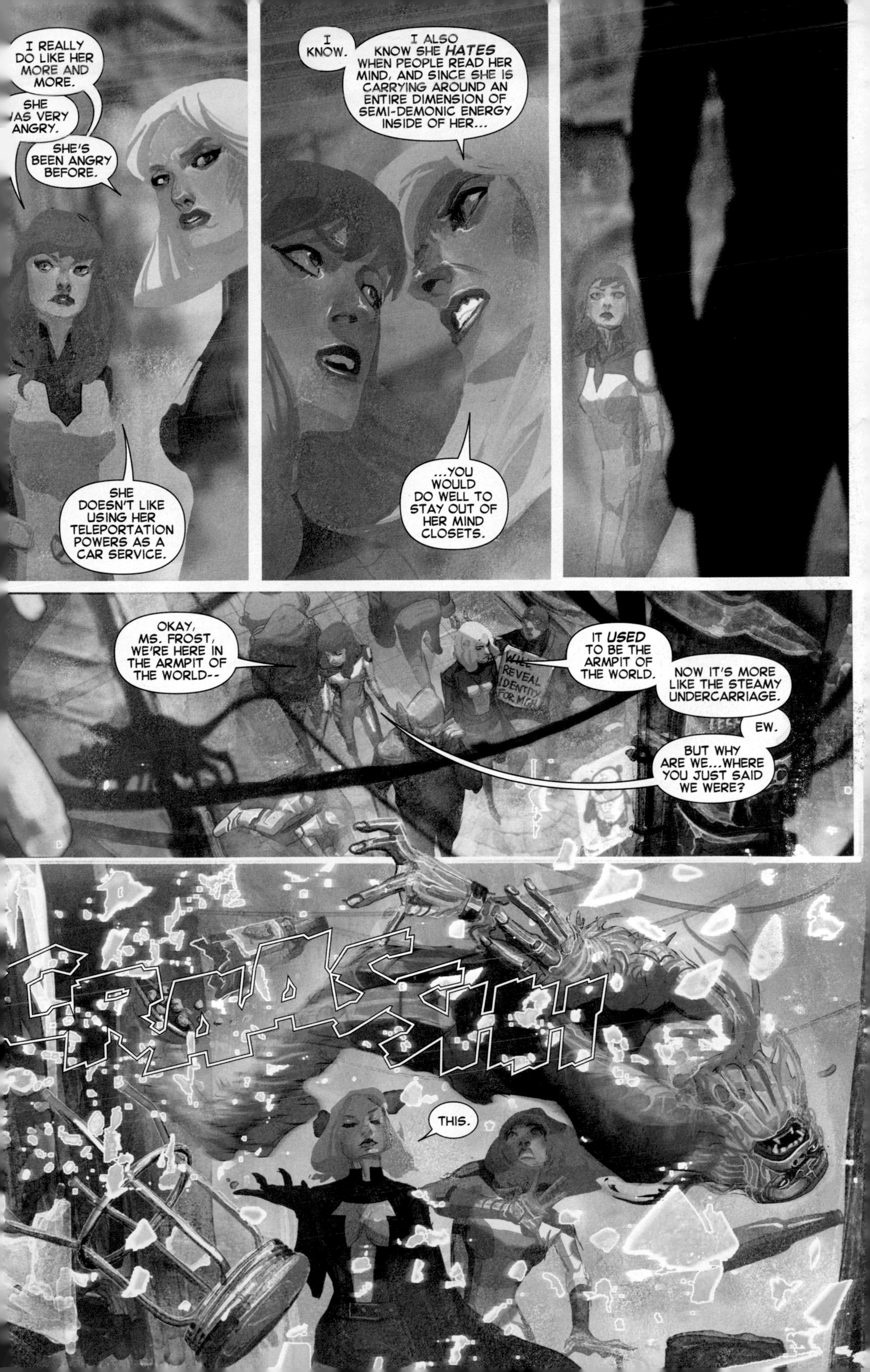
I REALLY DO LIKE HER MORE AND MORE.
SHE WAS VERY ANGRY.
SHE'S BEEN ANGRY BEFORE.
SHE DOESN'T LIKE USING HER TELEPORTATION POWERS AS A CAR SERVICE.
I KNOW.
I ALSO KNOW SHE HATES WHEN PEOPLE READ HER MIND, AND SINCE SHE IS CARRYING AROUND AN ENTIRE DIMENSION OF SEMI-DEMONIC ENERGY INSIDE OF HER...
...YOU WOULD DO WELL TO STAY OUT OF HER MIND CLOSETS.
OKAY, MS. FROST, WE'RE HERE IN THE ARMPIT OF THE WORLD--
WILL REVEAL IDENTITY FOR M
IT USED TO BE THE ARMPIT OF THE WORLD.
NOW IT'S MORE LIKE THE STEAMY UNDERCARRIAGE.
EW.
BUT WHY ARE WE...WHERE YOU JUST SAID WE WERE?
CRASSSH
THIS.

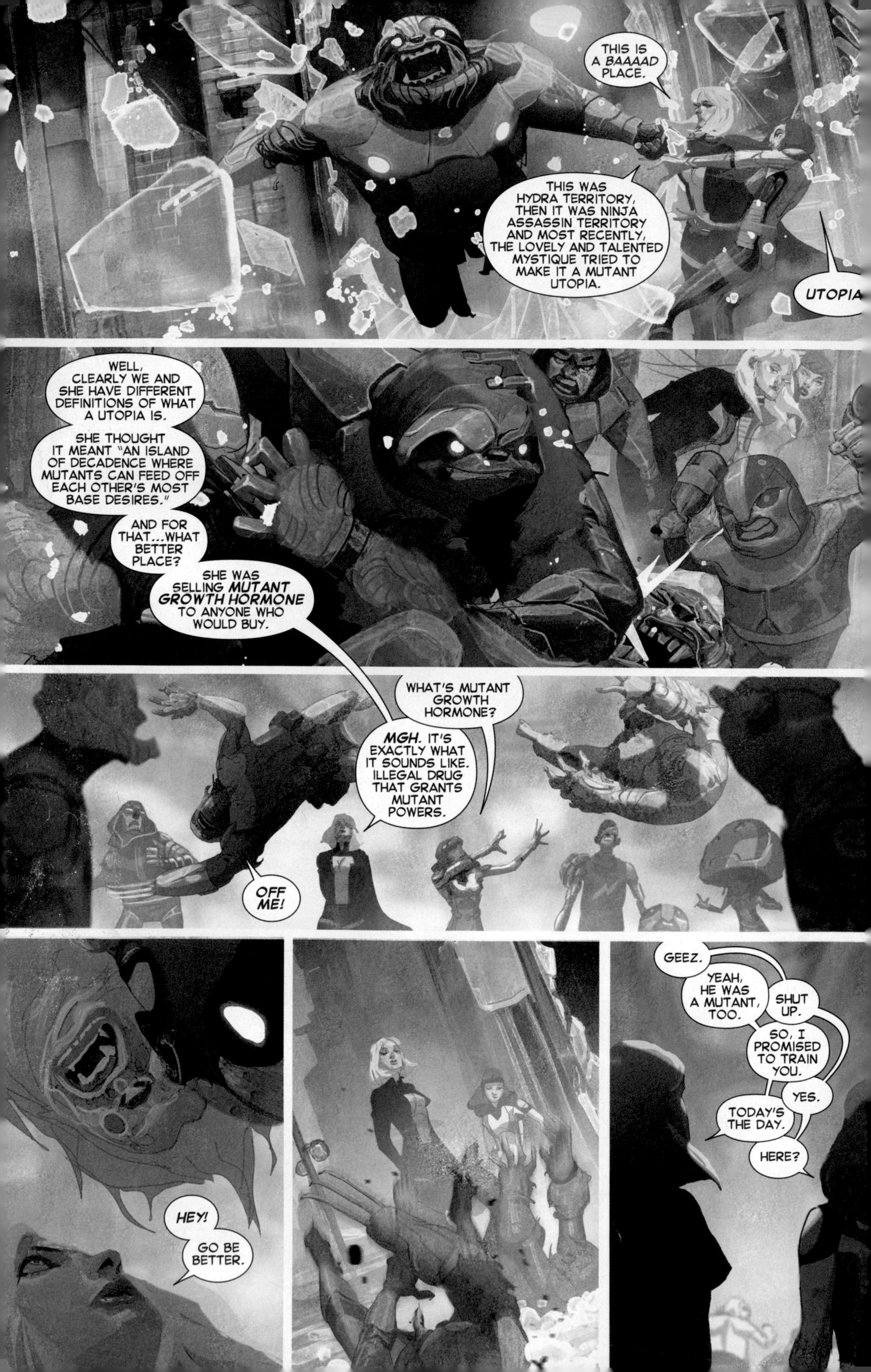
THIS IS A BAAAAD PLACE.
THIS WAS HYDRA TERRITORY, THEN IT WAS NINJA ASSASSIN TERRITORY AND MOST RECENTLY, THE LOVELY AND TALENTED MYSTIQUE TRIED TO MAKE IT A MUTANT UTOPIA.
UTOPIA
WELL, CLEARLY WE AND SHE HAVE DIFFERENT DEFINITIONS OF WHAT A UTOPIA IS.
SHE THOUGHT IT MEANT "AN ISLAND OF DECADENCE WHERE MUTANTS CAN FEED OFF EACH OTHER'S MOST BASE DESIRES."
AND FOR THAT...WHAT BETTER PLACE?
SHE WAS SELLING MUTANT GROWTH HORMONE TO ANYONE WHO WOULD BUY.
WHAT'S MUTANT GROWTH HORMONE?
MGH. IT'S EXACTLY WHAT IT SOUNDS LIKE. ILLEGAL DRUG THAT GRANTS MUTANT POWERS.
OFF ME!
HEY!
GO BE BETTER.
GEEZ.
YEAH, HE WAS A MUTANT, TOO.
SHUT UP.
SO, I PROMISED TO TRAIN YOU.
YES.
TODAY'S THE DAY.
HERE?

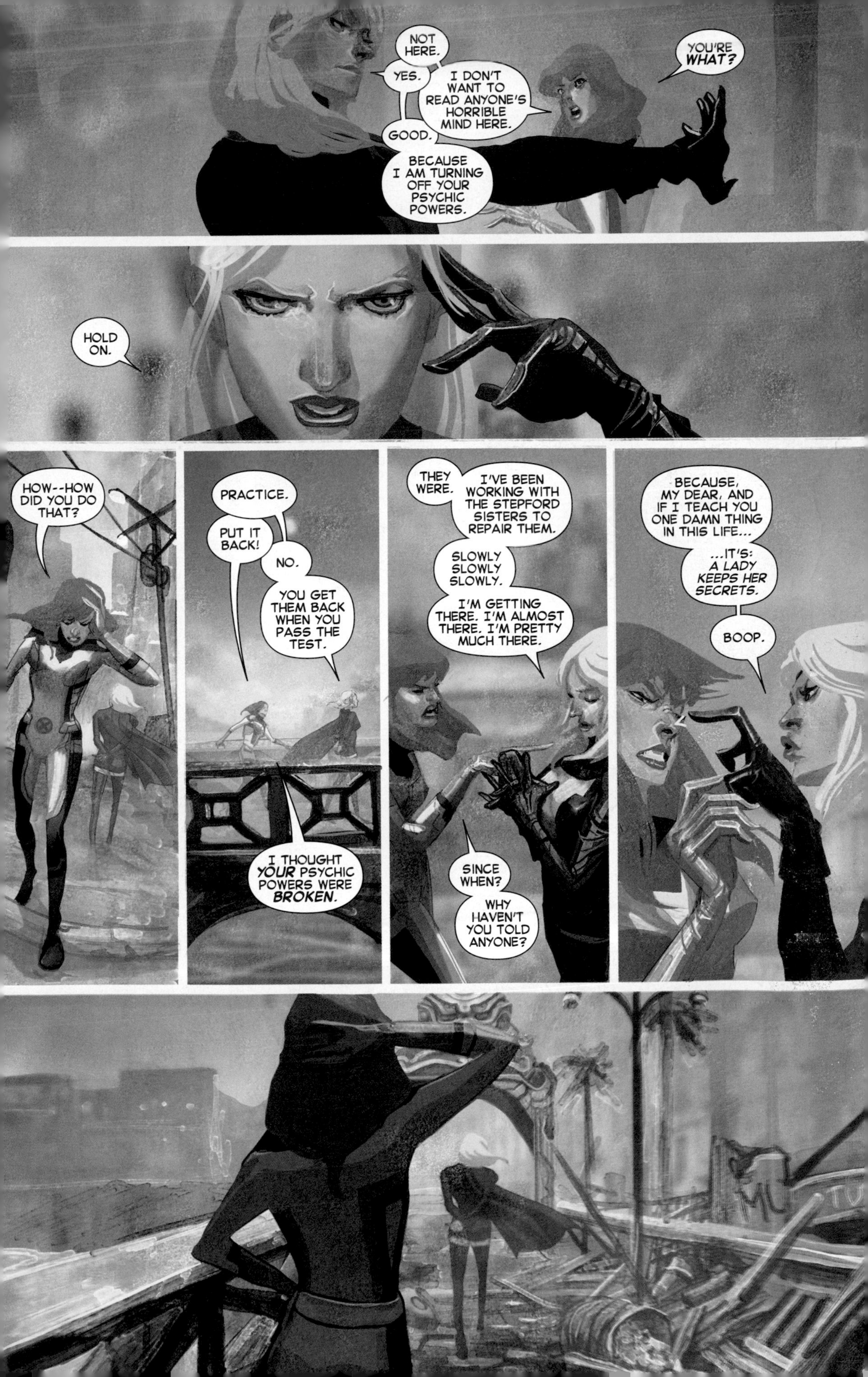
NOT HERE.
YES.
I DON'T WANT TO READ ANYONE'S HORRIBLE MIND HERE.
GOOD.
BECAUSE I AM TURNING OFF YOUR PSYCHIC POWERS.
YOU'RE *WHAT?*
HOLD ON.
HOW--HOW DID YOU DO THAT?
PRACTICE.
PUT IT BACK!
NO.
YOU GET THEM BACK WHEN YOU PASS THE TEST.
I THOUGHT *YOUR* PSYCHIC POWERS WERE *BROKEN*.
THEY WERE.
I'VE BEEN WORKING WITH THE STEPFORD SISTERS TO REPAIR THEM.
SLOWLY SLOWLY SLOWLY.
I'M GETTING THERE. I'M ALMOST THERE. I'M PRETTY MUCH THERE.
SINCE WHEN?
WHY HAVEN'T YOU TOLD ANYONE?
BECAUSE, MY DEAR, AND IF I TEACH YOU ONE DAMN THING IN THIS LIFE...
...IT'S: *A LADY KEEPS HER SECRETS.*
BOOP.

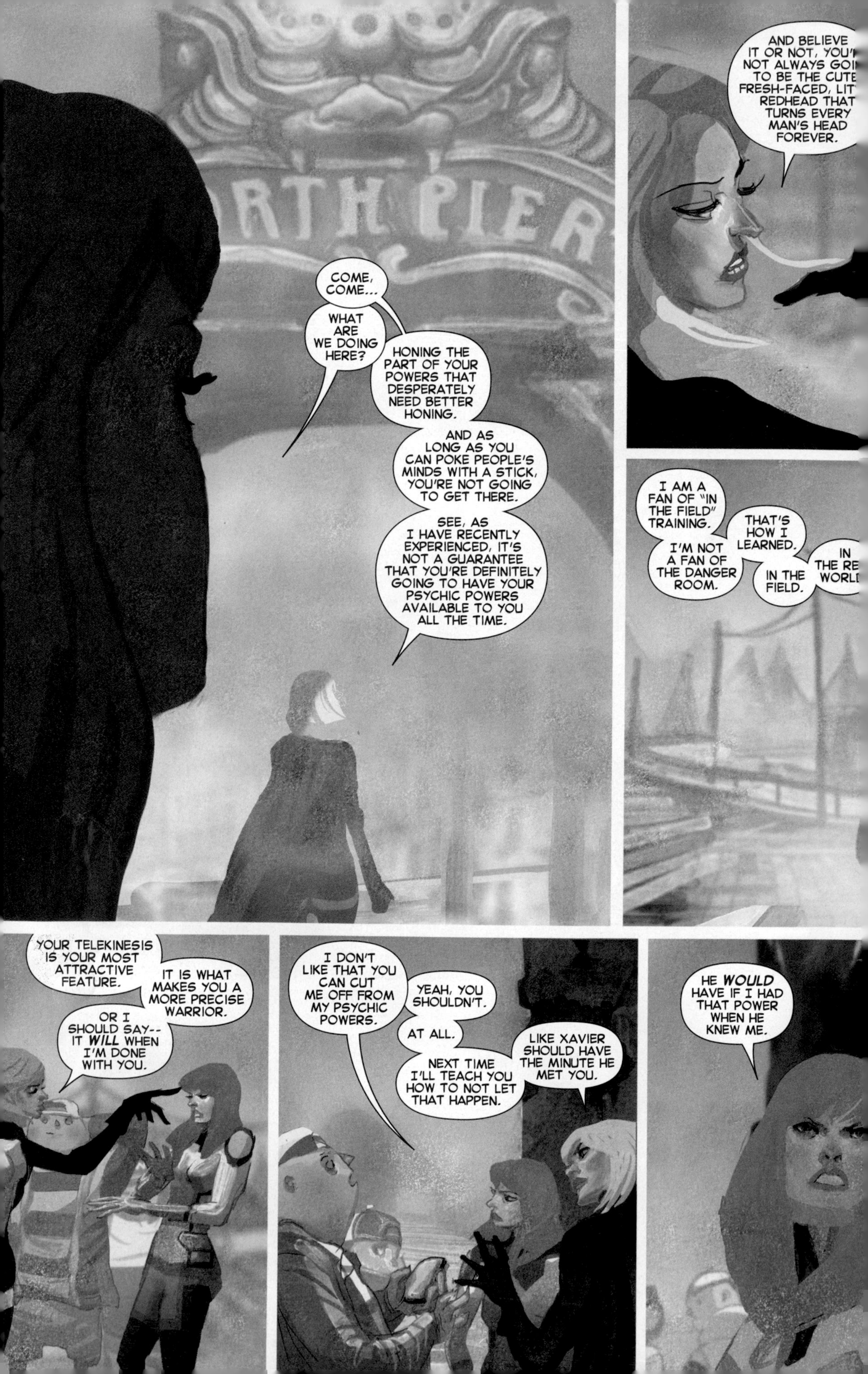

RTH PIER
COME, COME...
WHAT ARE WE DOING HERE?
HONING THE PART OF YOUR POWERS THAT DESPERATELY NEED BETTER HONING.
AND AS LONG AS YOU CAN POKE PEOPLE'S MINDS WITH A STICK, YOU'RE NOT GOING TO GET THERE.
SEE, AS I HAVE RECENTLY EXPERIENCED, IT'S NOT A GUARANTEE THAT YOU'RE DEFINITELY GOING TO HAVE YOUR PSYCHIC POWERS AVAILABLE TO YOU ALL THE TIME.
AND BELIEVE IT OR NOT, YOU'
NOT ALWAYS GOI
TO BE THE CUTE
FRESH-FACED, LIT
REDHEAD THAT TURNS EVERY MAN'S HEAD FOREVER.
I AM A FAN OF "IN THE FIELD" TRAINING.
I'M NOT A FAN OF THE DANGER ROOM.
THAT'S HOW I LEARNED.
IN THE FIELD.
IN
THE RE
WORLD
YOUR TELEKINESIS IS YOUR MOST ATTRACTIVE FEATURE.
IT IS WHAT MAKES YOU A MORE PRECISE WARRIOR.
OR I SHOULD SAY-- IT *WILL* WHEN I'M DONE WITH YOU.
I DON'T LIKE THAT YOU CAN CUT ME OFF FROM MY PSYCHIC POWERS.
YEAH, YOU SHOULDN'T.
AT ALL.
NEXT TIME I'LL TEACH YOU HOW TO NOT LET THAT HAPPEN.
LIKE XAVIER SHOULD HAVE THE MINUTE HE MET YOU.
HE *WOULD* HAVE IF I HAD THAT POWER WHEN HE KNEW ME.

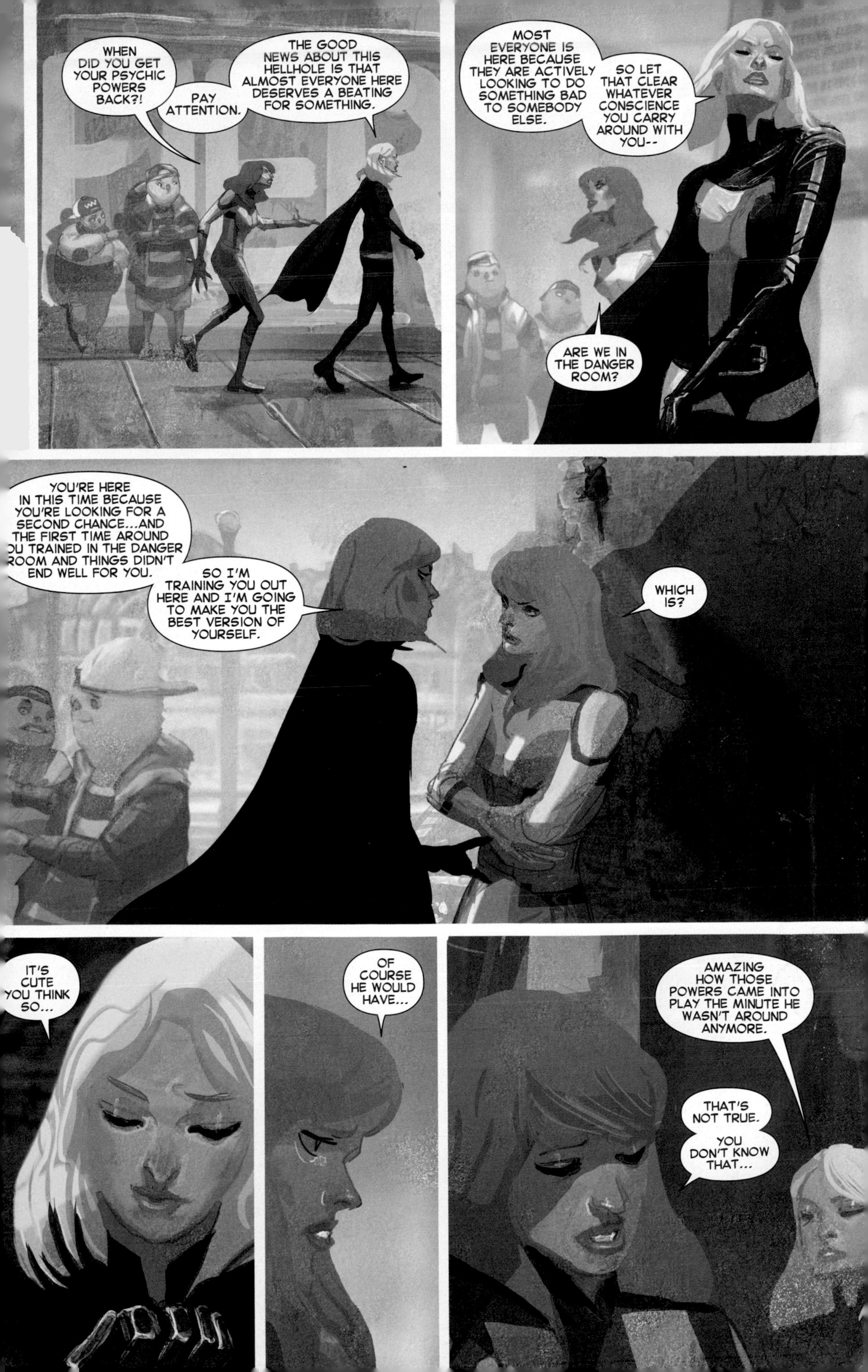
WHEN DID YOU GET YOUR PSYCHIC POWERS BACK?!
PAY ATTENTION.
THE GOOD NEWS ABOUT THIS HELLHOLE IS THAT ALMOST EVERYONE HERE DESERVES A BEATING FOR SOMETHING.
MOST EVERYONE IS HERE BECAUSE THEY ARE ACTIVELY LOOKING TO DO SOMETHING BAD TO SOMEBODY ELSE.
SO LET THAT CLEAR WHATEVER CONSCIENCE YOU CARRY AROUND WITH YOU--
ARE WE IN THE DANGER ROOM?
YOU'RE HERE IN THIS TIME BECAUSE YOU'RE LOOKING FOR A SECOND CHANCE...AND THE FIRST TIME AROUND YOU TRAINED IN THE DANGER ROOM AND THINGS DIDN'T END WELL FOR YOU.
SO I'M TRAINING YOU OUT HERE AND I'M GOING TO MAKE YOU THE BEST VERSION OF YOURSELF.
WHICH IS?
IT'S CUTE YOU THINK SO...
OF COURSE HE WOULD HAVE...
AMAZING HOW THOSE POWERS CAME INTO PLAY THE MINUTE HE WASN'T AROUND ANYMORE.
THAT'S NOT TRUE.
YOU DON'T KNOW THAT...

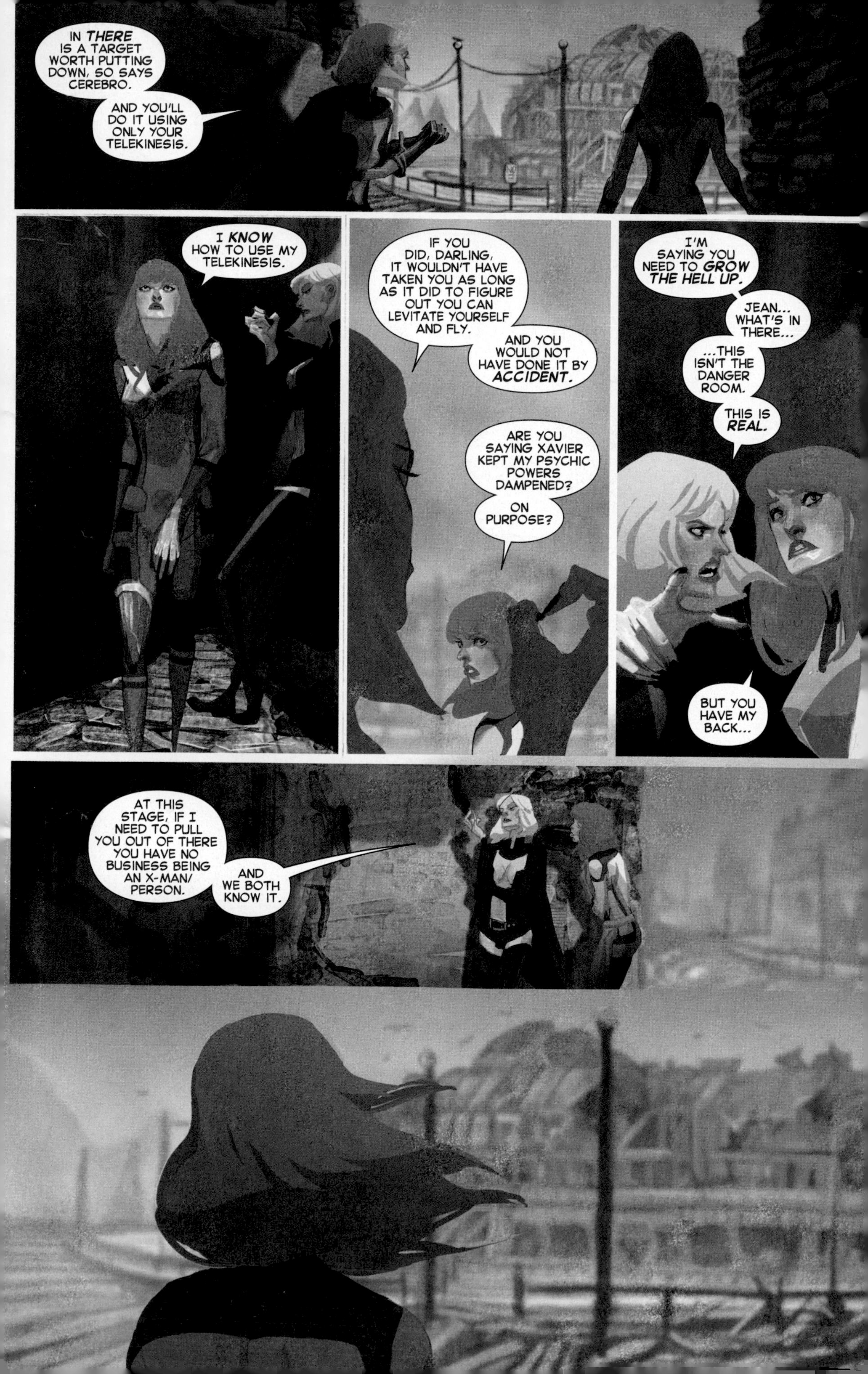

IN *THERE* IS A TARGET WORTH PUTTING DOWN, SO SAYS CEREBRO.
AND YOU'LL DO IT USING ONLY YOUR TELEKINESIS.
I *KNOW* HOW TO USE MY TELEKINESIS.
IF YOU DID, DARLING, IT WOULDN'T HAVE TAKEN YOU AS LONG AS IT DID TO FIGURE OUT YOU CAN LEVITATE YOURSELF AND FLY.
AND YOU WOULD NOT HAVE DONE IT BY *ACCIDENT.*
ARE YOU SAYING XAVIER KEPT MY PSYCHIC POWERS DAMPENED?
ON PURPOSE?
I'M SAYING YOU NEED TO *GROW THE HELL UP.*
JEAN... WHAT'S IN THERE...
...THIS ISN'T THE DANGER ROOM.
THIS IS *REAL.*
BUT YOU HAVE MY BACK...
AT THIS STAGE, IF I NEED TO PULL YOU OUT OF THERE YOU HAVE NO BUSINESS BEING AN X-MAN/ PERSON.
AND WE BOTH KNOW IT.

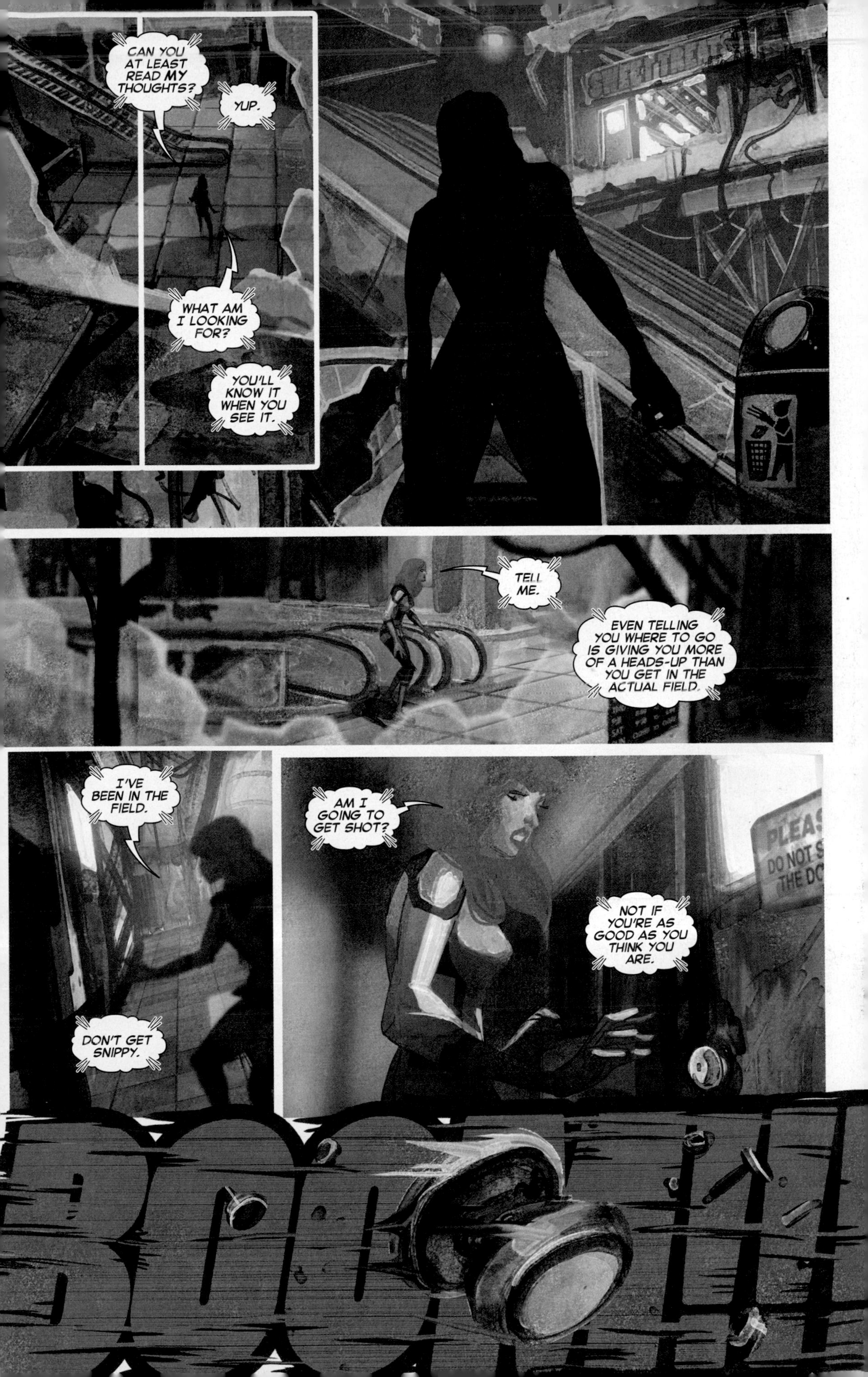
CAN YOU AT LEAST READ MY THOUGHTS?
YUP.
WHAT AM I LOOKING FOR?
YOU'LL KNOW IT WHEN YOU SEE IT.
TELL ME.
EVEN TELLING YOU WHERE TO GO IS GIVING YOU MORE OF A HEADS-UP THAN YOU GET IN THE ACTUAL FIELD.
I'VE BEEN IN THE FIELD.
DON'T GET SNIPPY.
AM I GOING TO GET SHOT?
NOT IF YOU'RE AS GOOD AS YOU THINK YOU ARE.

I KNOW THIS GUY... THE BLOB.
HE LOOKS BIGGER.
MUTANT GROWTH HORMONE...HE'S ADDICTED.
%#$&!
JEAN GREY?!
<HOLY %#$&!>
<WHAT THE HELL IS THIS?>*
PLEASE! DO NOT SLAM THE DOOR
* TRANSLATED FROM JAPANESE --UNCANNY X-ANDER!

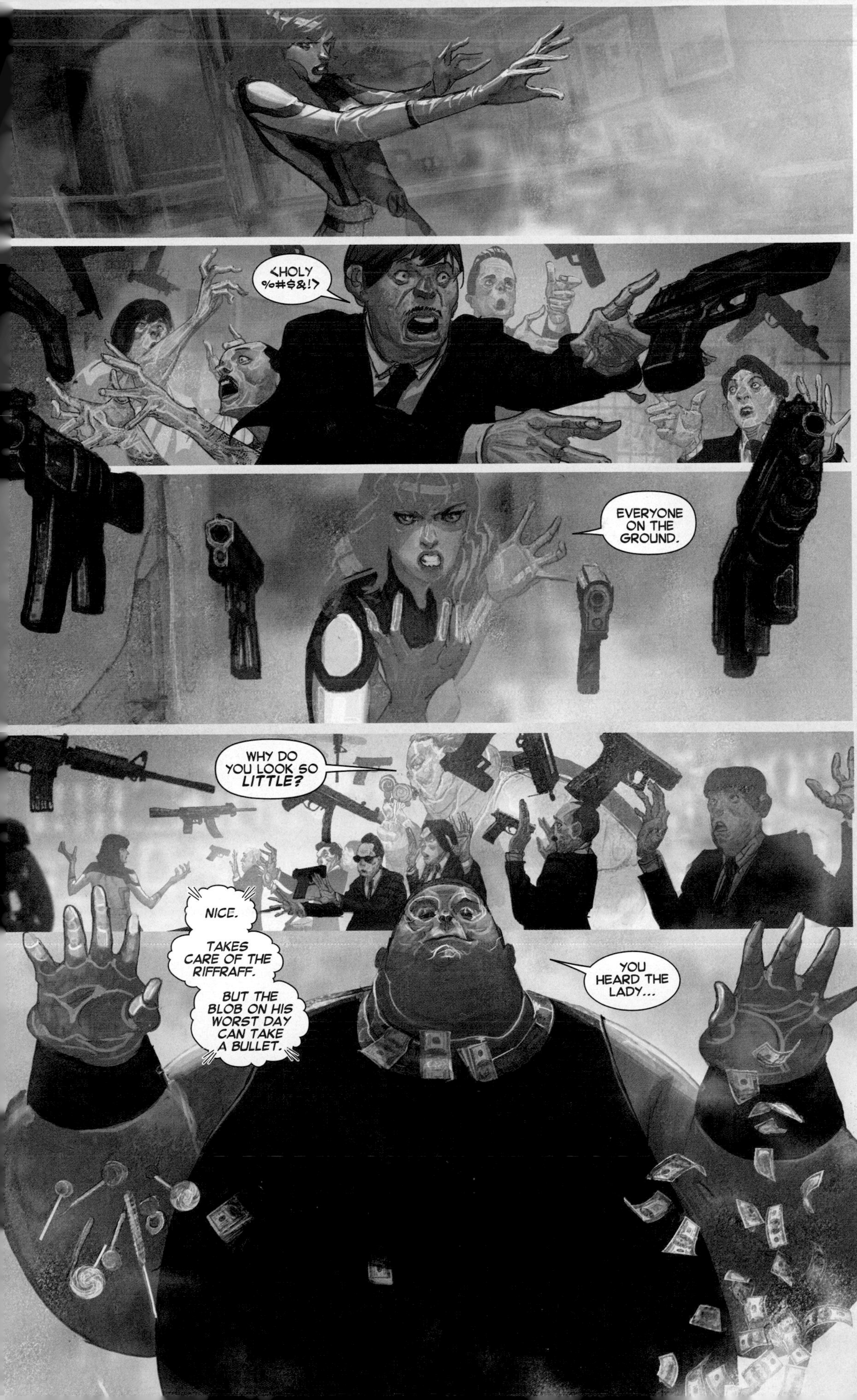

<HOLY %#$&!>
EVERYONE ON THE GROUND.
WHY DO YOU LOOK SO LITTLE?
NICE.
TAKES CARE OF THE RIFFRAFF.
BUT THE BLOB ON HIS WORST DAY CAN TAKE A BULLET.
YOU HEARD THE LADY...

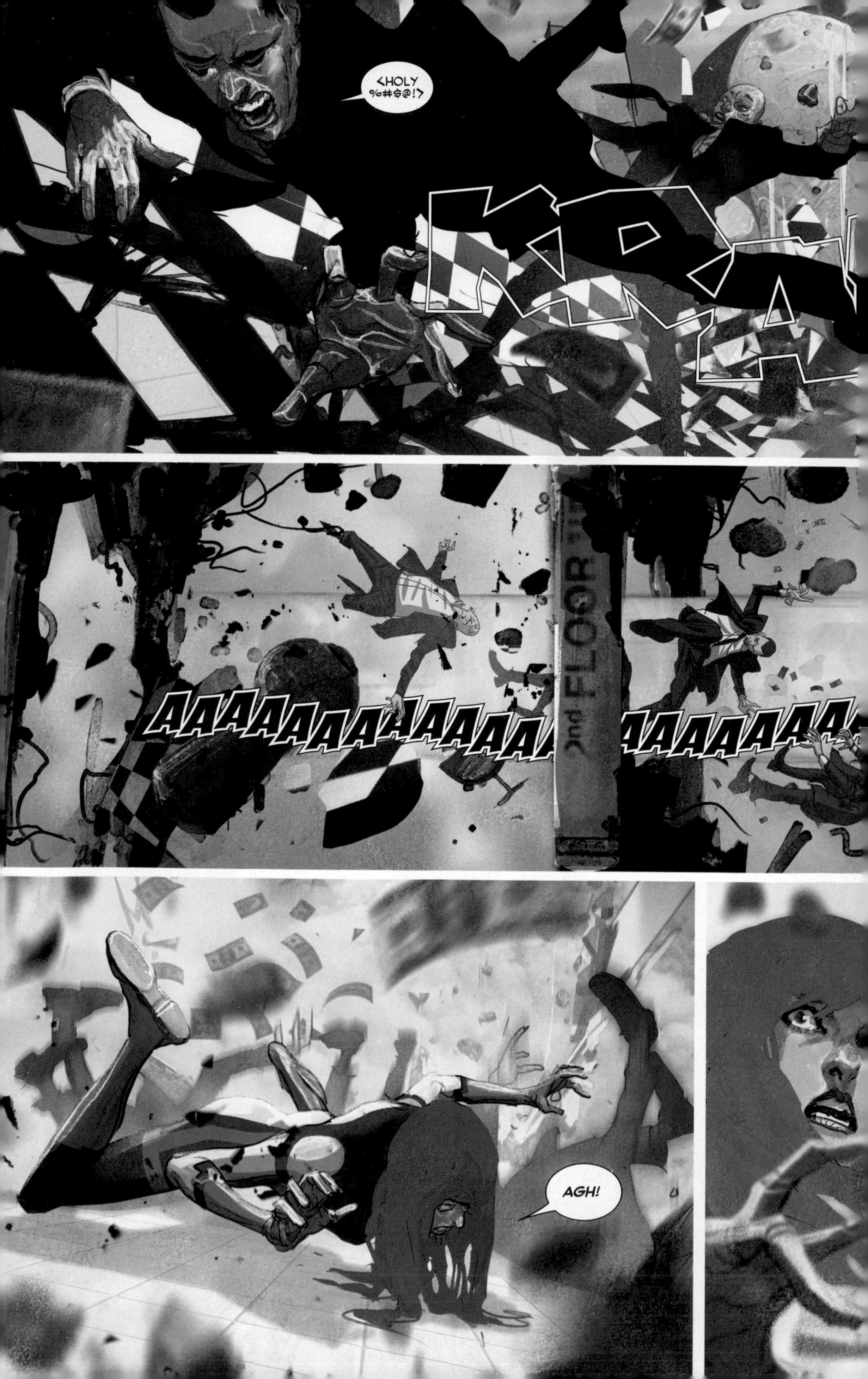

<HOLY %#$@!>
AAAAAAAAAAAAAAAAAAAAAAA
2nd FLOOR
AGH!

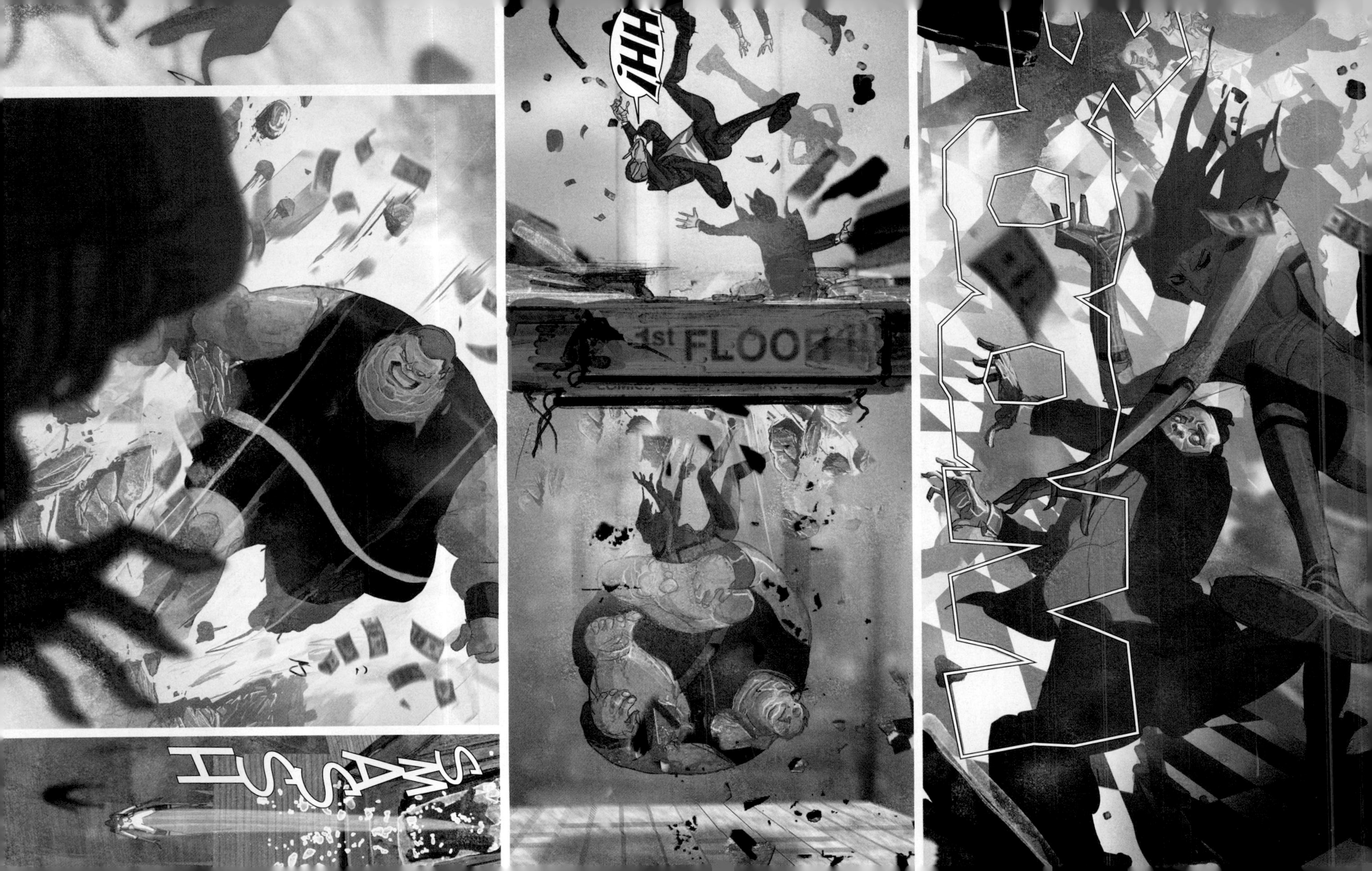
KOOM
HH!
1st FLOOR
SMASH

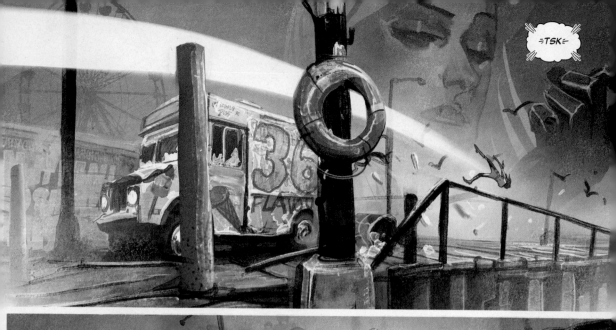

=TSK=

AGGH!

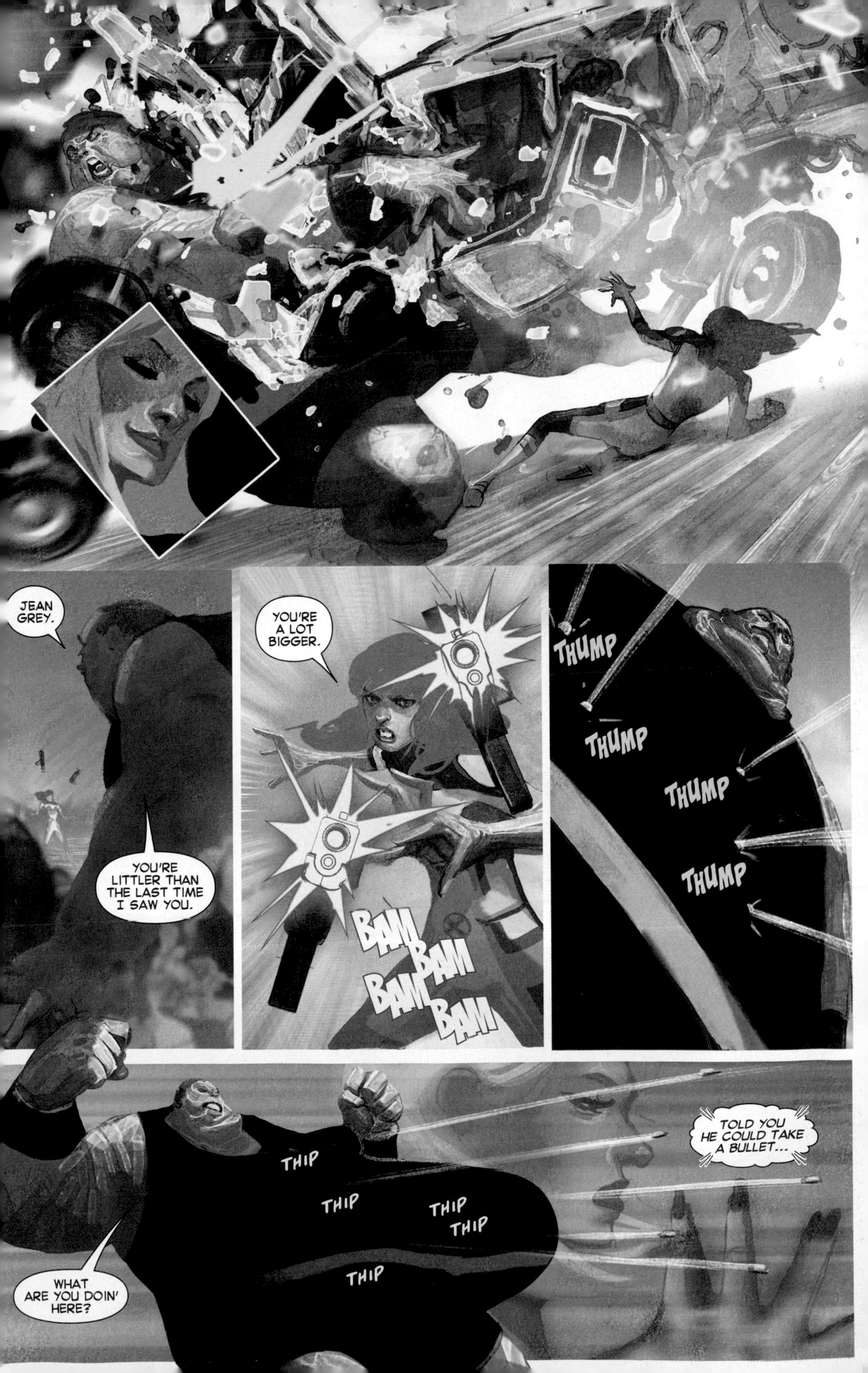
JEAN GREY.
YOU'RE LITTLER THAN THE LAST TIME I SAW YOU.
YOU'RE A LOT BIGGER.
BAM BAM BAM BAM
THUMP
THUMP
THUMP
THUMP
THIP
THIP
THIP
THIP
THIP
WHAT ARE YOU DOIN' HERE?
TOLD YOU HE COULD TAKE A BULLET...

SELLING MGH COMPOUND TO THE YAKUZA?

WHAT COULD YOU POSSIBLY CARE?

WHAT DO I *CARE*?

YEAH, SERIOUSLY, WHAT'S IT TO YA?

YOU'RE SELLING--I'M NOT HAVING THIS CONVERSATION.

YOU'RE BETRAYING OUR ENTIRE PEOPLE... FOR MONEY!

REMEMBER WHEN WE FIRST MET?

WE ASKED YOU TO JOIN THE X-MEN AND YOU THOUGHT YOU WERE SO MUCH BETTER THAN US.

IN RETROSPECT, DON'T YOU WISH YOU WOULD HAVE TAKEN US UP?

YEAH, SURE.

YOU X-MEN GOT IT ALL GOIN' ON. EVERYBODY LOVES YOU GUYS.

IT ALL WORKED OUT SO *WELL* FOR ALL OF YOU.

THAT'S FAIR.

BUT THIS HAS TO BE YOUR BOTTOM, BLOB.

IT'S A BOTTOM IF I EVER SAW ONE.

WHAT ARE YOU TALKIN' ABOUT? I AIN'T NEVER FELT BETTER!

YOU'RE DOWN HERE IN THIS ARMPIT SELLIN' OUR PEOPLE O TO WHOEVER WILL BUY.

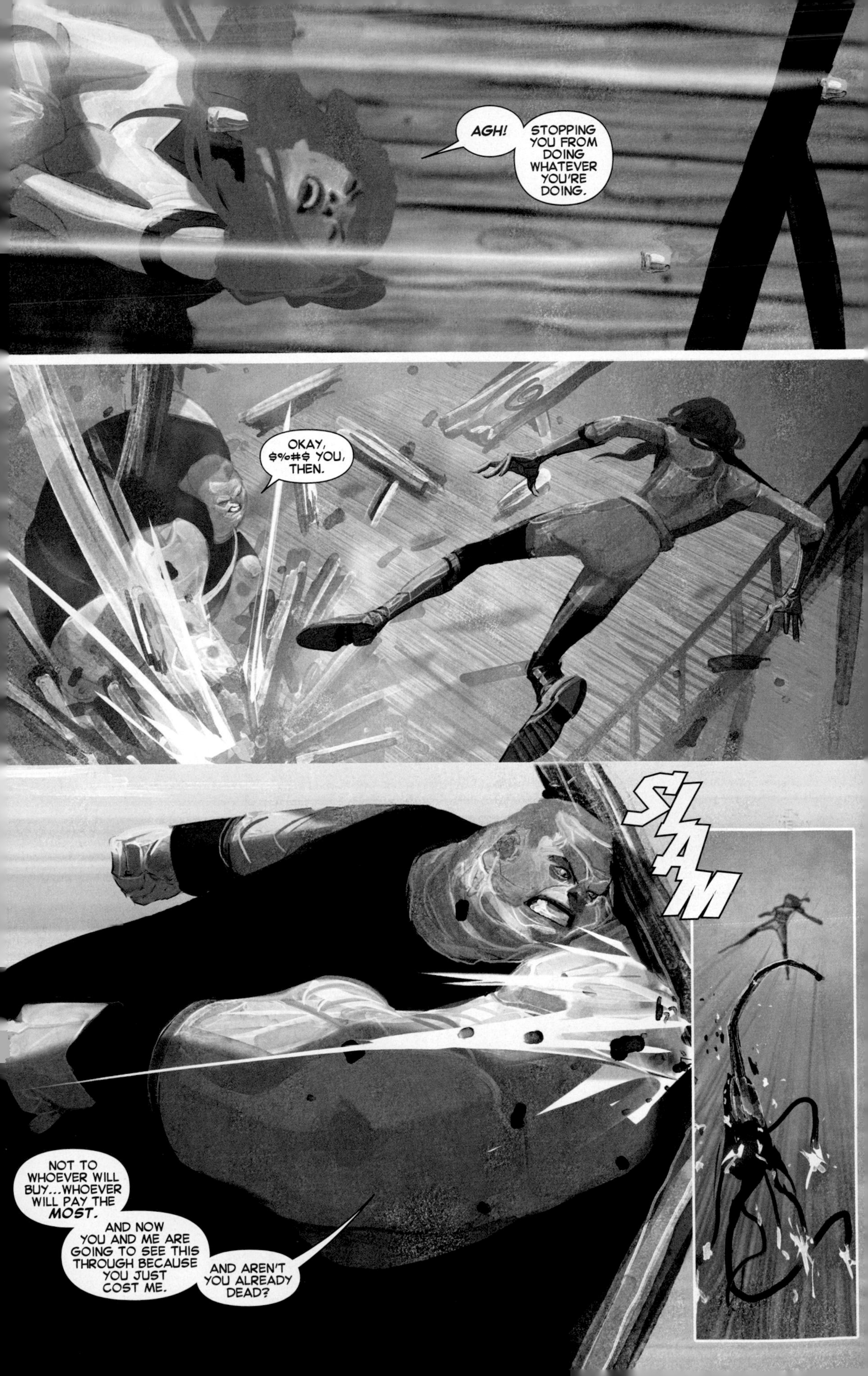
AGH!
STOPPING YOU FROM DOING WHATEVER YOU'RE DOING.
OKAY, $%#$ YOU, THEN.
SLAM
NOT TO WHOEVER WILL BUY...WHOEVER WILL PAY THE *MOST.*
AND NOW YOU AND ME ARE GOING TO SEE THIS THROUGH BECAUSE YOU JUST COST ME.
AND AREN'T YOU ALREADY DEAD?

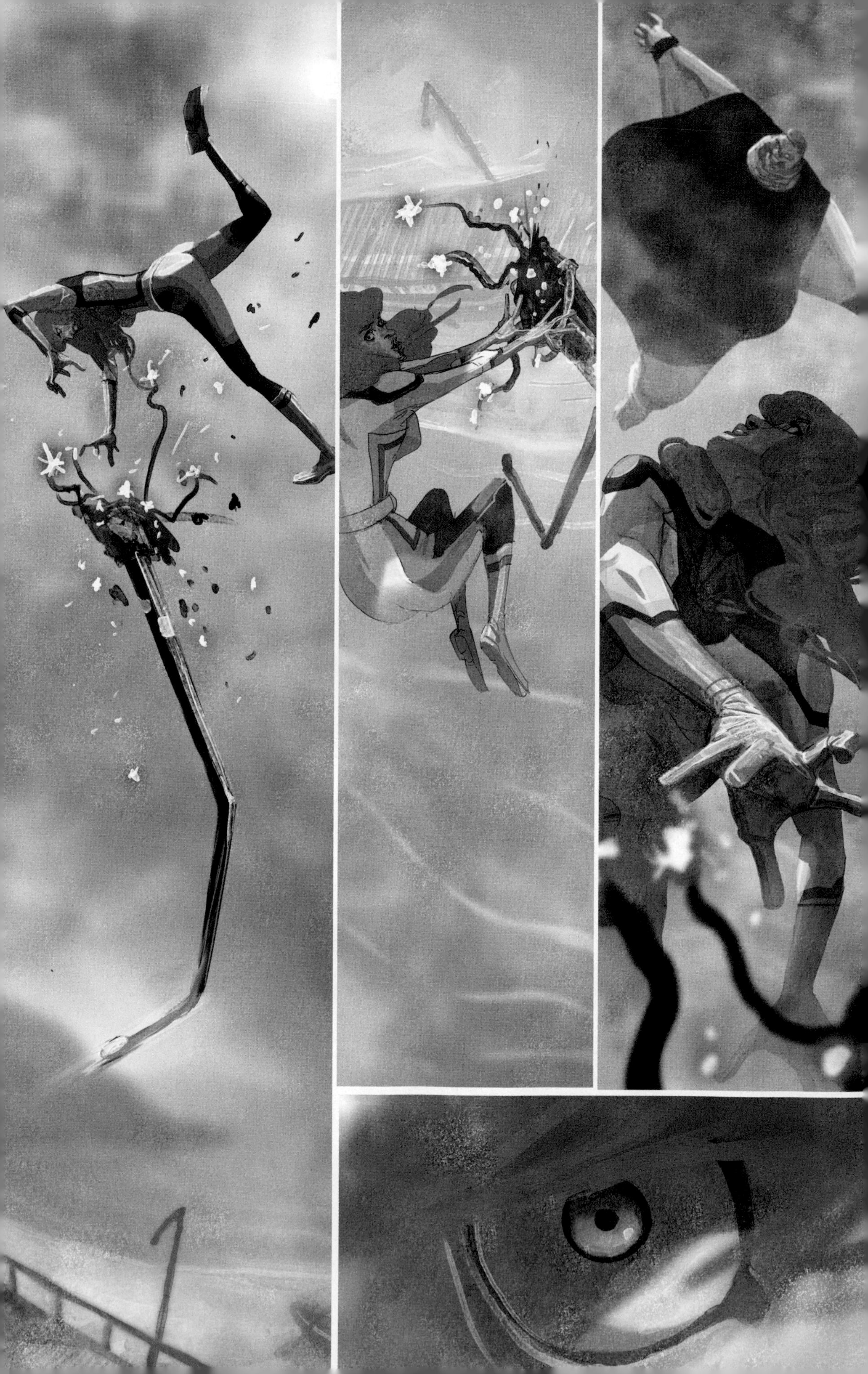

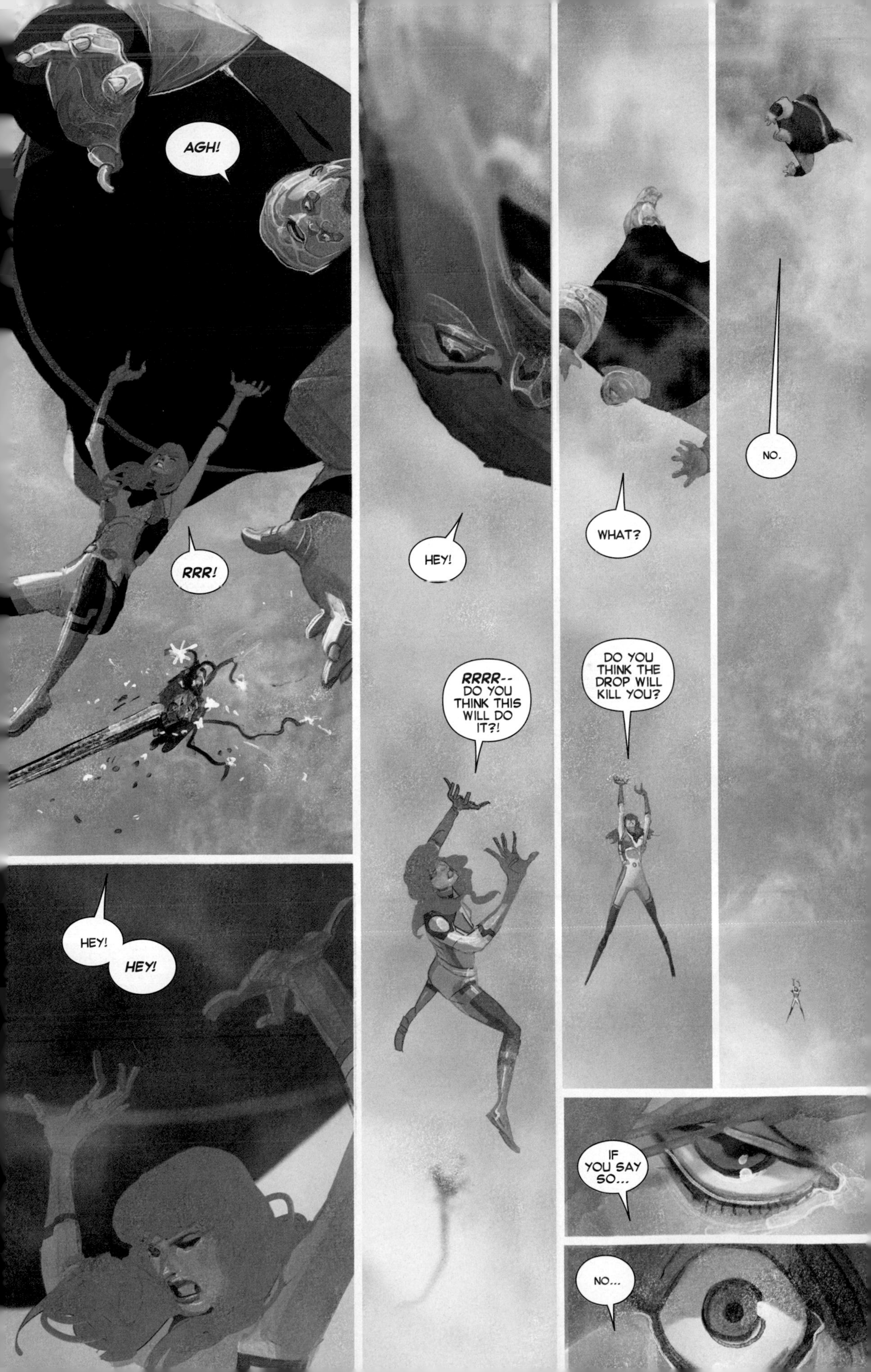
AGH!
RRR!
HEY!
HEY!
HEY!
RRRR-- DO YOU THINK THIS WILL DO IT?!
WHAT?
DO YOU THINK THE DROP WILL KILL YOU?
NO.
IF YOU SAY SO...
NO...

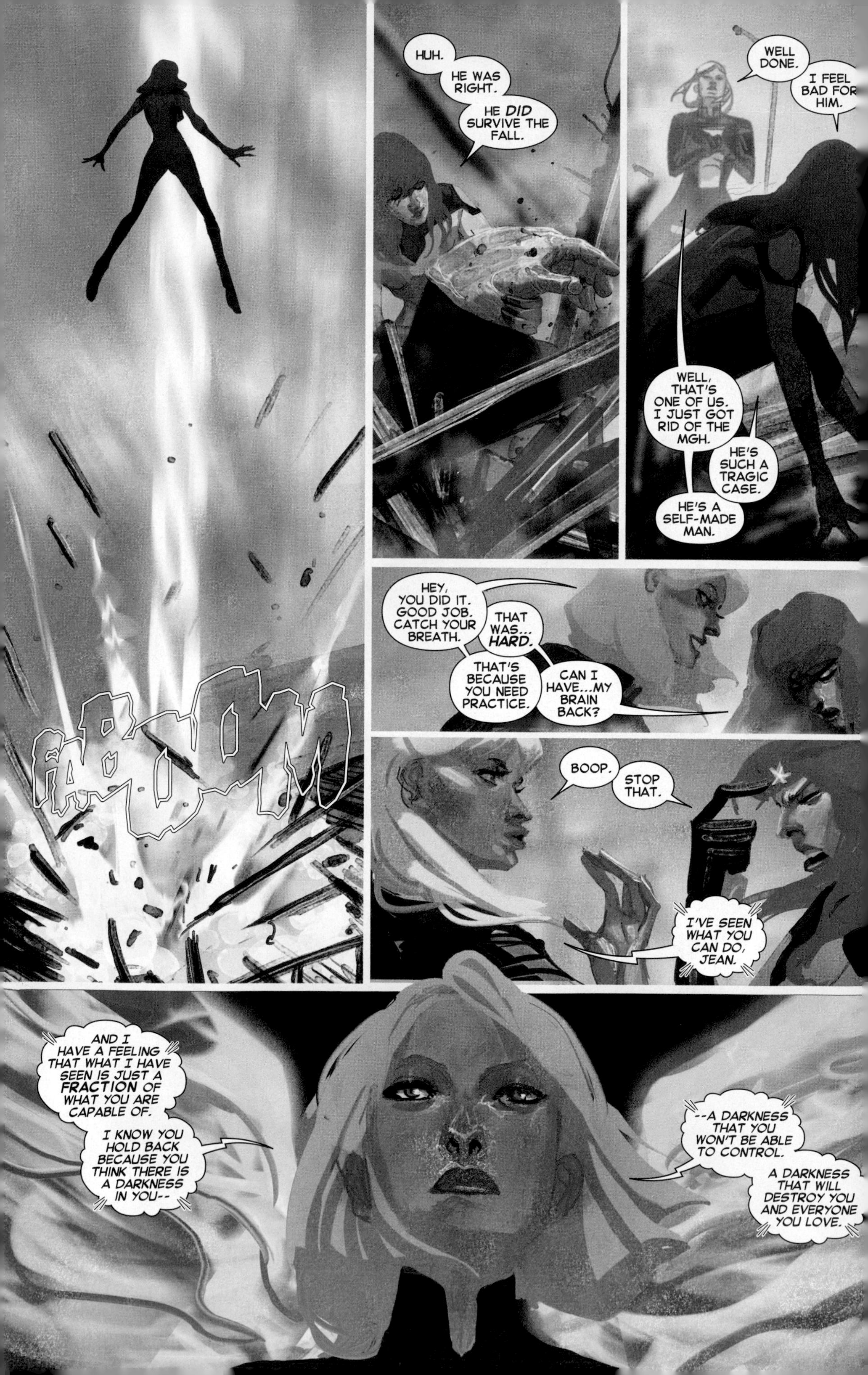
FRA-BOOOM
HUH.
HE WAS RIGHT.
HE *DID* SURVIVE THE FALL.
WELL DONE.
I FEEL BAD FOR HIM.
WELL, THAT'S ONE OF US. I JUST GOT RID OF THE MGH.
HE'S SUCH A TRAGIC CASE.
HE'S A SELF-MADE MAN.
HEY, YOU DID IT. GOOD JOB. CATCH YOUR BREATH.
THAT WAS... ***HARD.***
THAT'S BECAUSE YOU NEED PRACTICE.
CAN I HAVE...MY BRAIN BACK?
BOOP.
STOP THAT.
I'VE SEEN WHAT YOU CAN DO, JEAN.
AND I HAVE A FEELING THAT WHAT I HAVE SEEN IS JUST A **FRACTION** OF WHAT YOU ARE CAPABLE OF.
I KNOW YOU HOLD BACK BECAUSE YOU THINK THERE IS A DARKNESS IN YOU--
--A DARKNESS THAT YOU WON'T BE ABLE TO CONTROL.
A DARKNESS THAT WILL DESTROY YOU AND EVERYONE YOU LOVE.

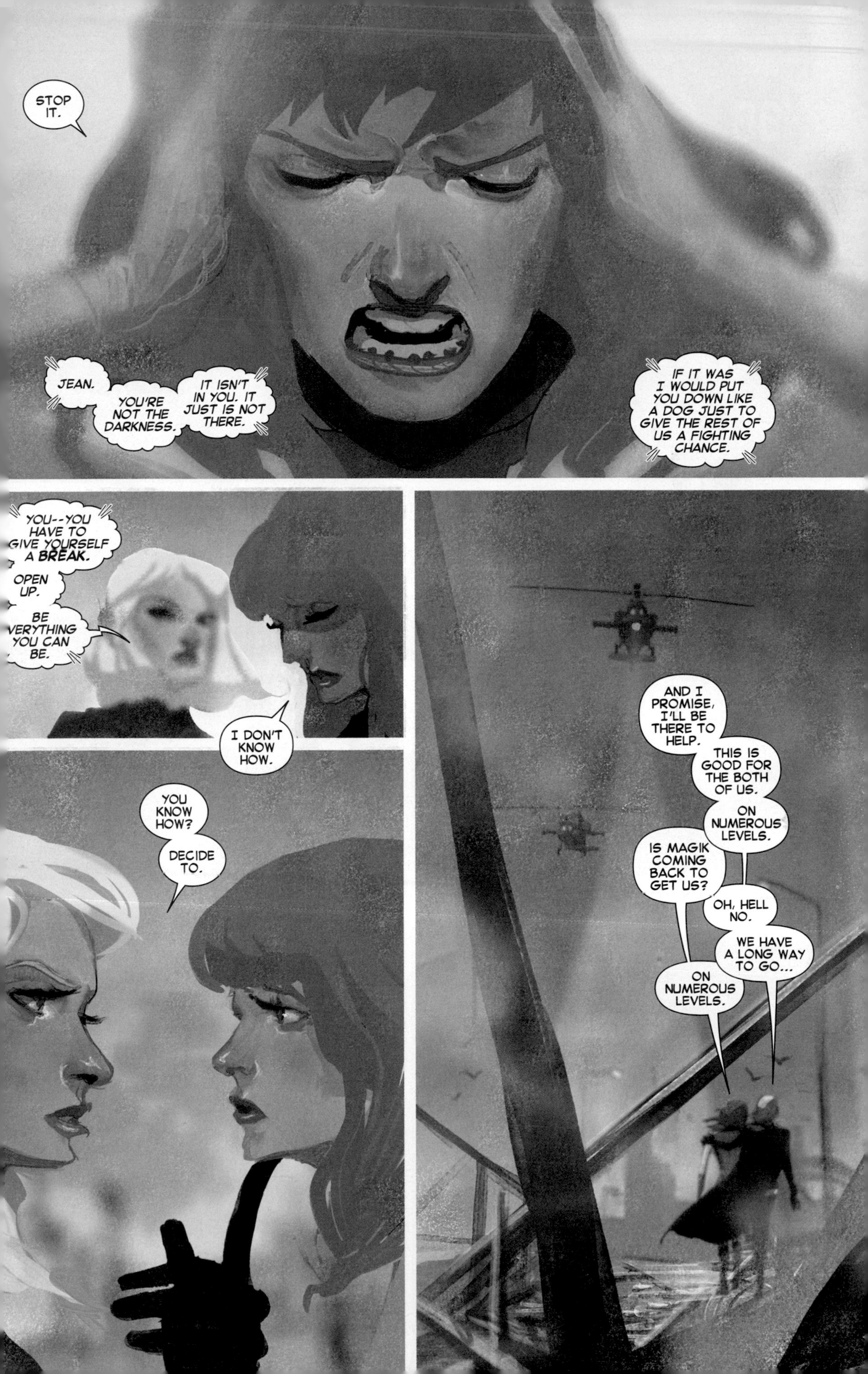
STOP IT.
JEAN.
YOU'RE NOT THE DARKNESS.
IT ISN'T IN YOU. IT JUST IS NOT THERE.
IF IT WAS I WOULD PUT YOU DOWN LIKE A DOG JUST TO GIVE THE REST OF US A FIGHTING CHANCE.
YOU--YOU HAVE TO GIVE YOURSELF A BREAK.
OPEN UP.
BE EVERYTHING YOU CAN BE.
I DON'T KNOW HOW.
YOU KNOW HOW?
DECIDE TO.
AND I PROMISE, I'LL BE THERE TO HELP.
THIS IS GOOD FOR THE BOTH OF US.
ON NUMEROUS LEVELS.
IS MAGIK COMING BACK TO GET US?
OH, HELL NO.
WE HAVE A LONG WAY TO GO...
ON NUMEROUS LEVELS.

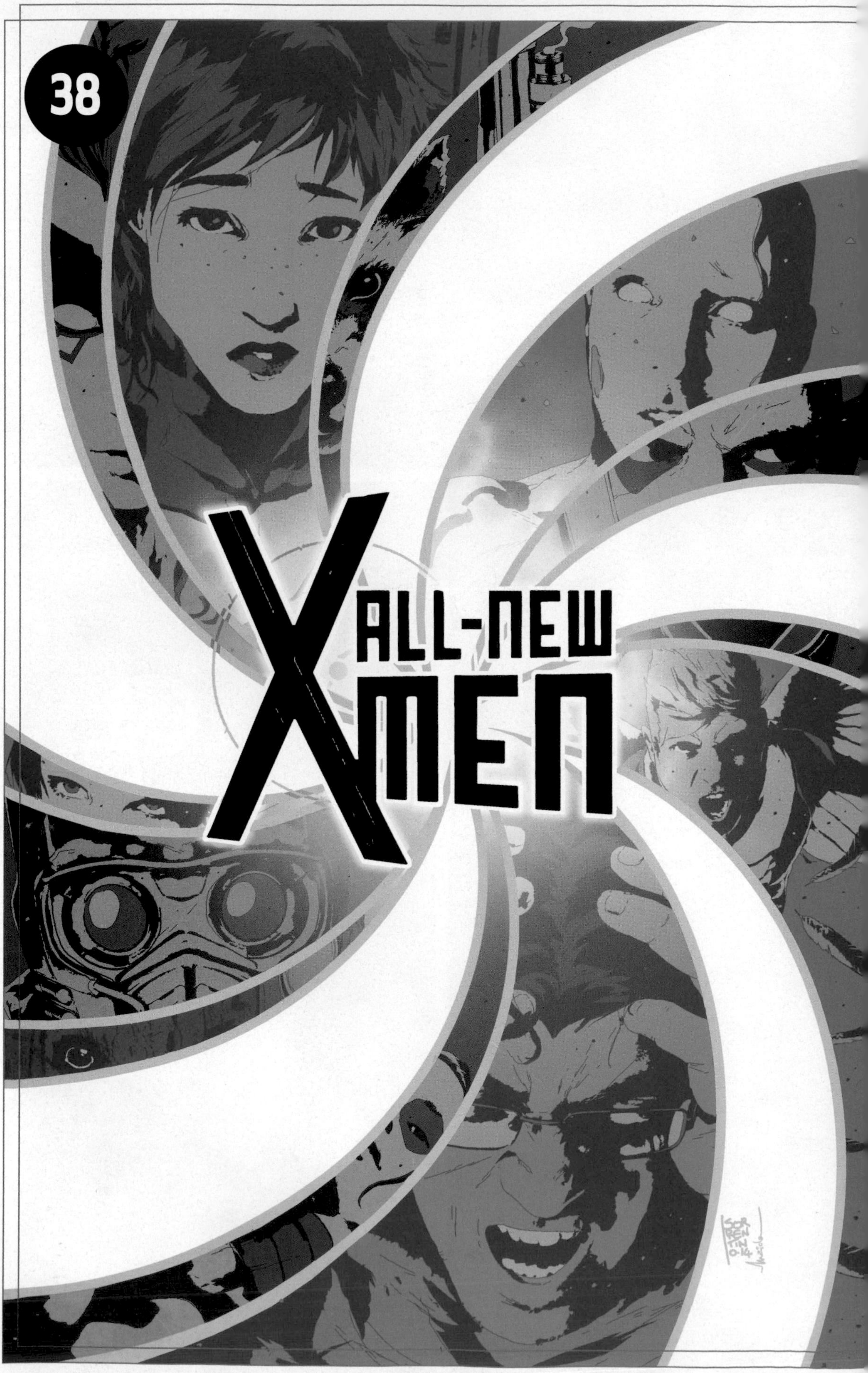
38
ALL-NEW
X
MEN

GUARDIANS OF THE GALAXY & X-MEN

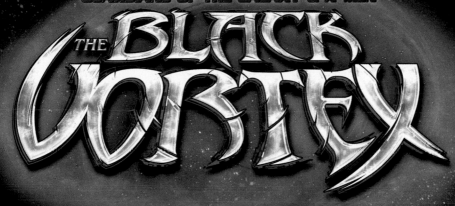

THE BLACK VORTEX

Previously in *The Black Vortex*...

Billions of years ago, an ancient race named the Viscardi were gifted an object of immense cosmic power by a Celestial. This artifact, known as the Black Vortex, transformed the user, imbuing them with cosmic energy. However, the power of this object caused the Viscardi to turn on each other, annihilating their own race from within.

Presently, Peter Quill and Kitty Pryde have recently discovered that the sadistic Mister Knife is actually Peter's father, J'Son, the deposed Emperor of Spartax. Finding that Knife had recovered the Black Vortex, they were forced to act. Peter and Kitty stole the artifact and recruited the Guardians of the Galaxy and the X-Men to help battle Mister Knife. But the group was soon attacked by Knife's enhanced henchmen, the Slaughter Lords, forcing Gamora to use the Black Vortex to fend them off. To escape their pursuers, Storm had Magik teleport the group to Spartax's moon. As the group argued over what to do with the Vortex, the elder Beast and Angel chose to submit to the Vortex. Now cosmically aware, the three enhanced heroes set themselves above the others, taking the Black Vortex and rocketing away with a new mission — to reshape the universe in their image. But those they left behind did not have long to react, as Knife's flying fortress appeared in the sky, firing a massive blast directly at the moon!

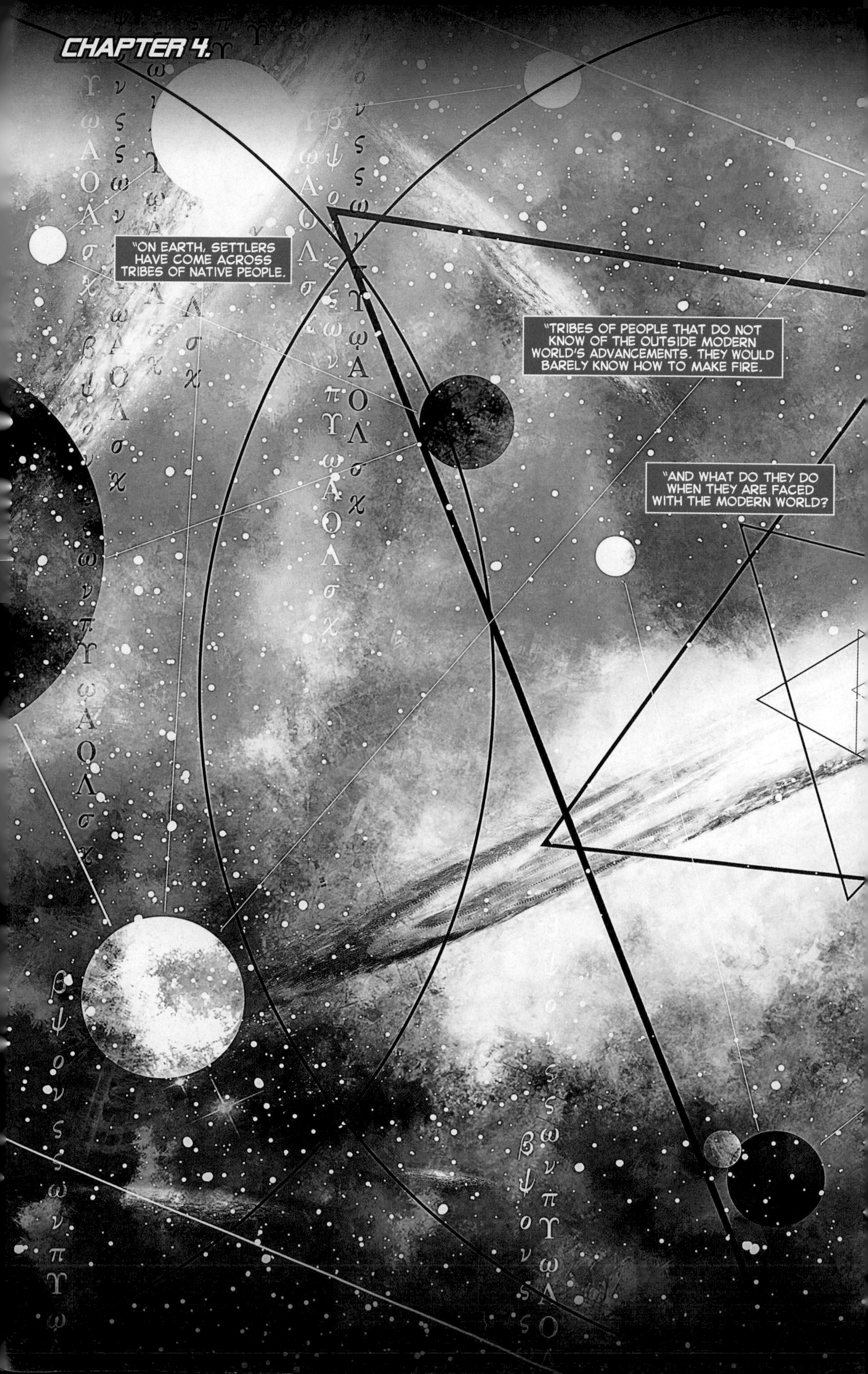
CHAPTER 4.
"ON EARTH, SETTLERS HAVE COME ACROSS TRIBES OF NATIVE PEOPLE.
"TRIBES OF PEOPLE THAT DO NOT KNOW OF THE OUTSIDE MODERN WORLD'S ADVANCEMENTS. THEY WOULD BARELY KNOW HOW TO MAKE FIRE.
"AND WHAT DO THEY DO WHEN THEY ARE FACED WITH THE MODERN WORLD?

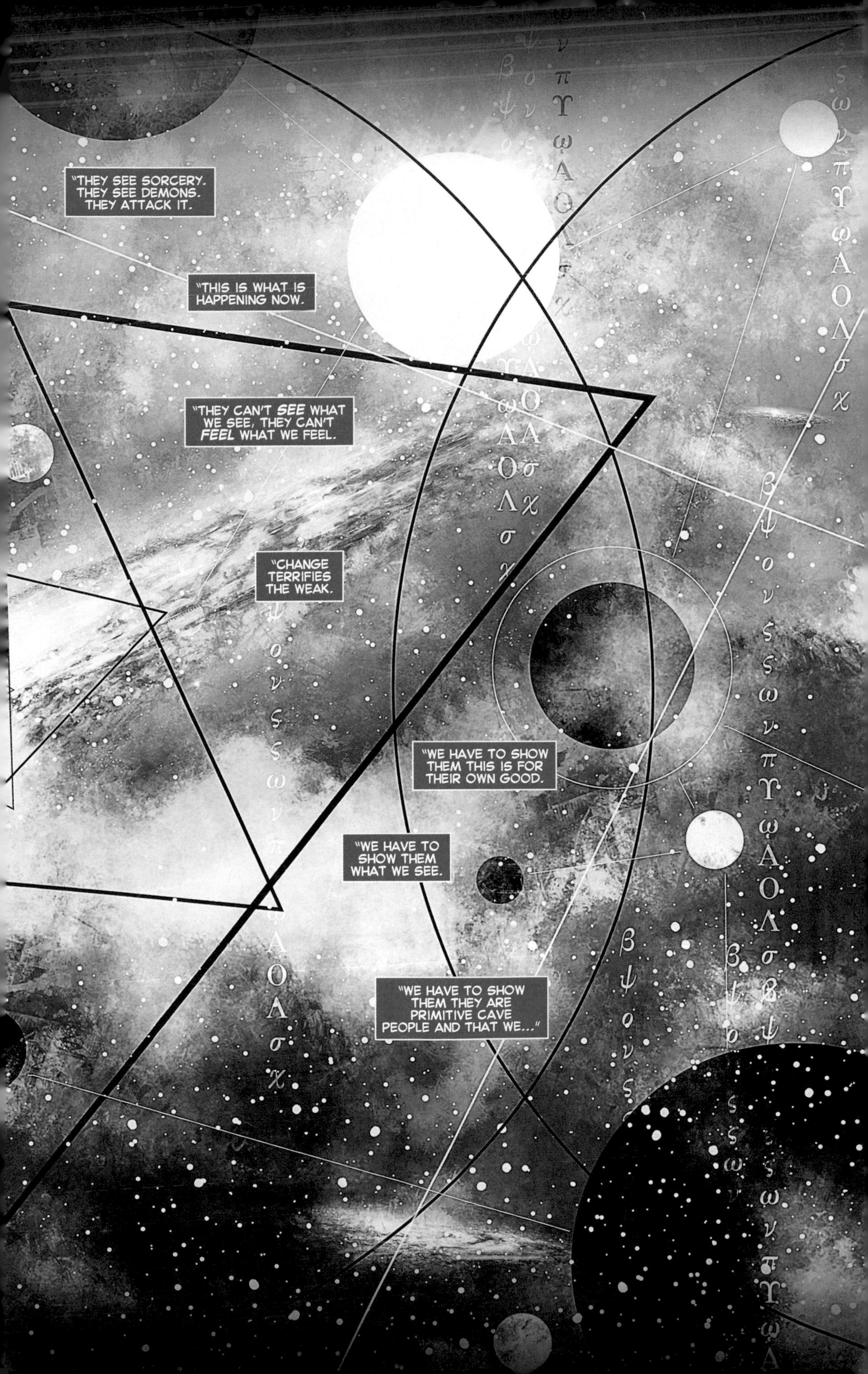
"THEY SEE SORCERY. THEY SEE DEMONS. THEY ATTACK IT.
"THIS IS WHAT IS HAPPENING NOW.
"THEY CAN'T SEE WHAT WE SEE, THEY CAN'T FEEL WHAT WE FEEL.
"CHANGE TERRIFIES THE WEAK.
"WE HAVE TO SHOW THEM THIS IS FOR THEIR OWN GOOD.
"WE HAVE TO SHOW THEM WHAT WE SEE.
"WE HAVE TO SHOW THEM THEY ARE PRIMITIVE CAVE PEOPLE AND THAT WE..."

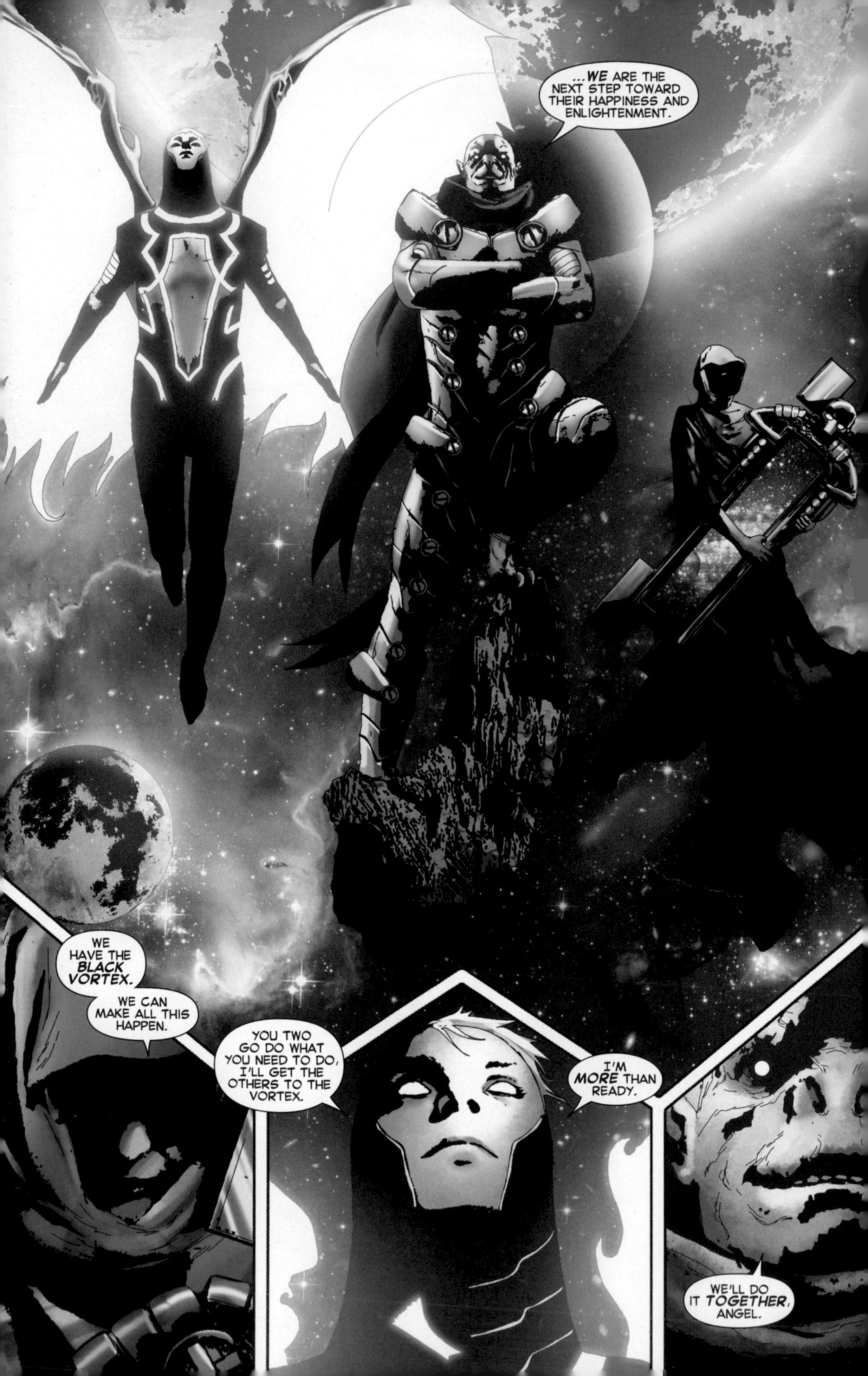
...WE ARE THE NEXT STEP TOWARD THEIR HAPPINESS AND ENLIGHTENMENT.
WE HAVE THE BLACK VORTEX.
WE CAN MAKE ALL THIS HAPPEN.
YOU TWO GO DO WHAT YOU NEED TO DO, I'LL GET THE OTHERS TO THE VORTEX.
I'M MORE THAN READY.
WE'LL DO IT TOGETHER, ANGEL.

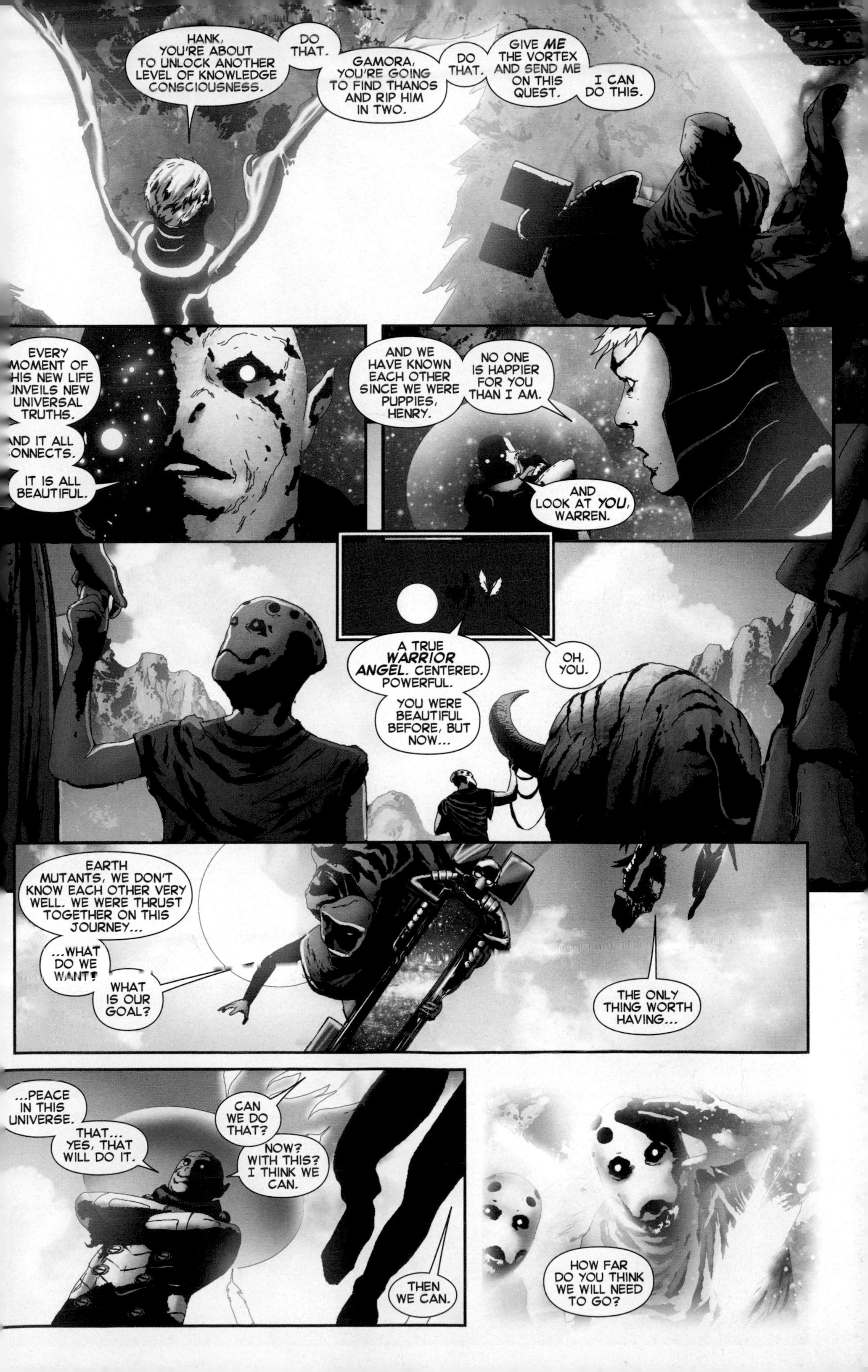
HANK, YOU'RE ABOUT TO UNLOCK ANOTHER LEVEL OF KNOWLEDGE CONSCIOUSNESS.
DO THAT.
GAMORA, YOU'RE GOING TO FIND THANOS AND RIP HIM IN TWO.
DO THAT.
GIVE ME THE VORTEX AND SEND ME ON THIS QUEST.
I CAN DO THIS.
EVERY MOMENT OF THIS NEW LIFE UNVEILS NEW UNIVERSAL TRUTHS.
AND IT ALL CONNECTS.
IT IS ALL BEAUTIFUL.
AND WE HAVE KNOWN EACH OTHER SINCE WE WERE PUPPIES, HENRY.
NO ONE IS HAPPIER FOR YOU THAN I AM.
AND LOOK AT YOU, WARREN.
A TRUE WARRIOR ANGEL. CENTERED. POWERFUL.
YOU WERE BEAUTIFUL BEFORE, BUT NOW...
OH, YOU.
EARTH MUTANTS, WE DON'T KNOW EACH OTHER VERY WELL. WE WERE THRUST TOGETHER ON THIS JOURNEY...
...WHAT DO WE WANT?
WHAT IS OUR GOAL?
THE ONLY THING WORTH HAVING...
...PEACE IN THIS UNIVERSE.
THAT... YES, THAT WILL DO IT.
CAN WE DO THAT?
NOW? WITH THIS? I THINK WE CAN.
THEN WE CAN.
HOW FAR DO YOU THINK WE WILL NEED TO GO?

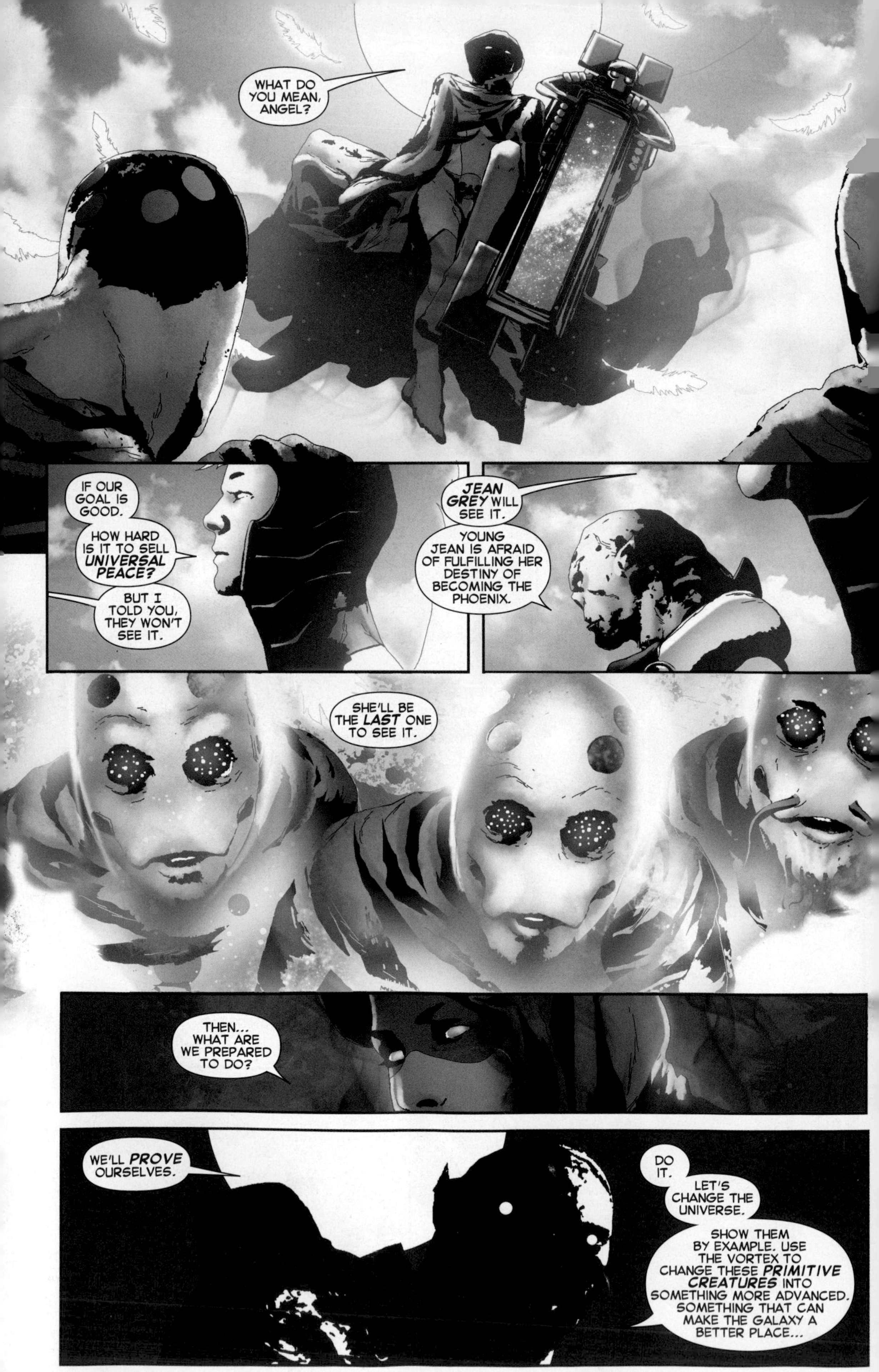
WHAT DO YOU MEAN, ANGEL?
IF OUR GOAL IS GOOD.
HOW HARD IS IT TO SELL UNIVERSAL PEACE?
BUT I TOLD YOU, THEY WON'T SEE IT.
JEAN GREY WILL SEE IT.
YOUNG JEAN IS AFRAID OF FULFILLING HER DESTINY OF BECOMING THE PHOENIX.
SHE'LL BE THE LAST ONE TO SEE IT.
THEN... WHAT ARE WE PREPARED TO DO?
WE'LL PROVE OURSELVES.
DO IT.
LET'S CHANGE THE UNIVERSE.
SHOW THEM BY EXAMPLE. USE THE VORTEX TO CHANGE THESE PRIMITIVE CREATURES INTO SOMETHING MORE ADVANCED. SOMETHING THAT CAN MAKE THE GALAXY A BETTER PLACE...

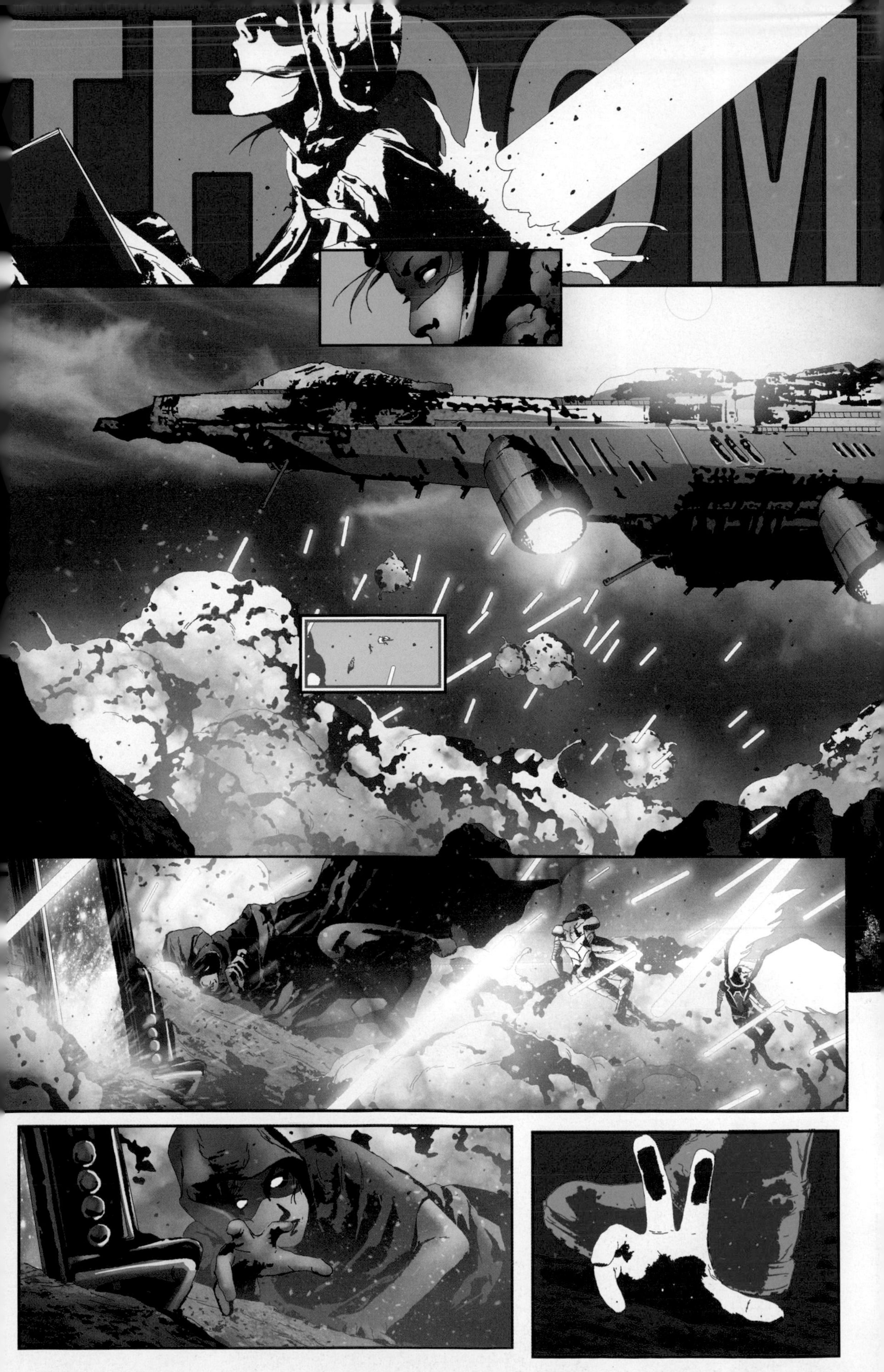

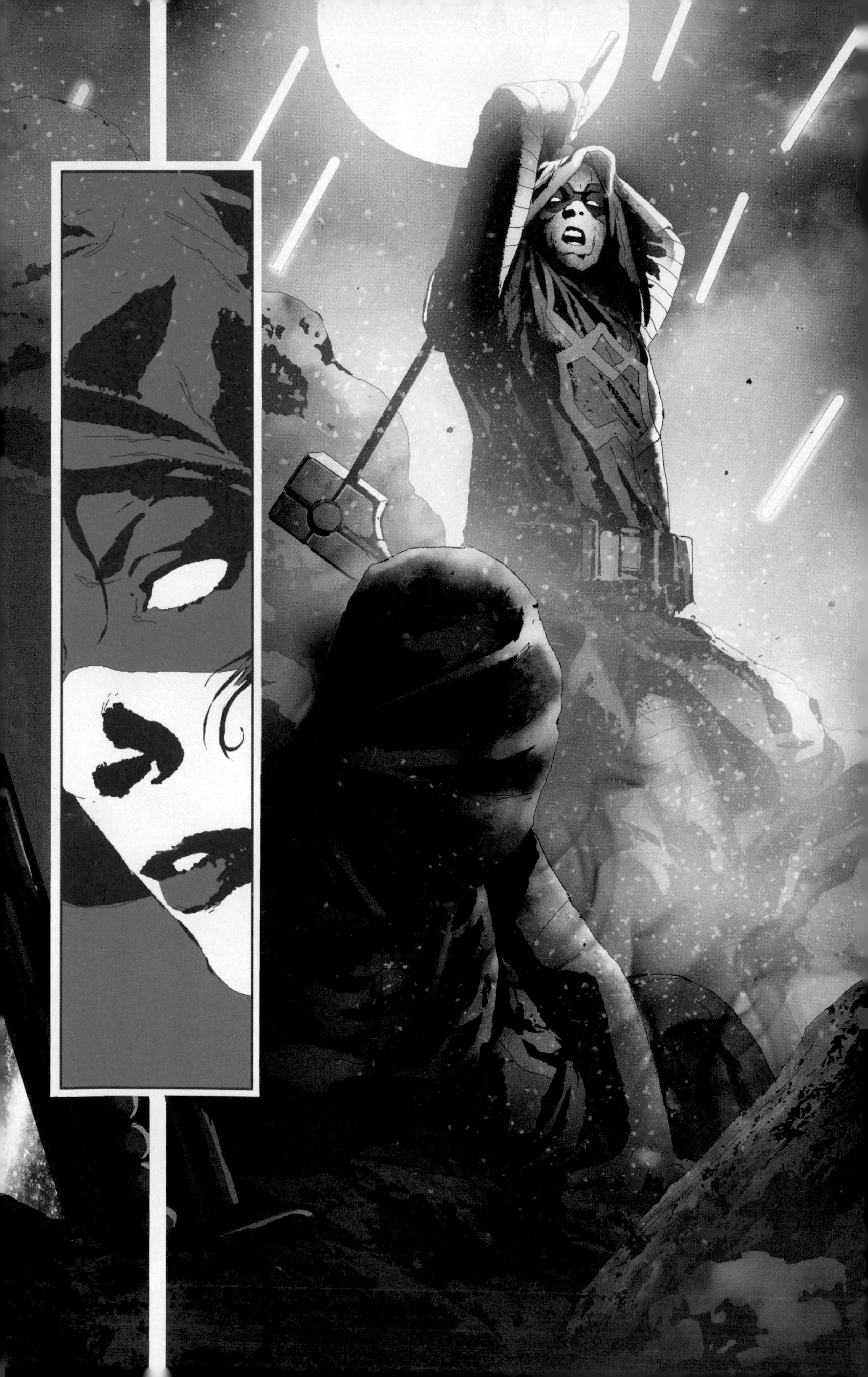

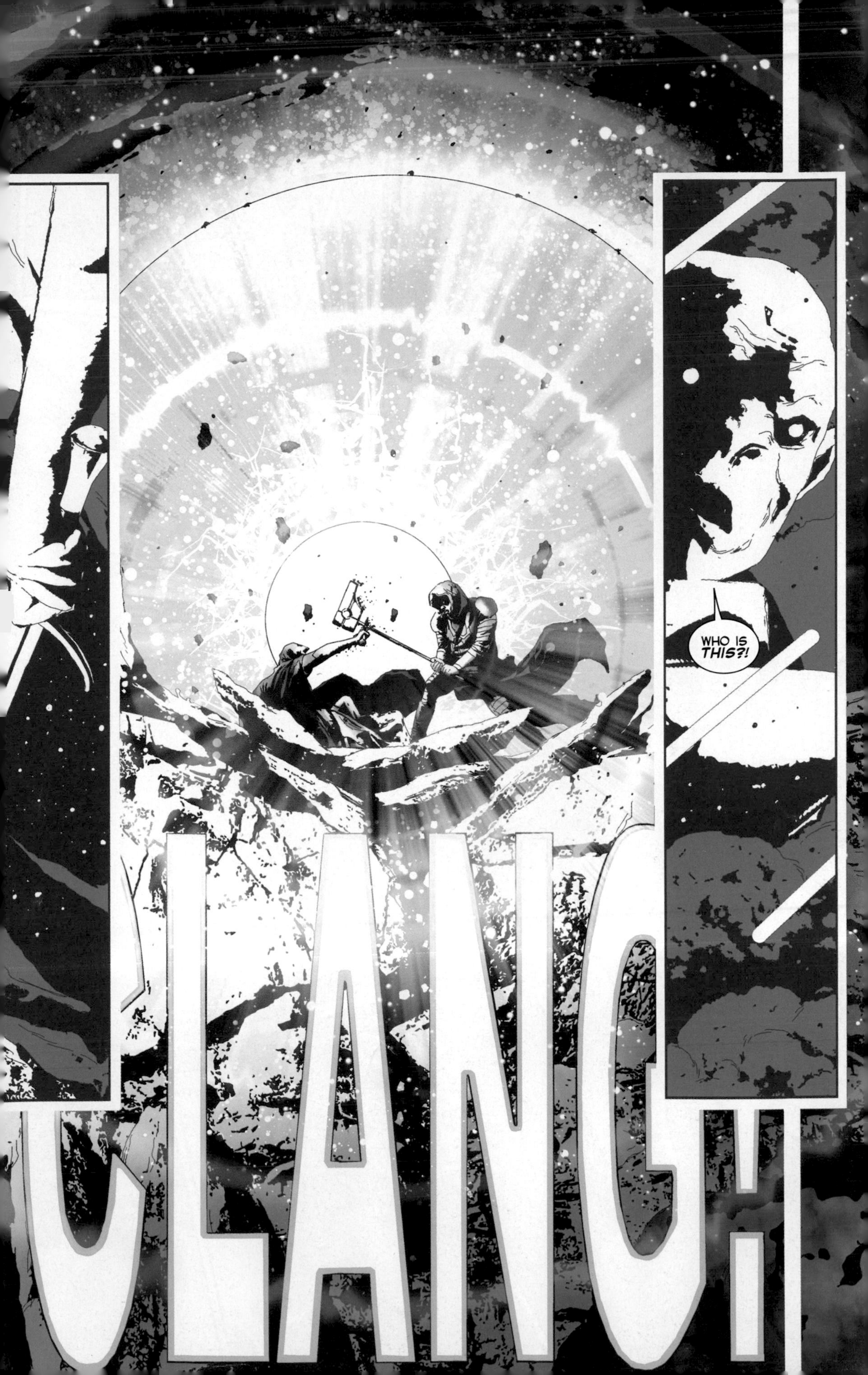
WHO IS THIS?!
CLANG!

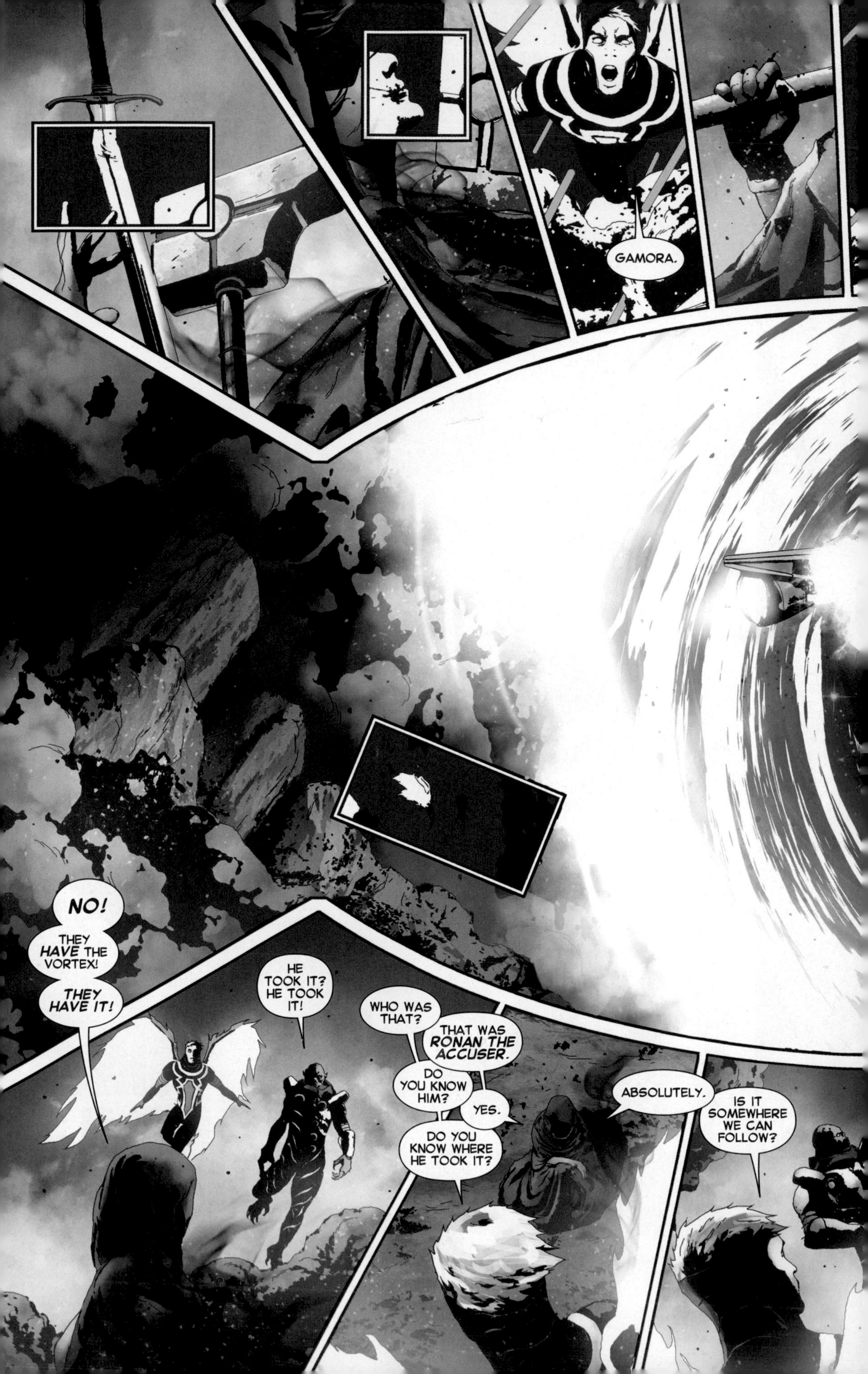
GAMORA.
NO!
THEY HAVE THE VORTEX!
THEY HAVE IT!
HE TOOK IT? HE TOOK IT!
WHO WAS THAT?
THAT WAS RONAN THE ACCUSER.
DO YOU KNOW HIM?
YES.
DO YOU KNOW WHERE HE TOOK IT?
ABSOLUTELY.
IS IT SOMEWHERE WE CAN FOLLOW?

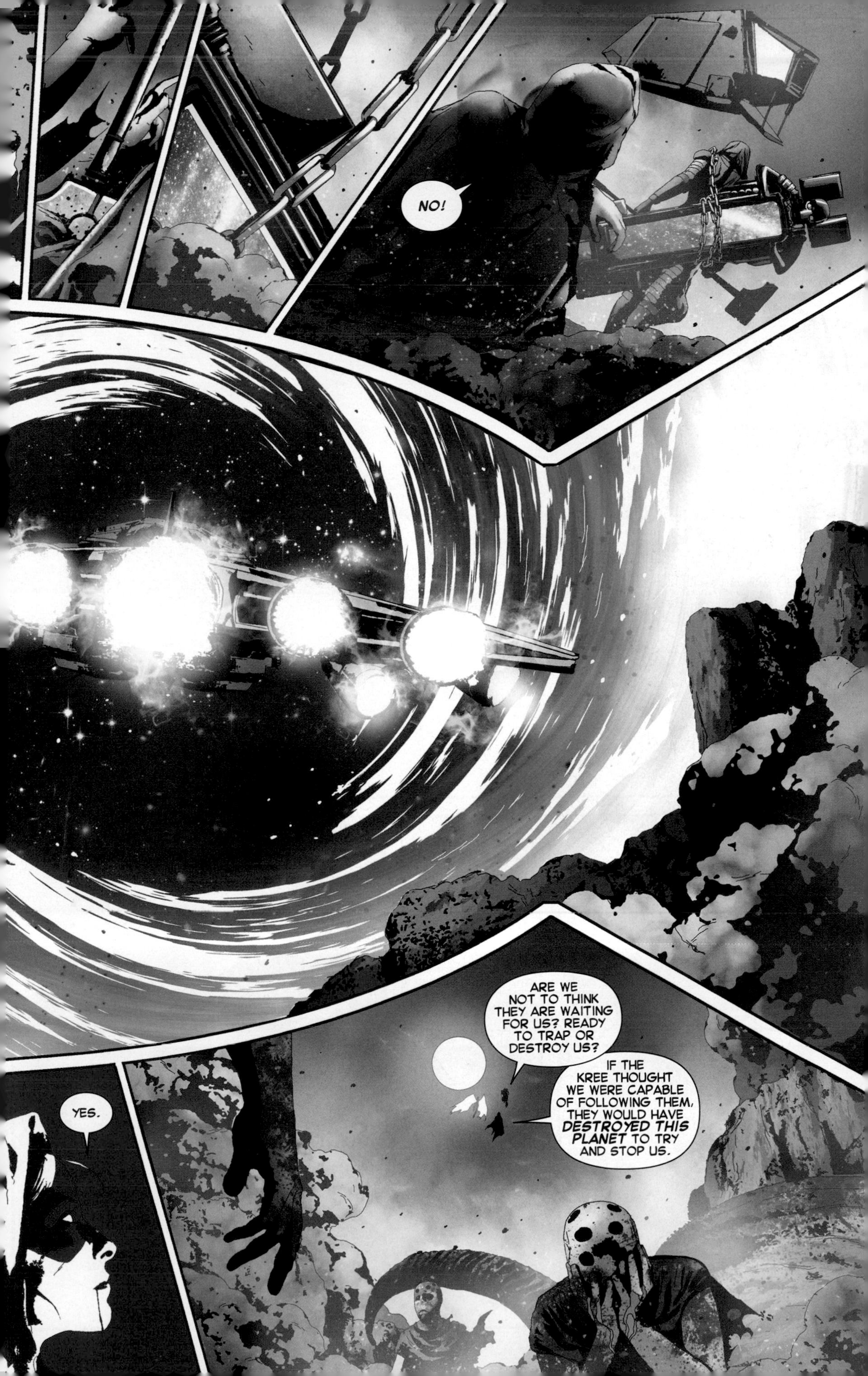
NO!
ARE WE NOT TO THINK THEY ARE WAITING FOR US? READY TO TRAP OR DESTROY US?
IF THE KREE THOUGHT WE WERE CAPABLE OF FOLLOWING THEM, THEY WOULD HAVE **DESTROYED THIS PLANET** TO TRY AND STOP US.
YES.

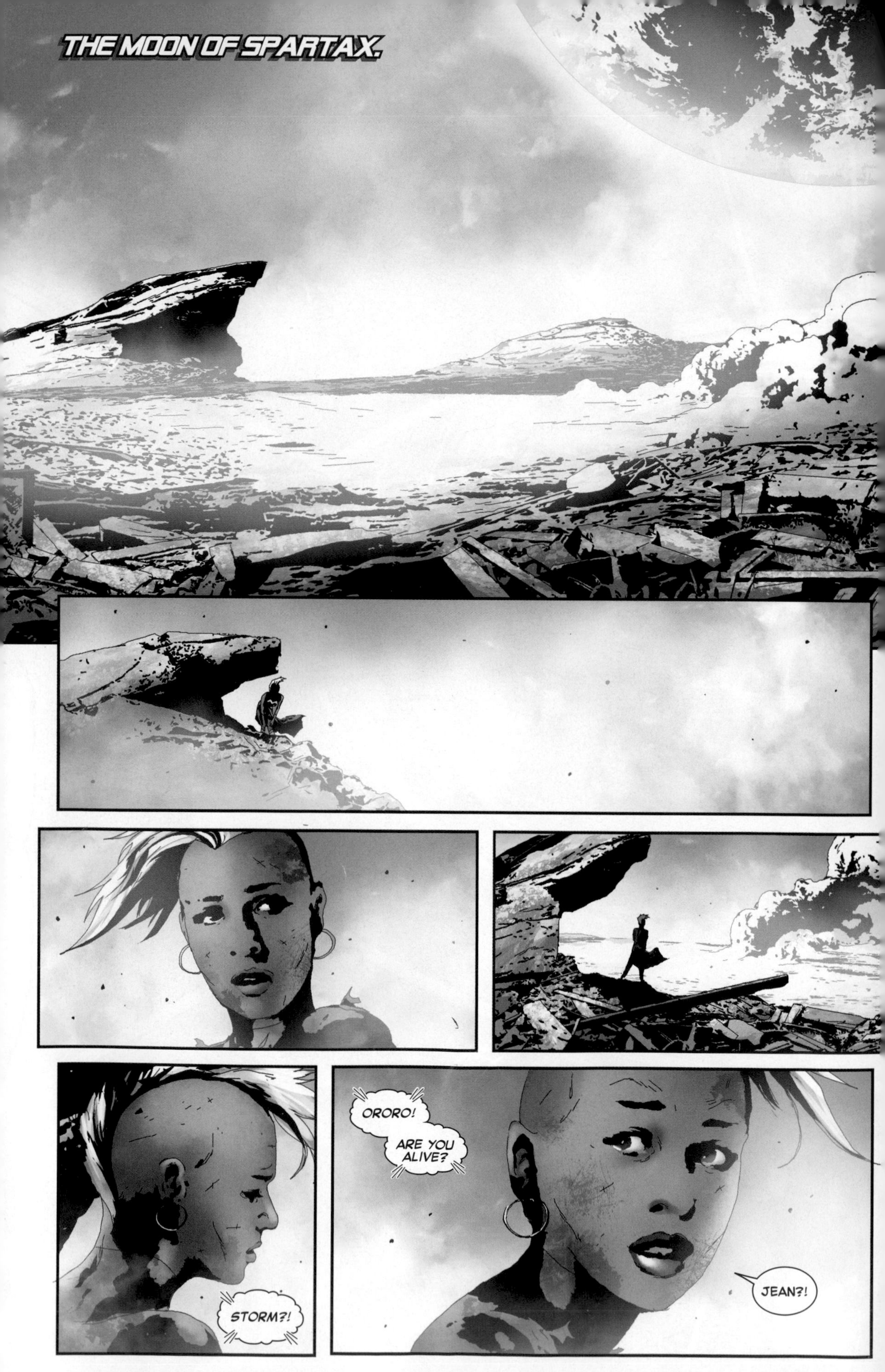
THE MOON OF SPARTAX.
ORORO!
ARE YOU ALIVE?
STORM?!
JEAN?!

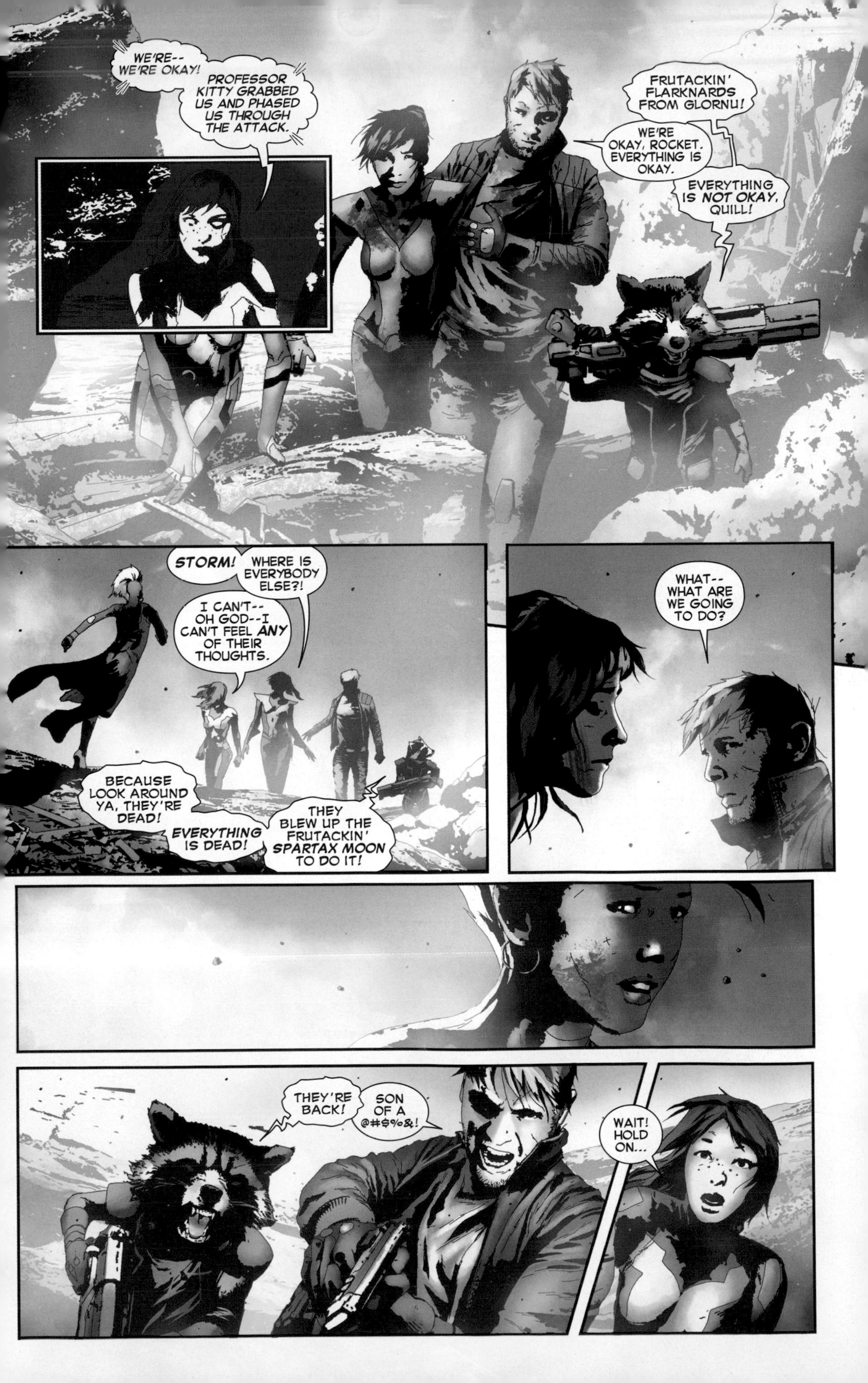

WE'RE-- WE'RE OKAY!
PROFESSOR KITTY GRABBED US AND PHASED US THROUGH THE ATTACK.
FRUTACKIN' FLARKNARDS FROM GLORNU!
WE'RE OKAY, ROCKET. EVERYTHING IS OKAY.
EVERYTHING IS NOT OKAY, QUILL!
STORM!
WHERE IS EVERYBODY ELSE?!
I CAN'T-- OH GOD--I CAN'T FEEL ANY OF THEIR THOUGHTS.
BECAUSE LOOK AROUND YA, THEY'RE DEAD!
EVERYTHING IS DEAD!
THEY BLEW UP THE FRUTACKIN' SPARTAX MOON TO DO IT!
WHAT-- WHAT ARE WE GOING TO DO?
THEY'RE BACK!
SON OF A @#$%&!
WAIT! HOLD ON...

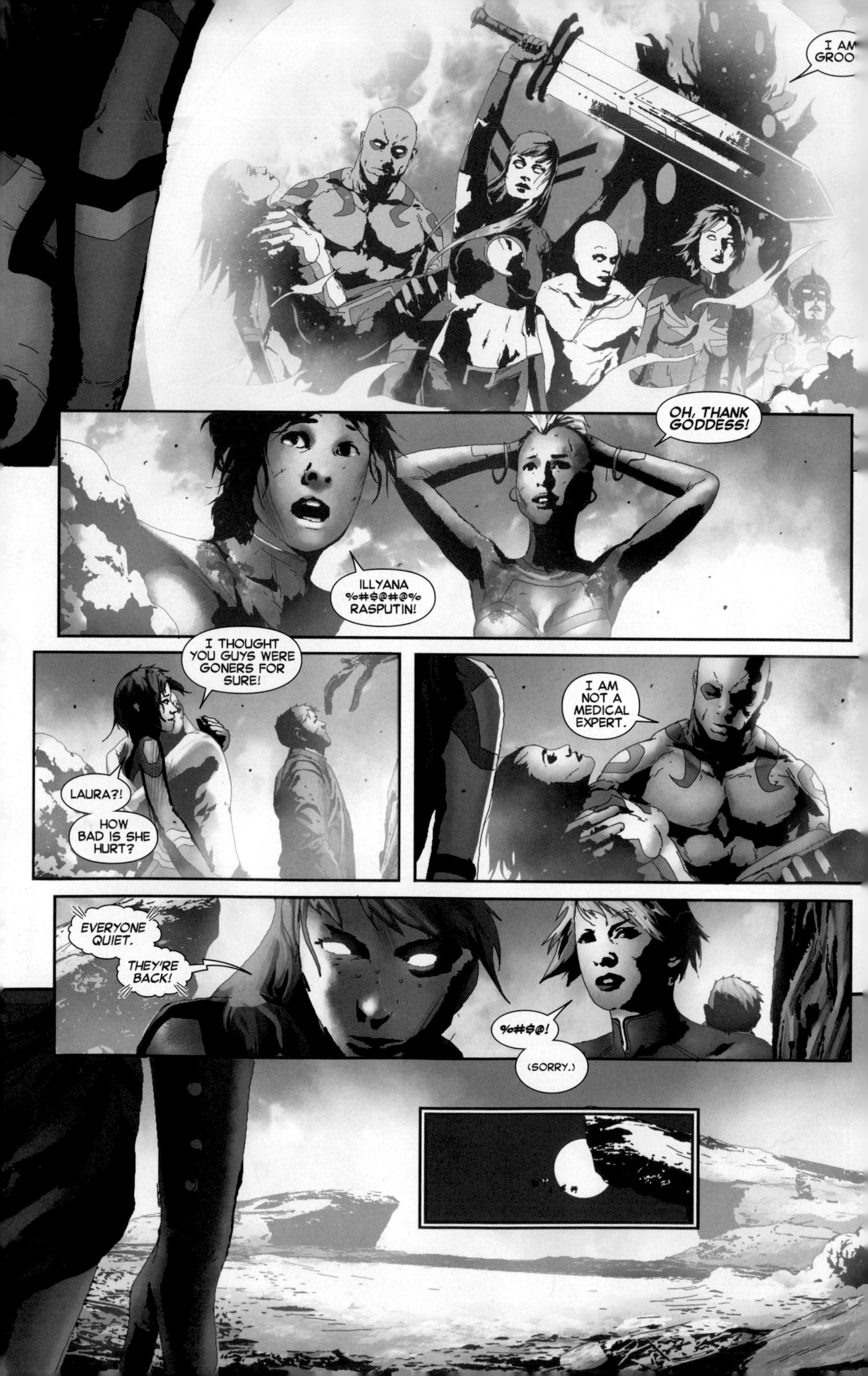
I AM GROO
OH, THANK GODDESS!
ILLYANA %#$@#@% RASPUTIN!
I THOUGHT YOU GUYS WERE GONERS FOR SURE!
LAURA?!
HOW BAD IS SHE HURT?
I AM NOT A MEDICAL EXPERT.
EVERYONE QUIET.
THEY'RE BACK!
%#$@!
(SORRY.)

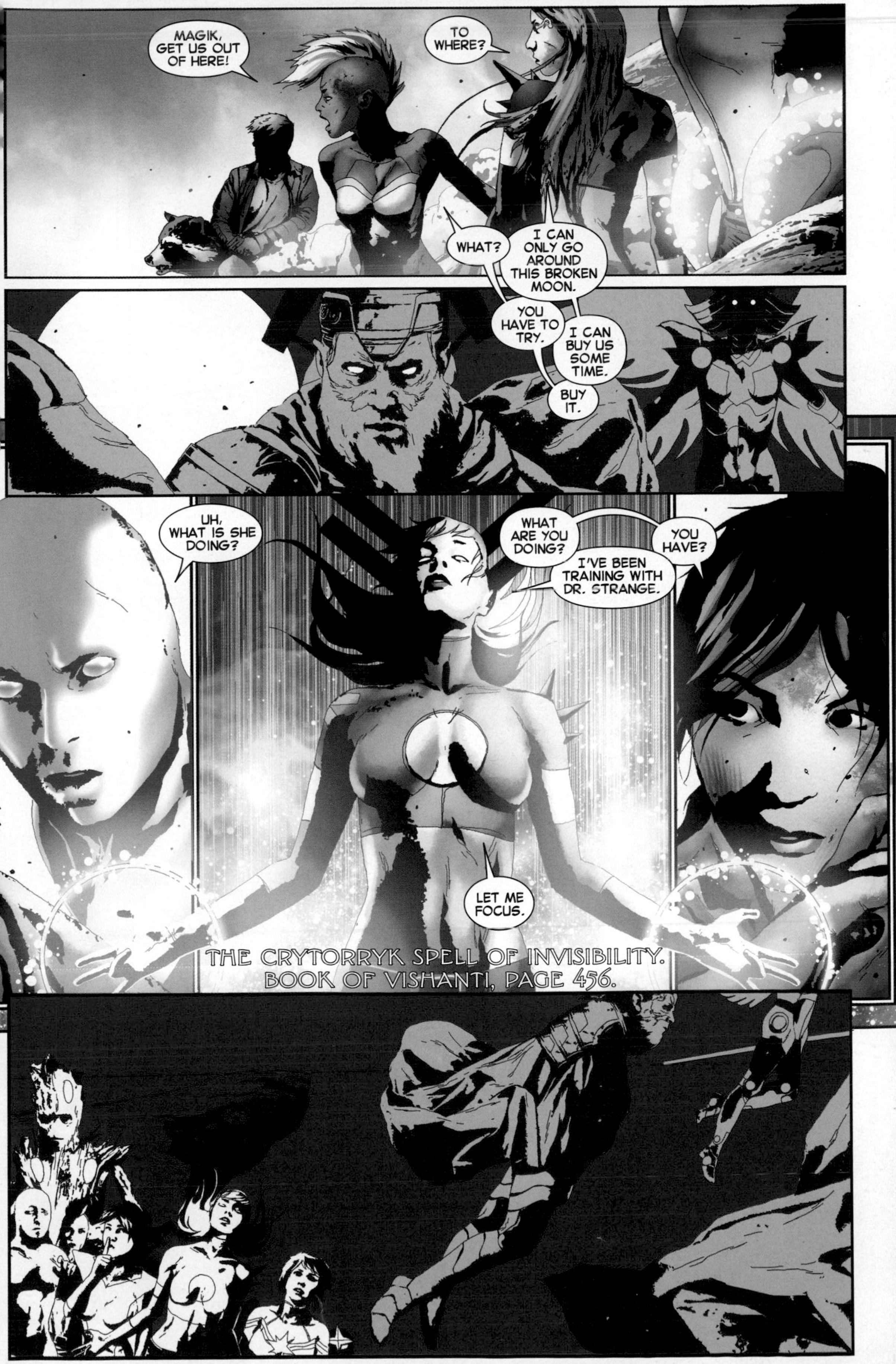
MAGIK, GET US OUT OF HERE!
TO WHERE?
WHAT?
I CAN ONLY GO AROUND THIS BROKEN MOON.
YOU HAVE TO TRY.
I CAN BUY US SOME TIME.
BUY IT.
UH, WHAT IS SHE DOING?
WHAT ARE YOU DOING?
I'VE BEEN TRAINING WITH DR. STRANGE.
YOU HAVE?
LET ME FOCUS.
THE CRYTORRYK SPELL OF INVISIBILITY. BOOK OF VISHANTI, PAGE 456.

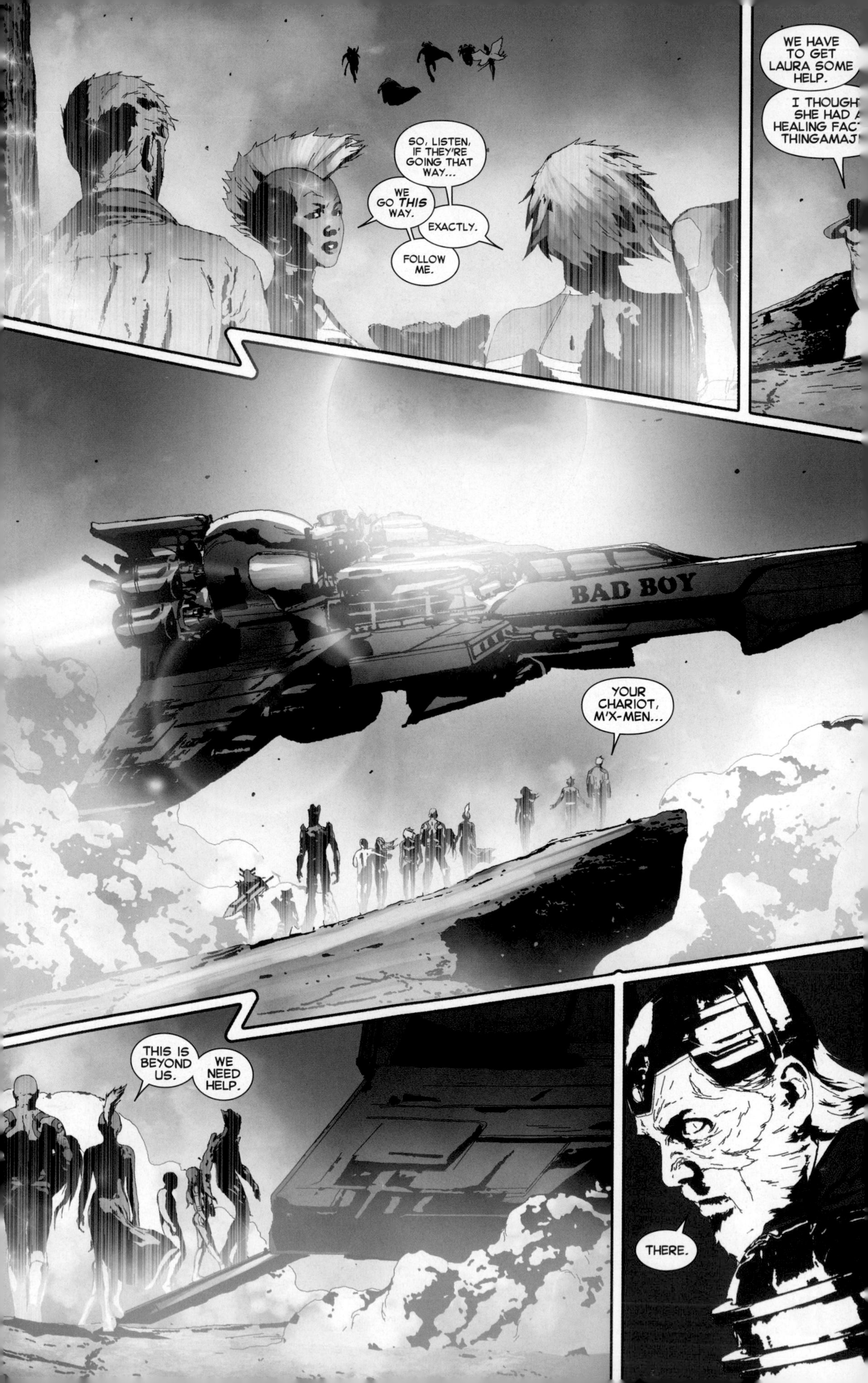
SO, LISTEN, IF THEY'RE GOING THAT WAY...
WE GO THIS WAY.
EXACTLY.
FOLLOW ME.
WE HAVE TO GET LAURA SOME HELP.
BAD BOY
YOUR CHARIOT, M'X-MEN...
THIS IS BEYOND US.
WE NEED HELP.
THERE.

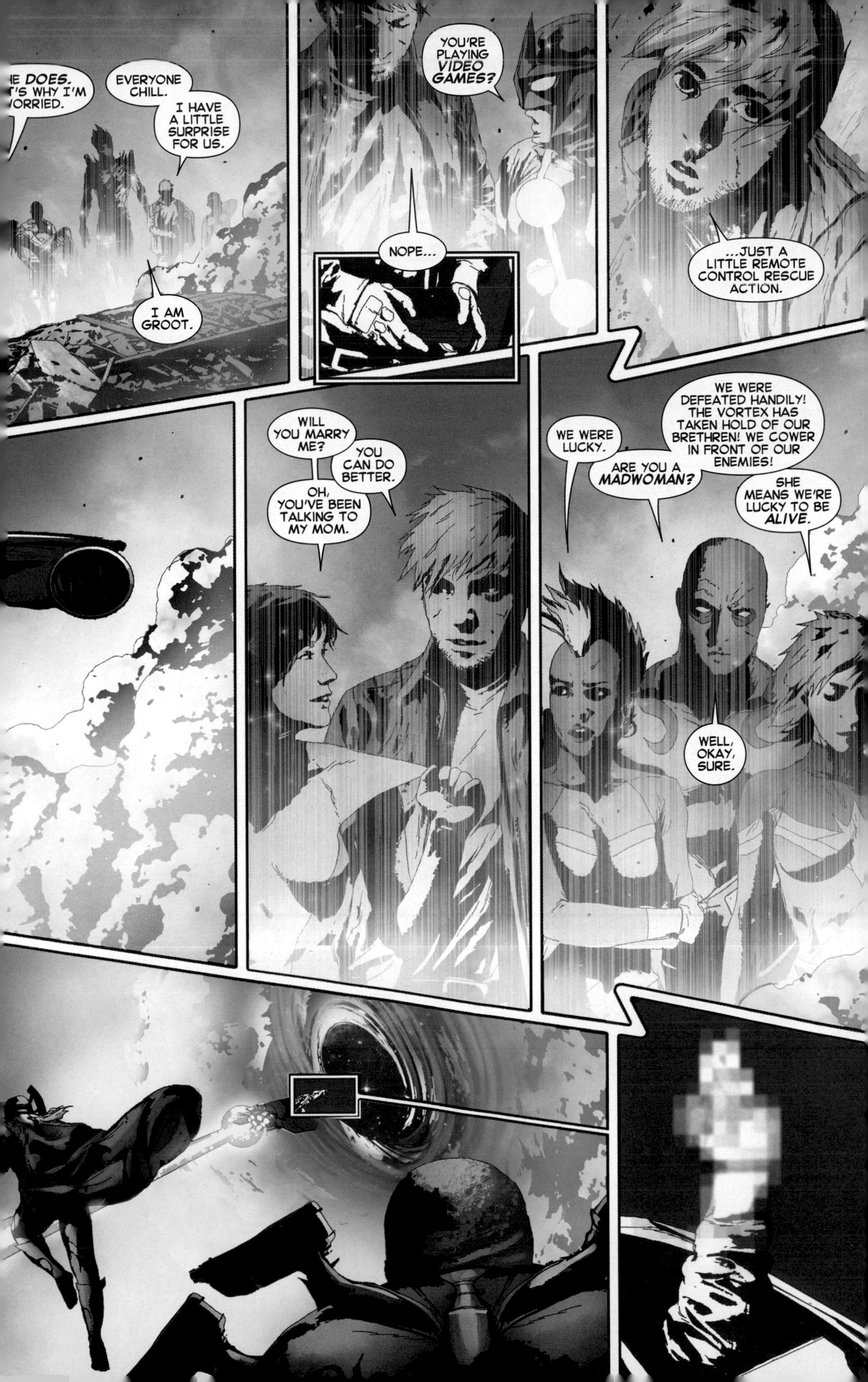
HE DOES. IT'S WHY I'M WORRIED.
EVERYONE CHILL.
I HAVE A LITTLE SURPRISE FOR US.
I AM GROOT.
YOU'RE PLAYING VIDEO GAMES?
NOPE...
...JUST A LITTLE REMOTE CONTROL RESCUE ACTION.
WILL YOU MARRY ME?
YOU CAN DO BETTER.
OH, YOU'VE BEEN TALKING TO MY MOM.
WE WERE LUCKY.
WE WERE DEFEATED HANDILY! THE VORTEX HAS TAKEN HOLD OF OUR BRETHREN! WE COWER IN FRONT OF OUR ENEMIES!
ARE YOU A MADWOMAN?
SHE MEANS WE'RE LUCKY TO BE ALIVE.
WELL, OKAY, SURE.

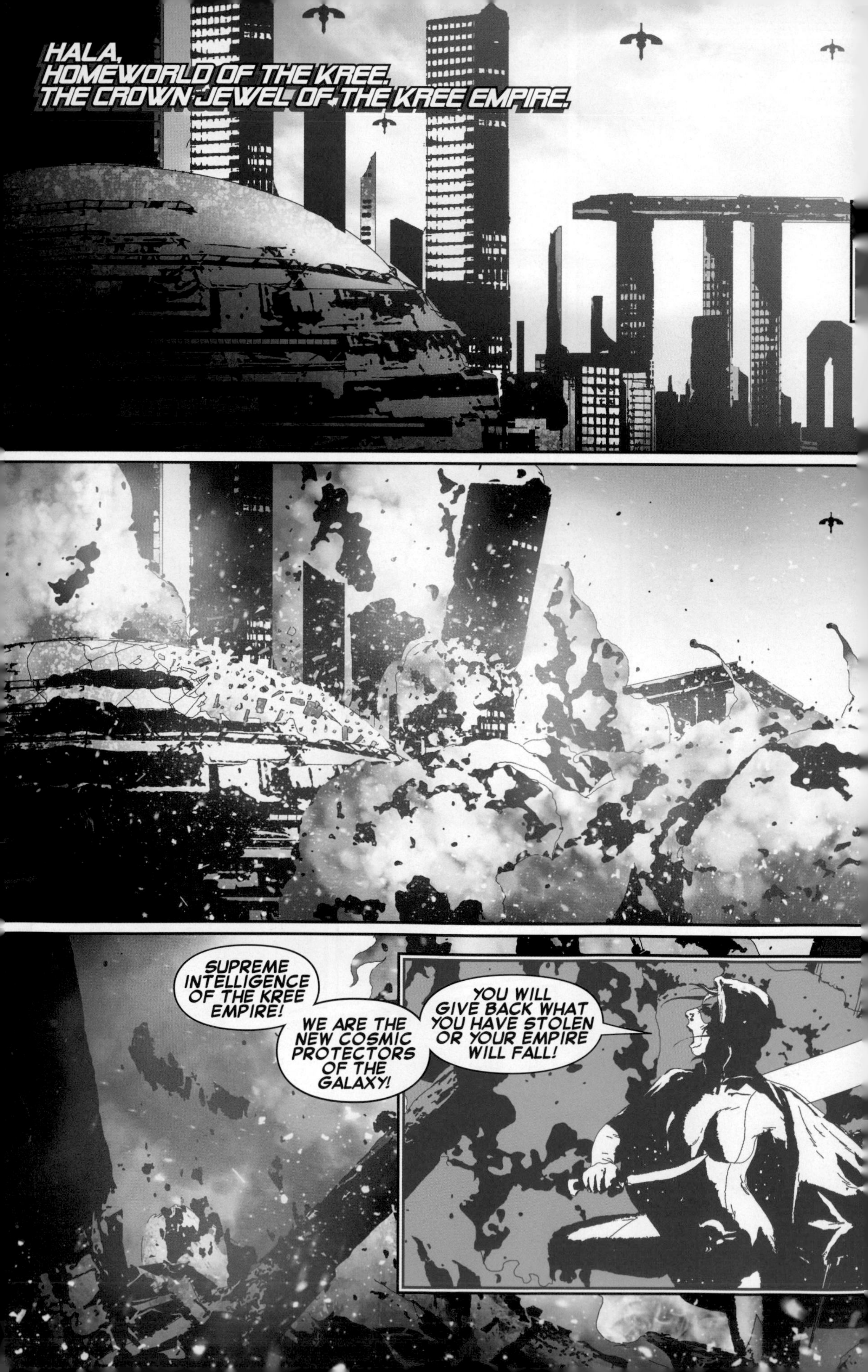
HALA,
HOMEWORLD OF THE KREE.
THE CROWN JEWEL OF THE KREE EMPIRE.
SUPREME INTELLIGENCE OF THE KREE EMPIRE!
WE ARE THE NEW COSMIC PROTECTORS OF THE GALAXY!
YOU WILL GIVE BACK WHAT YOU HAVE STOLEN OR YOUR EMPIRE WILL FALL!

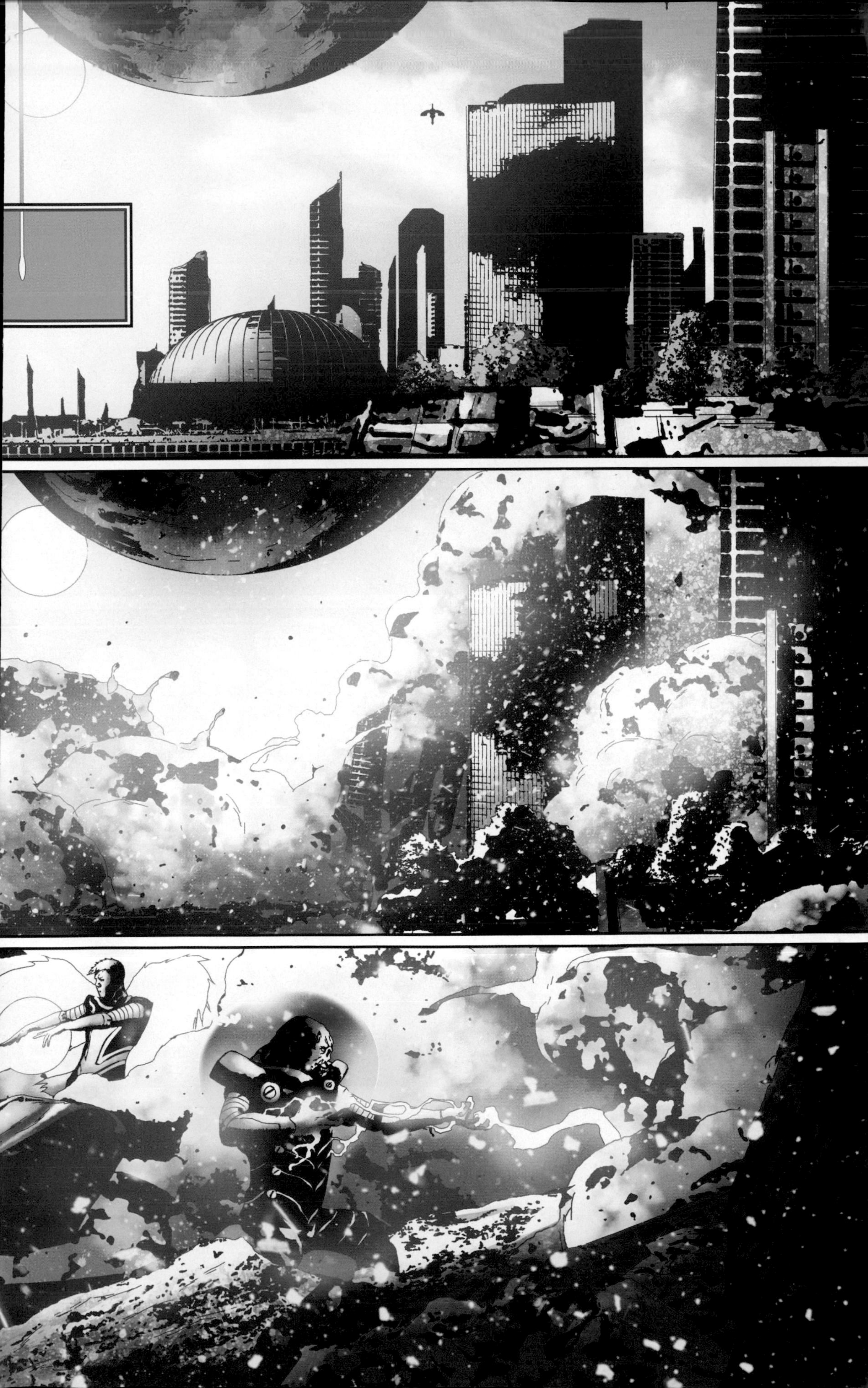

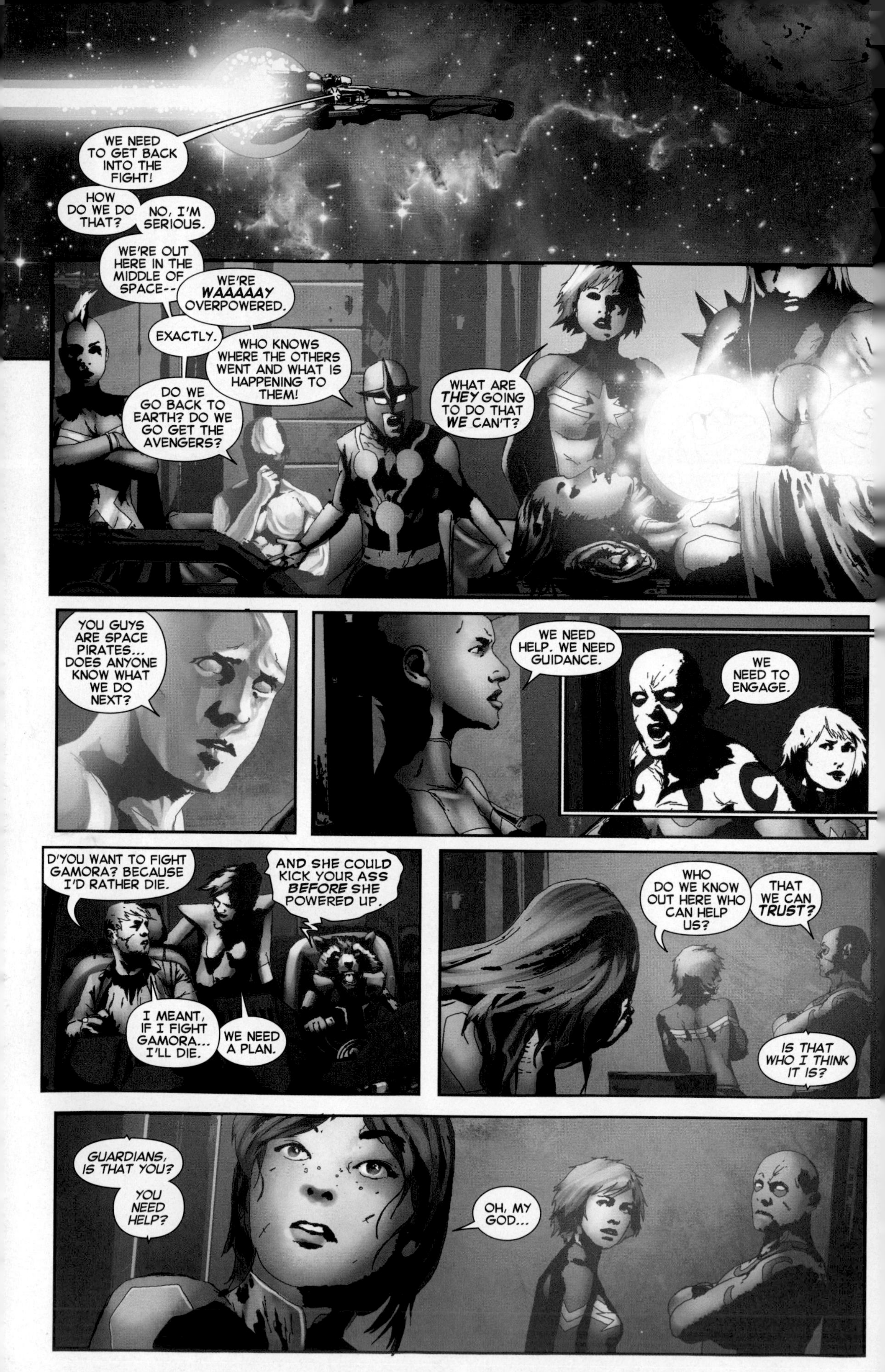
WE NEED TO GET BACK INTO THE FIGHT!
HOW DO WE DO THAT?
NO, I'M SERIOUS.
WE'RE OUT HERE IN THE MIDDLE OF SPACE--
WE'RE WAAAAAY OVERPOWERED.
EXACTLY.
WHO KNOWS WHERE THE OTHERS WENT AND WHAT IS HAPPENING TO THEM!
DO WE GO BACK TO EARTH? DO WE GO GET THE AVENGERS?
WHAT ARE THEY GOING TO DO THAT WE CAN'T?
YOU GUYS ARE SPACE PIRATES... DOES ANYONE KNOW WHAT WE DO NEXT?
WE NEED HELP. WE NEED GUIDANCE.
WE NEED TO ENGAGE.
D'YOU WANT TO FIGHT GAMORA? BECAUSE I'D RATHER DIE.
AND SHE COULD KICK YOUR ASS BEFORE SHE POWERED UP.
I MEANT, IF I FIGHT GAMORA... I'LL DIE.
WE NEED A PLAN.
WHO DO WE KNOW OUT HERE WHO CAN HELP US?
THAT WE CAN TRUST?
IS THAT WHO I THINK IT IS?
GUARDIANS, IS THAT YOU?
YOU NEED HELP?
OH, MY GOD...

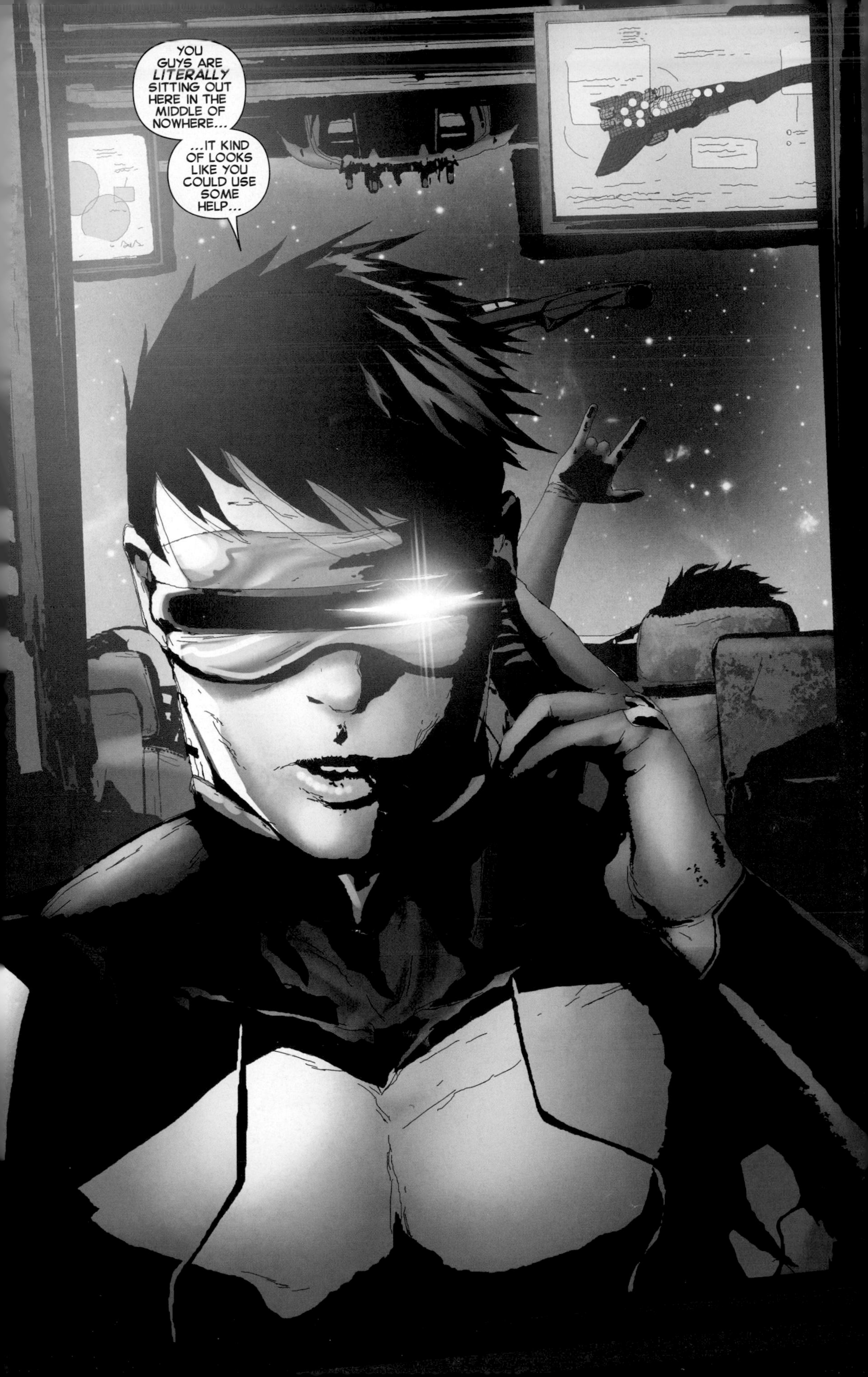
YOU GUYS ARE LITERALLY SITTING OUT HERE IN THE MIDDLE OF NOWHERE...
...IT KIND OF LOOKS LIKE YOU COULD USE SOME HELP...

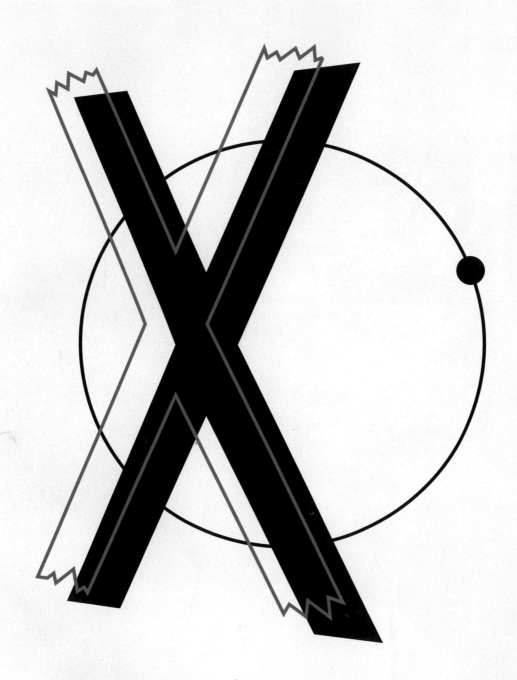

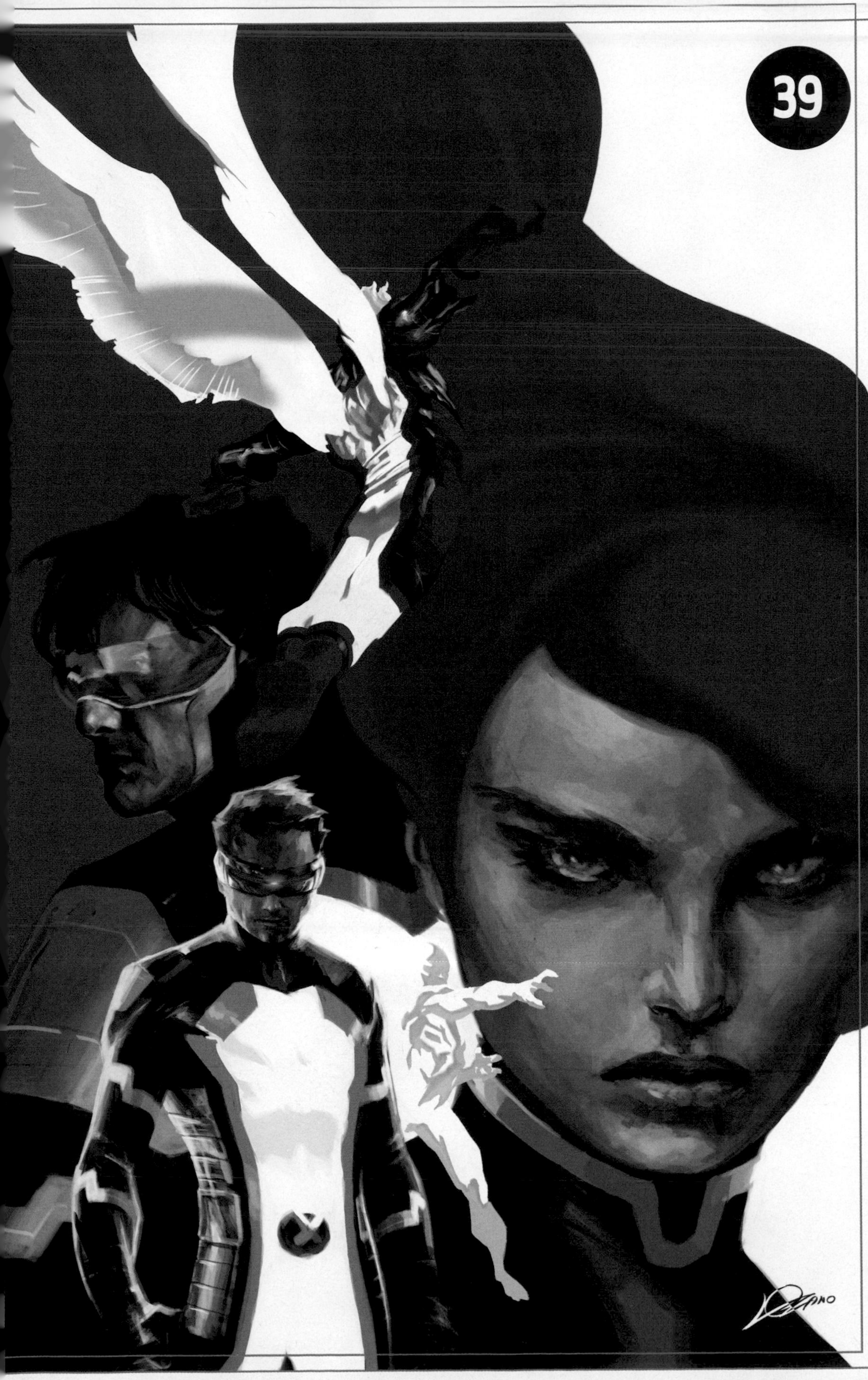
39

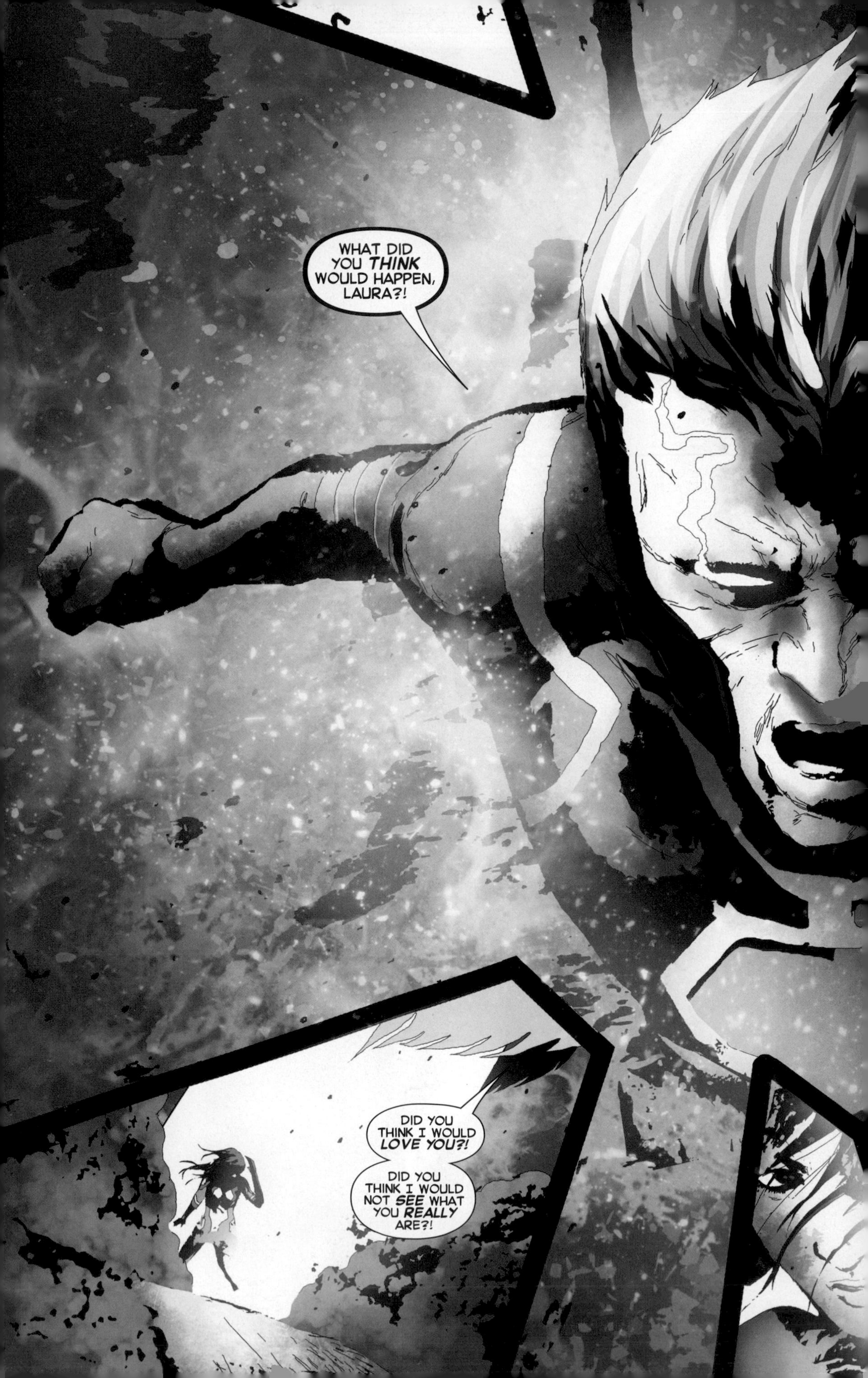
WHAT DID YOU THINK WOULD HAPPEN, LAURA?!
DID YOU THINK I WOULD LOVE YOU?!
DID YOU THINK I WOULD NOT SEE WHAT YOU REALLY ARE?!

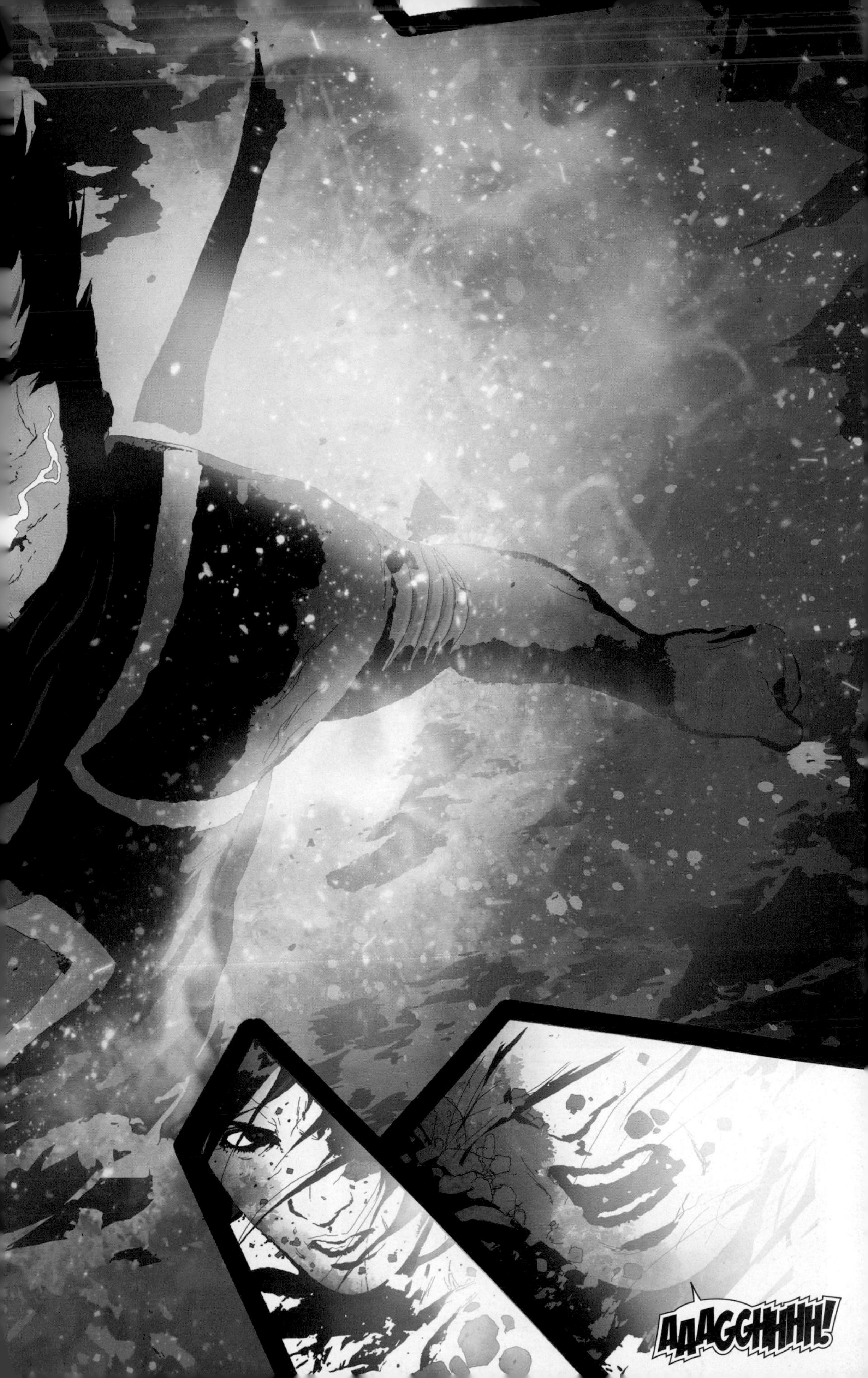
AAAGGHHHH!

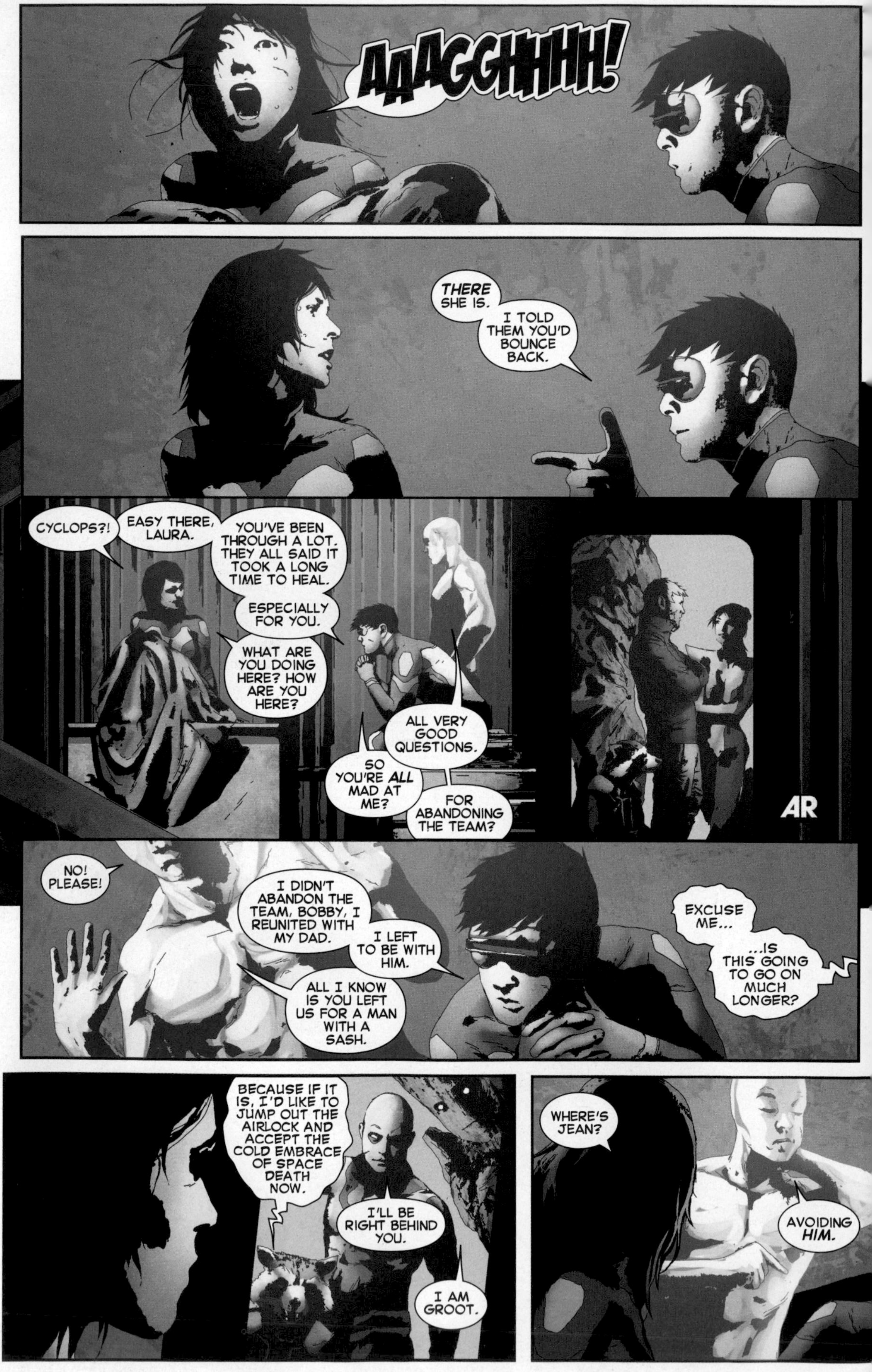
AAAGGHHHH!
THERE SHE IS.
I TOLD THEM YOU'D BOUNCE BACK.
CYCLOPS?!
EASY THERE, LAURA.
YOU'VE BEEN THROUGH A LOT. THEY ALL SAID IT TOOK A LONG TIME TO HEAL.
ESPECIALLY FOR YOU.
WHAT ARE YOU DOING HERE? HOW ARE YOU HERE?
ALL VERY GOOD QUESTIONS.
SO YOU'RE ALL MAD AT ME?
FOR ABANDONING THE TEAM?
AR
NO! PLEASE!
I DIDN'T ABANDON THE TEAM, BOBBY, I REUNITED WITH MY DAD.
I LEFT TO BE WITH HIM.
ALL I KNOW IS YOU LEFT US FOR A MAN WITH A SASH.
EXCUSE ME...
...IS THIS GOING TO GO ON MUCH LONGER?
BECAUSE IF IT IS, I'D LIKE TO JUMP OUT THE AIRLOCK AND ACCEPT THE COLD EMBRACE OF SPACE DEATH NOW.
I'LL BE RIGHT BEHIND YOU.
I AM GROOT.
WHERE'S JEAN?
AVOIDING HIM.

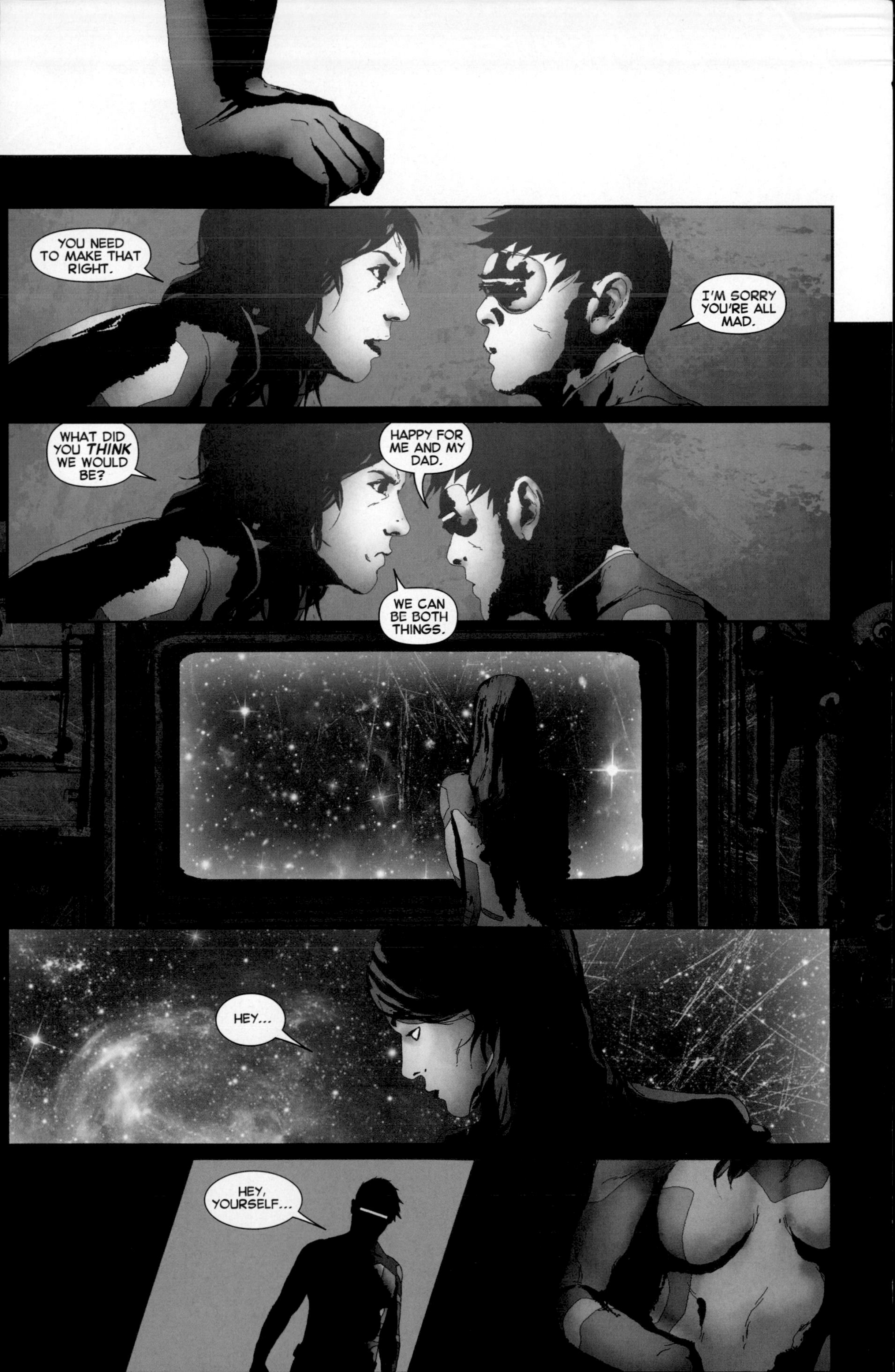
YOU NEED TO MAKE THAT RIGHT.
I'M SORRY YOU'RE ALL MAD.
WHAT DID YOU *THINK* WE WOULD BE?
HAPPY FOR ME AND MY DAD.
WE CAN BE BOTH THINGS.
HEY...
HEY, YOURSELF...

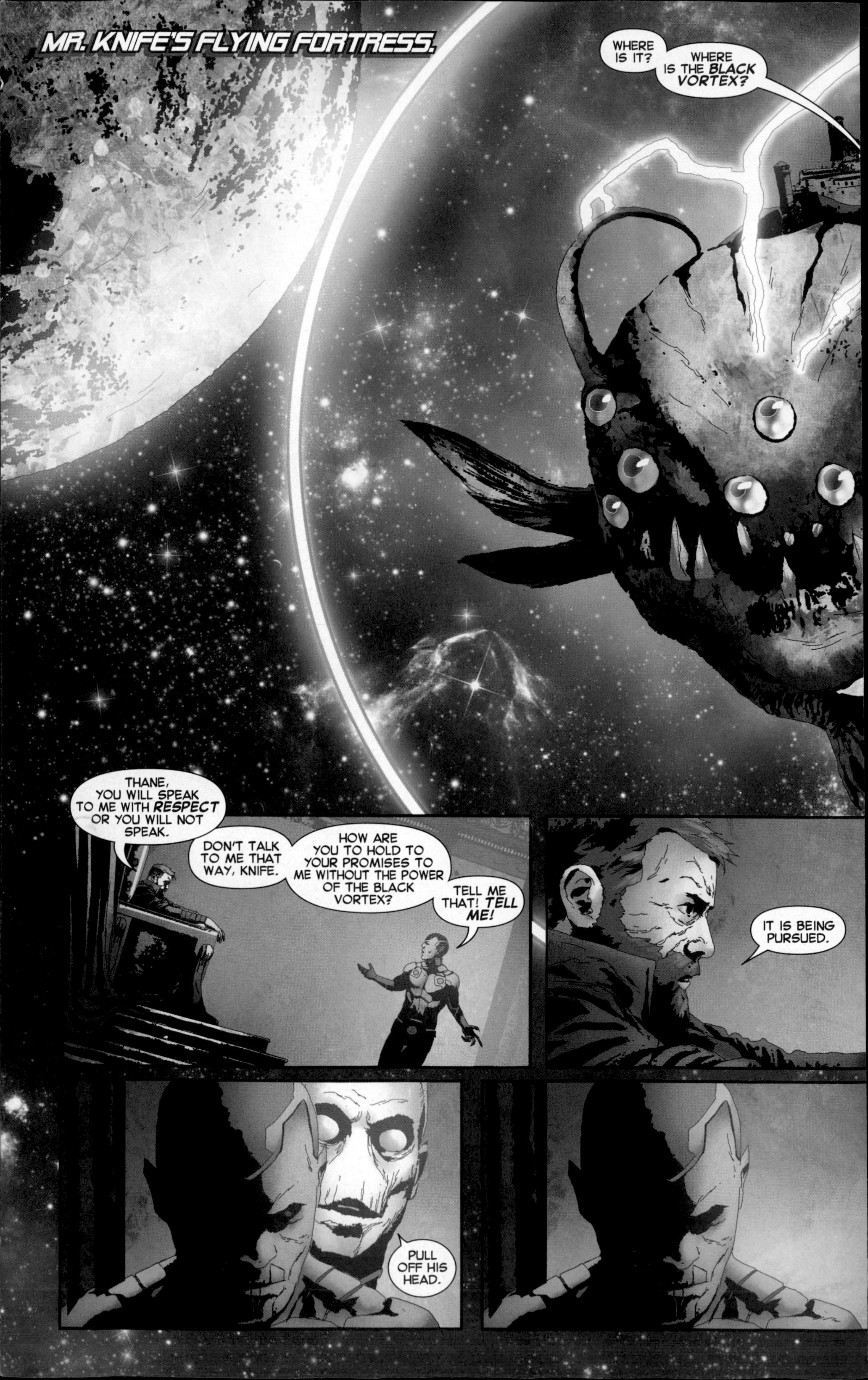
MR. KNIFE'S FLYING FORTRESS.
WHERE IS IT?
WHERE IS THE BLACK VORTEX?
THANE, YOU WILL SPEAK TO ME WITH RESPECT OR YOU WILL NOT SPEAK.
DON'T TALK TO ME THAT WAY, KNIFE.
HOW ARE YOU TO HOLD TO YOUR PROMISES TO ME WITHOUT THE POWER OF THE BLACK VORTEX?
TELL ME THAT! TELL ME!
IT IS BEING PURSUED.
PULL OFF HIS HEAD.

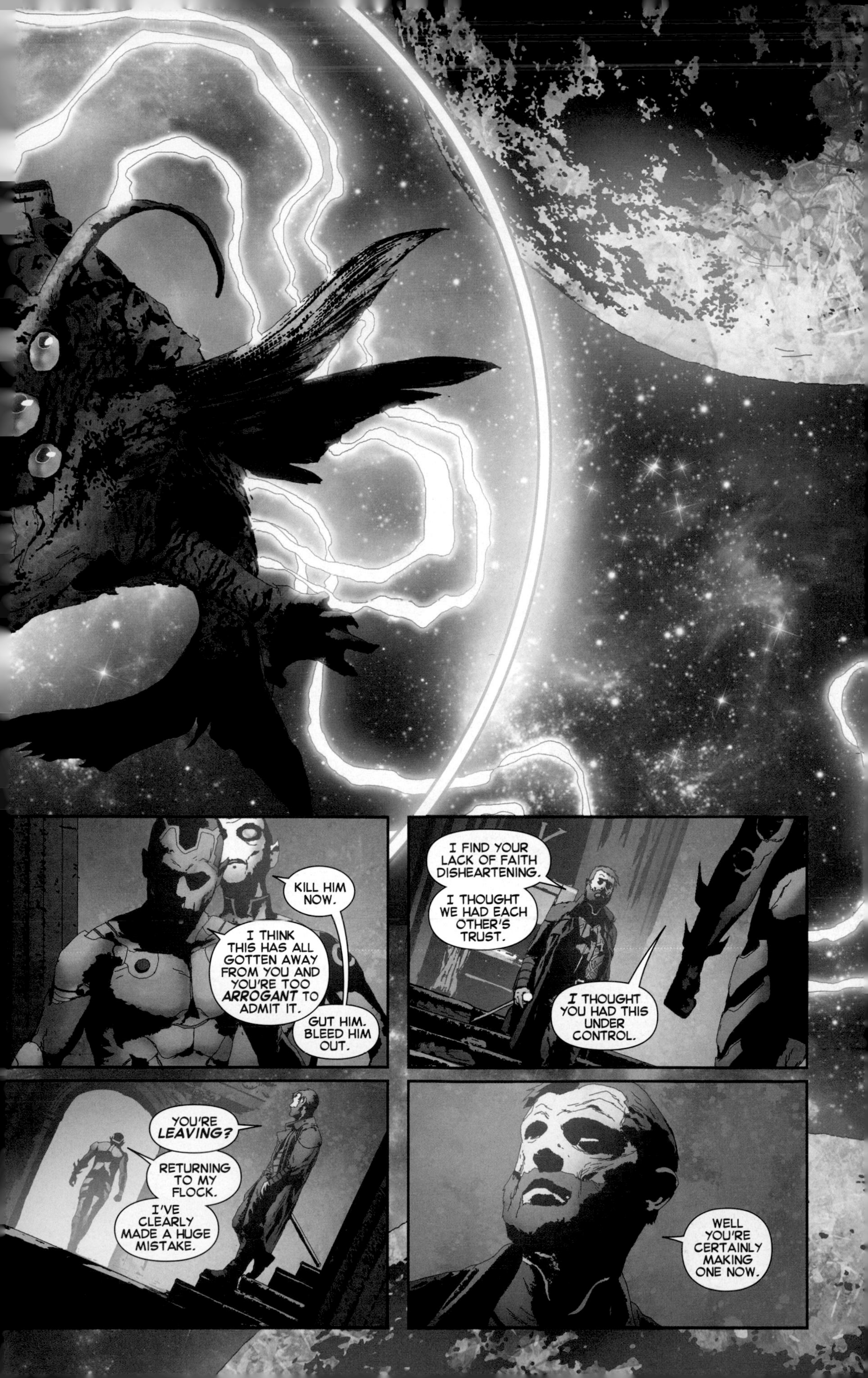

KILL HIM NOW.
I THINK THIS HAS ALL GOTTEN AWAY FROM YOU AND YOU'RE TOO ARROGANT TO ADMIT IT.
GUT HIM. BLEED HIM OUT.
I FIND YOUR LACK OF FAITH DISHEARTENING.
I THOUGHT WE HAD EACH OTHER'S TRUST.
I THOUGHT YOU HAD THIS UNDER CONTROL.
YOU'RE LEAVING?
RETURNING TO MY FLOCK.
I'VE CLEARLY MADE A HUGE MISTAKE.
WELL YOU'RE CERTAINLY MAKING ONE NOW.

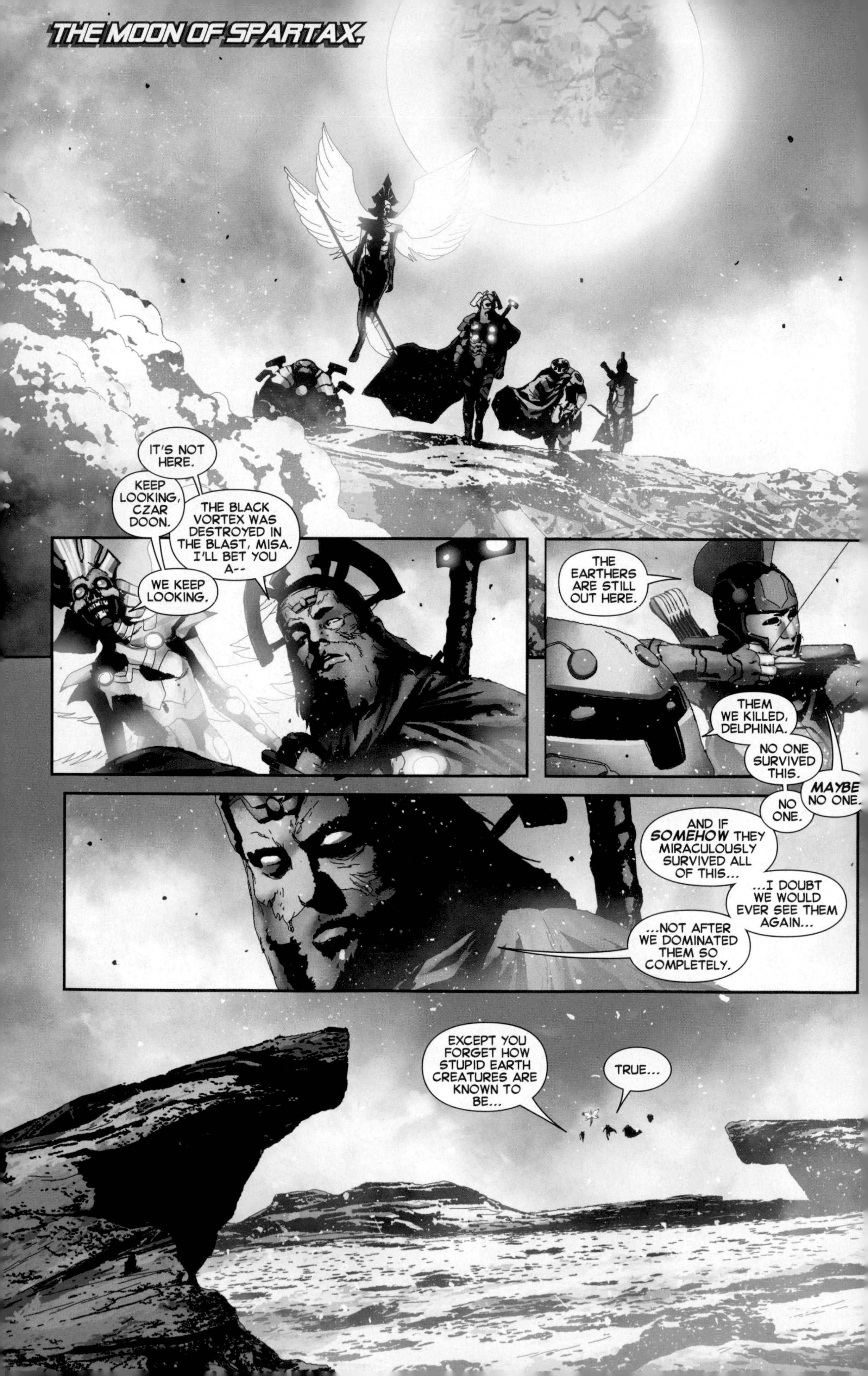
THE MOON OF SPARTAX.
IT'S NOT HERE.
KEEP LOOKING, CZAR DOON.
THE BLACK VORTEX WAS DESTROYED IN THE BLAST, MISA. I'LL BET YOU A--
WE KEEP LOOKING.
THE EARTHERS ARE STILL OUT HERE.
THEM WE KILLED, DELPHINIA.
NO ONE SURVIVED THIS.
NO ONE.
MAYBE NO ONE.
AND IF SOMEHOW THEY MIRACULOUSLY SURVIVED ALL OF THIS...
...I DOUBT WE WOULD EVER SEE THEM AGAIN...
...NOT AFTER WE DOMINATED THEM SO COMPLETELY.
EXCEPT YOU FORGET HOW STUPID EARTH CREATURES ARE KNOWN TO BE...
TRUE...

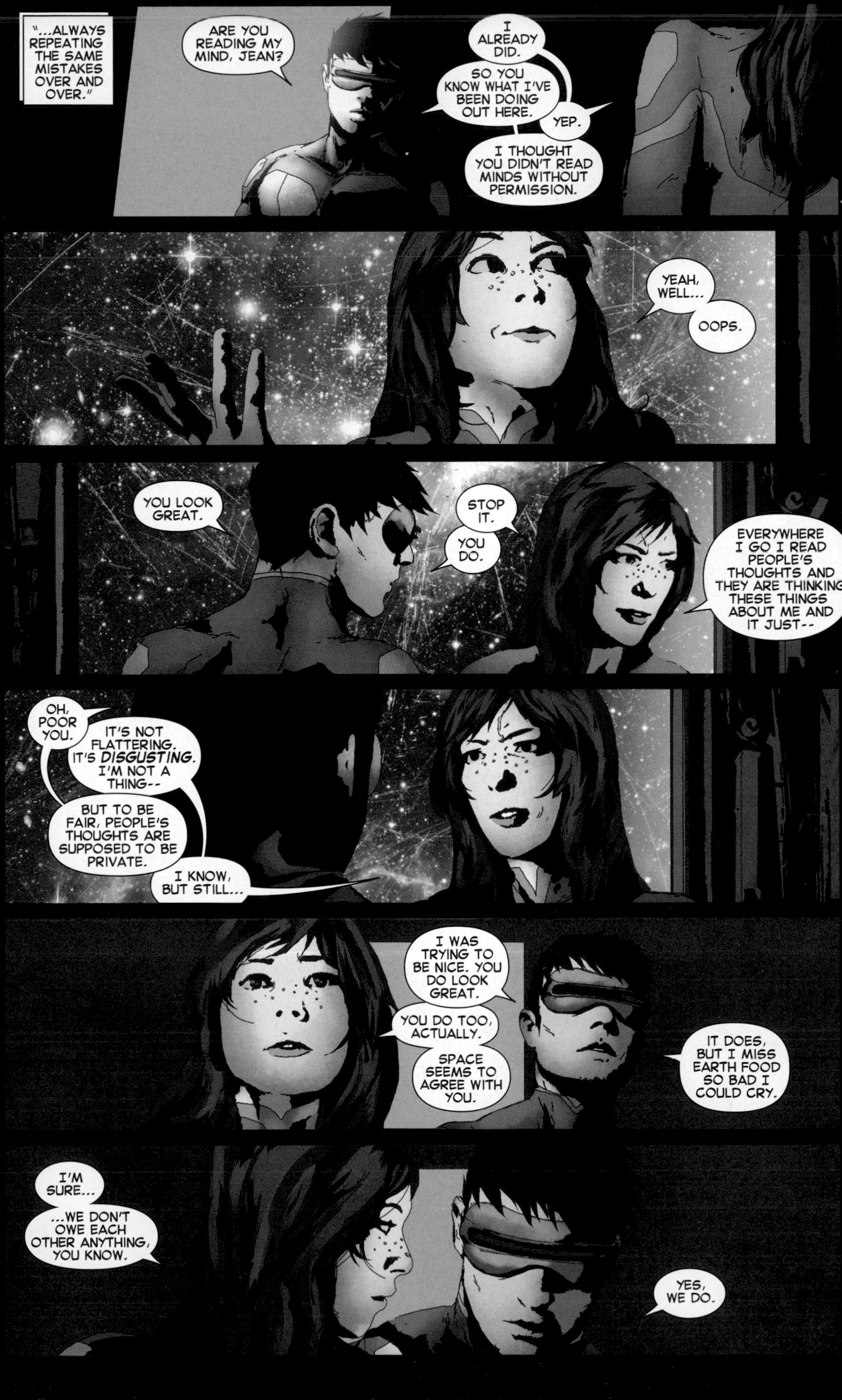
"...ALWAYS REPEATING THE SAME MISTAKES OVER AND OVER."
ARE YOU READING MY MIND, JEAN?
I ALREADY DID.
SO YOU KNOW WHAT I'VE BEEN DOING OUT HERE.
YEP.
I THOUGHT YOU DIDN'T READ MINDS WITHOUT PERMISSION.
YEAH, WELL...
OOPS.
YOU LOOK GREAT.
STOP IT.
YOU DO.
EVERYWHERE I GO I READ PEOPLE'S THOUGHTS AND THEY ARE THINKING THESE THINGS ABOUT ME AND IT JUST--
OH, POOR YOU.
IT'S NOT FLATTERING. IT'S *DISGUSTING*. I'M NOT A THING--
BUT TO BE FAIR, PEOPLE'S THOUGHTS ARE SUPPOSED TO BE PRIVATE.
I KNOW, BUT STILL...
I WAS TRYING TO BE NICE. YOU DO LOOK GREAT.
YOU DO TOO, ACTUALLY.
SPACE SEEMS TO AGREE WITH YOU.
IT DOES, BUT I MISS EARTH FOOD SO BAD I COULD CRY.
I'M SURE...
...WE DON'T OWE EACH OTHER ANYTHING, YOU KNOW.
YES, WE DO.

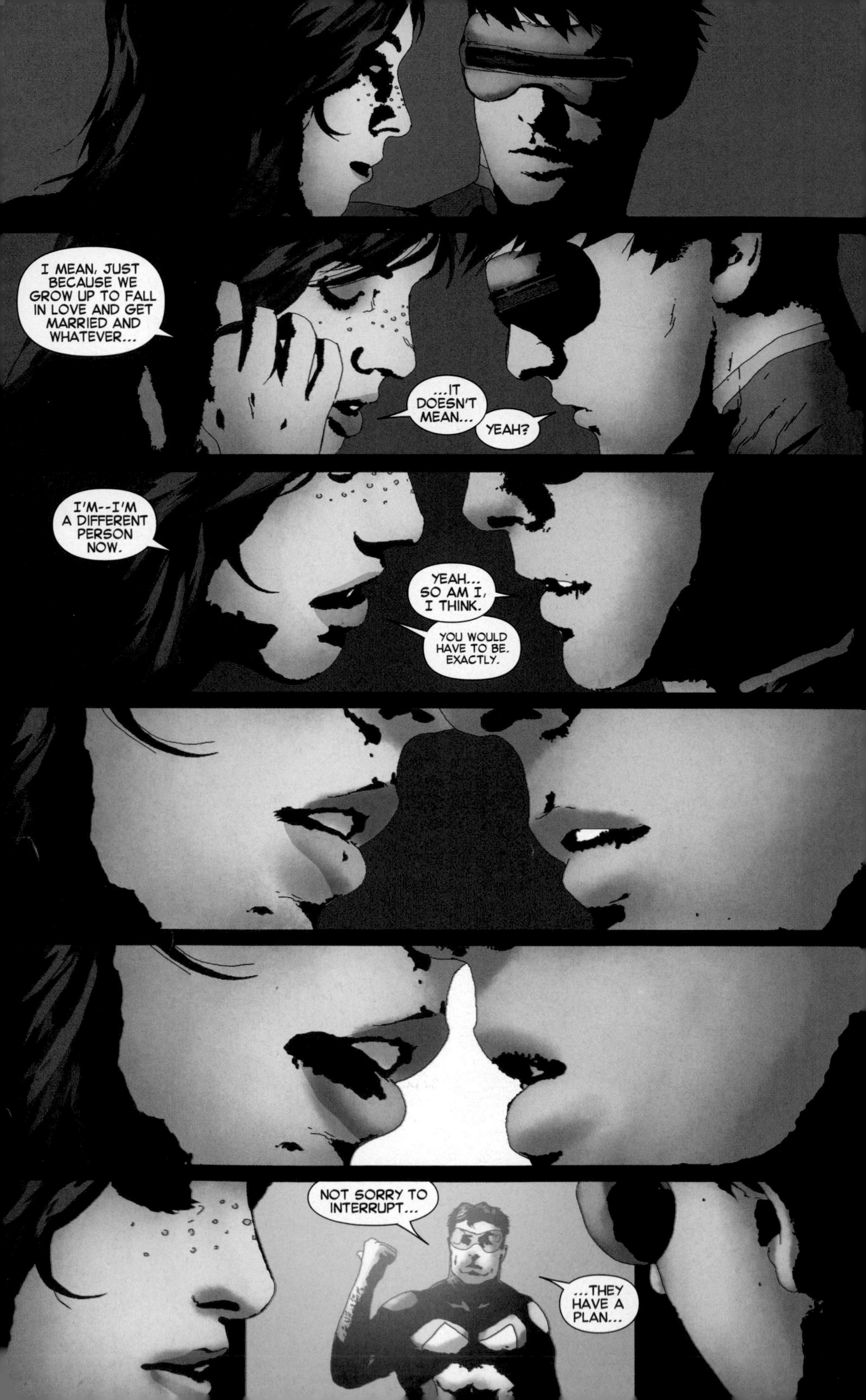

I MEAN, JUST BECAUSE WE GROW UP TO FALL IN LOVE AND GET MARRIED AND WHATEVER...
...IT DOESN'T MEAN...
YEAH?
I'M--I'M A DIFFERENT PERSON NOW.
YEAH... SO AM I, I THINK.
YOU WOULD HAVE TO BE. EXACTLY.
NOT SORRY TO INTERRUPT...
...THEY HAVE A PLAN...

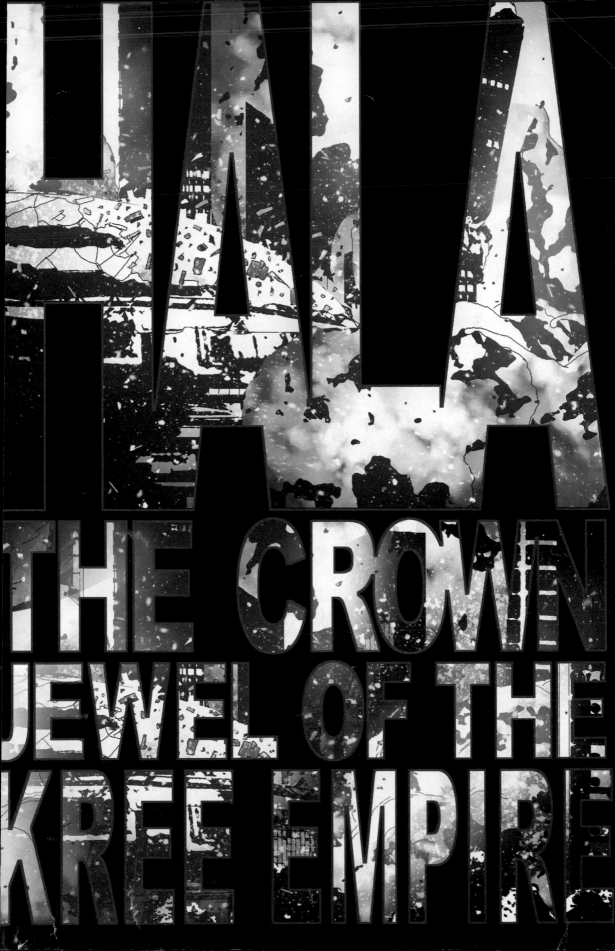

HALA
THE CROWN
JEWEL OF THE
KREE EMPIRE

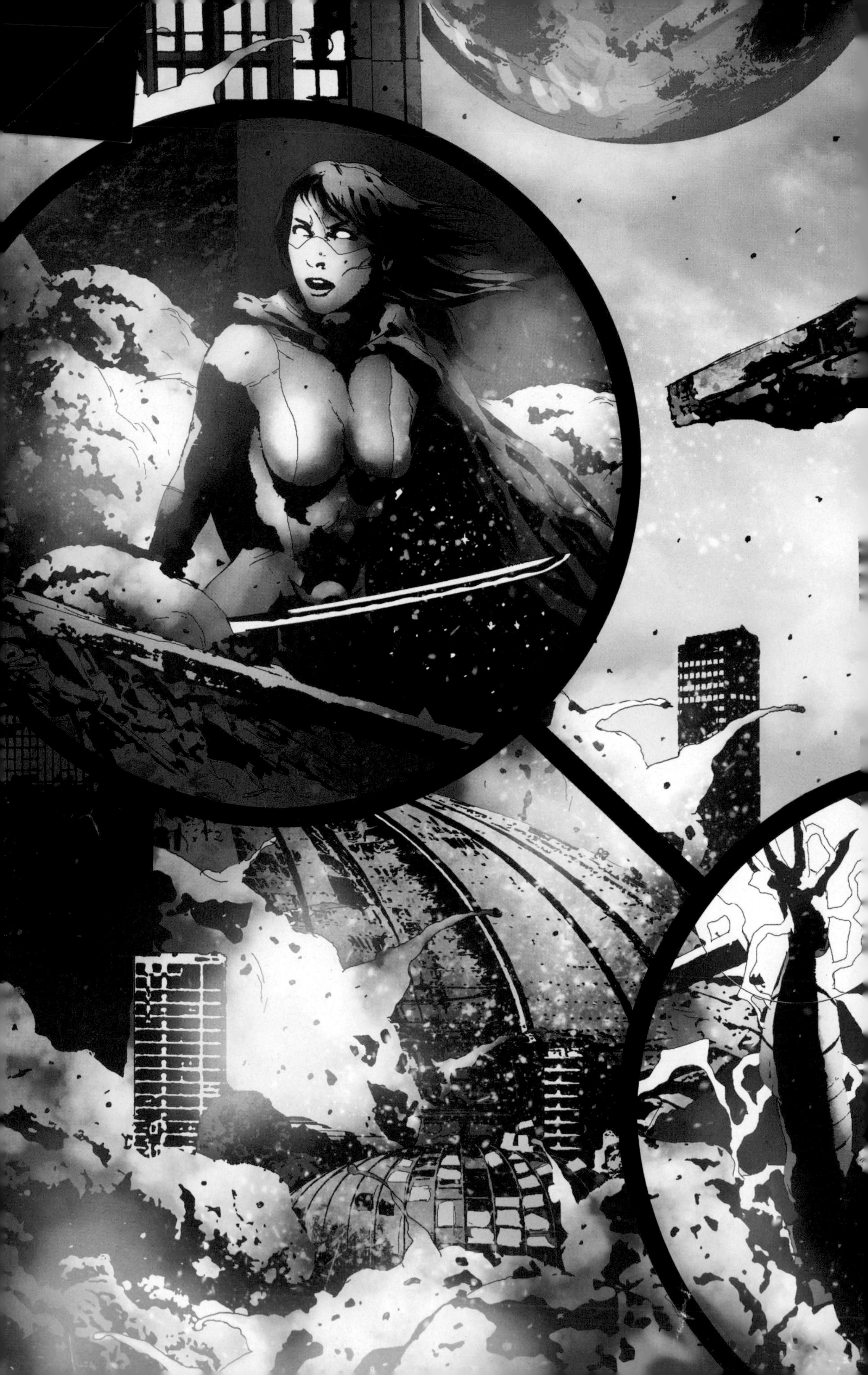

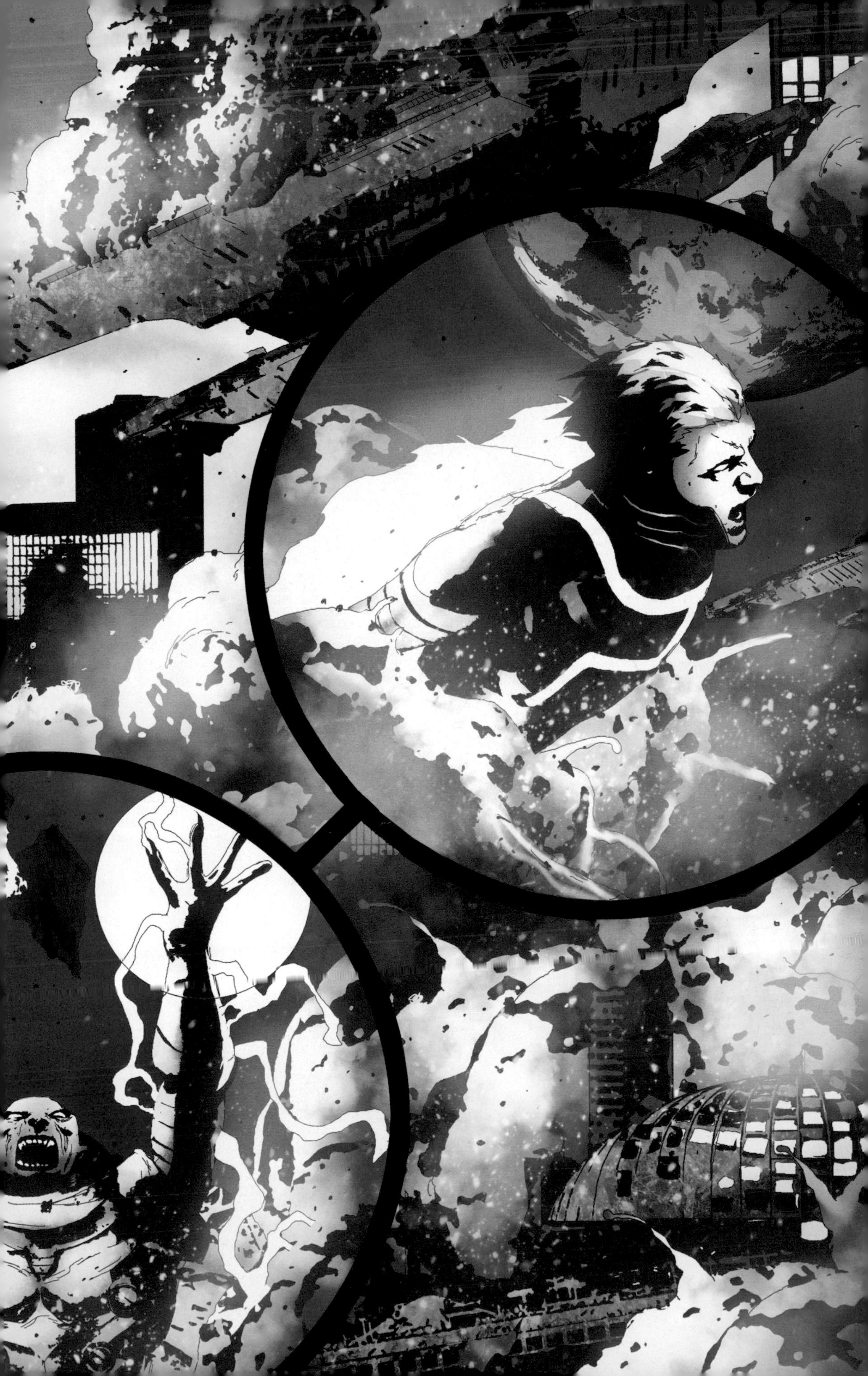

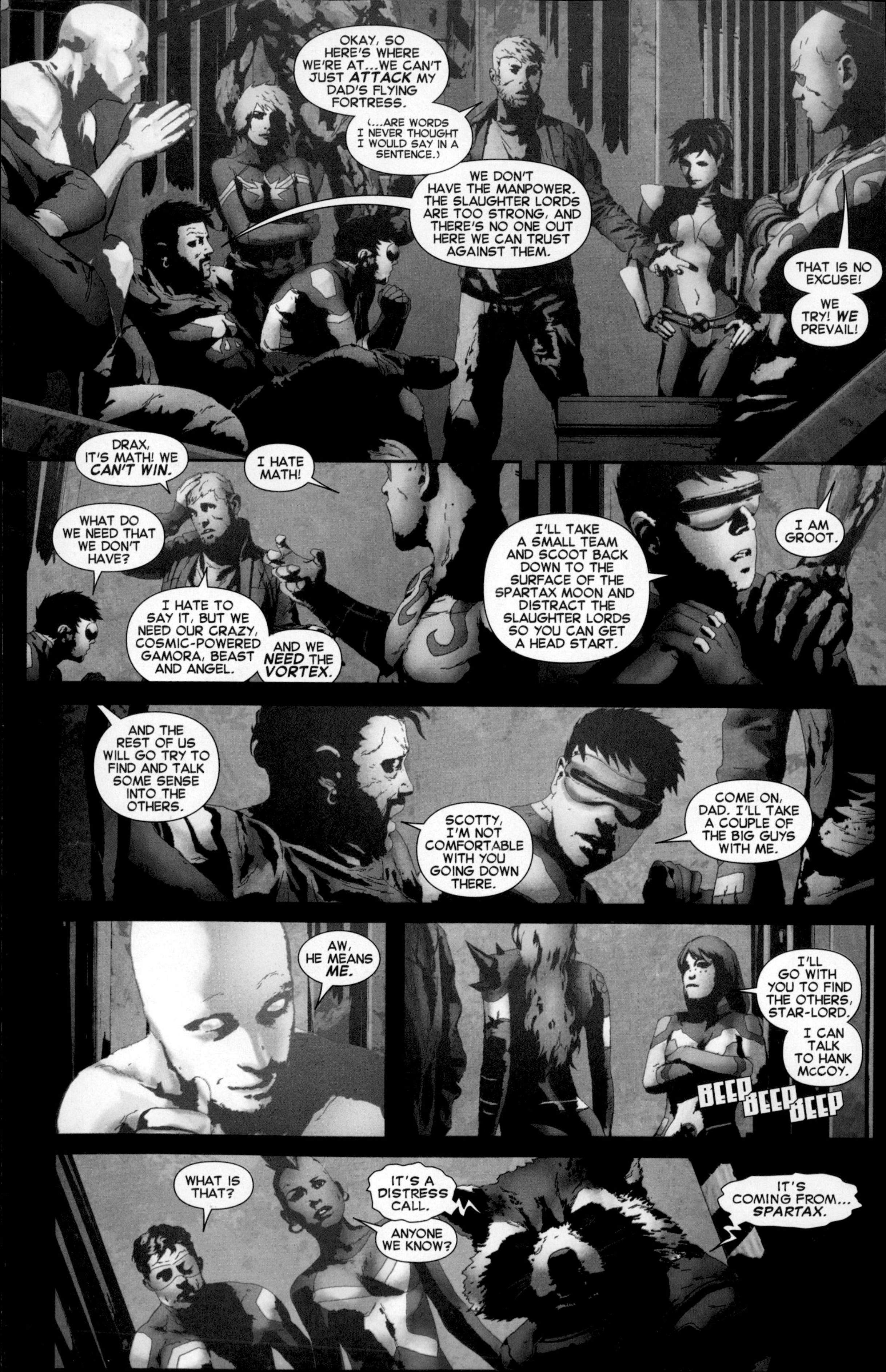
OKAY, SO HERE'S WHERE WE'RE AT...WE CAN'T JUST ATTACK MY DAD'S FLYING FORTRESS.
(...ARE WORDS I NEVER THOUGHT I WOULD SAY IN A SENTENCE.)
WE DON'T HAVE THE MANPOWER. THE SLAUGHTER LORDS ARE TOO STRONG, AND THERE'S NO ONE OUT HERE WE CAN TRUST AGAINST THEM.
THAT IS NO EXCUSE!
WE TRY! WE PREVAIL!
DRAX, IT'S MATH! WE CAN'T WIN.
I HATE MATH!
WHAT DO WE NEED THAT WE DON'T HAVE?
I HATE TO SAY IT, BUT WE NEED OUR CRAZY, COSMIC-POWERED GAMORA, BEAST AND ANGEL.
AND WE NEED THE VORTEX.
I AM GROOT.
I'LL TAKE A SMALL TEAM AND SCOOT BACK DOWN TO THE SURFACE OF THE SPARTAX MOON AND DISTRACT THE SLAUGHTER LORDS SO YOU CAN GET A HEAD START.
AND THE REST OF US WILL GO TRY TO FIND AND TALK SOME SENSE INTO THE OTHERS.
SCOTTY, I'M NOT COMFORTABLE WITH YOU GOING DOWN THERE.
COME ON, DAD. I'LL TAKE A COUPLE OF THE BIG GUYS WITH ME.
AW, HE MEANS ME.
I'LL GO WITH YOU TO FIND THE OTHERS, STAR-LORD.
I CAN TALK TO HANK McCOY.
BEEP BEEP BEEP
WHAT IS THAT?
IT'S A DISTRESS CALL.
ANYONE WE KNOW?
IT'S COMING FROM... SPARTAX.

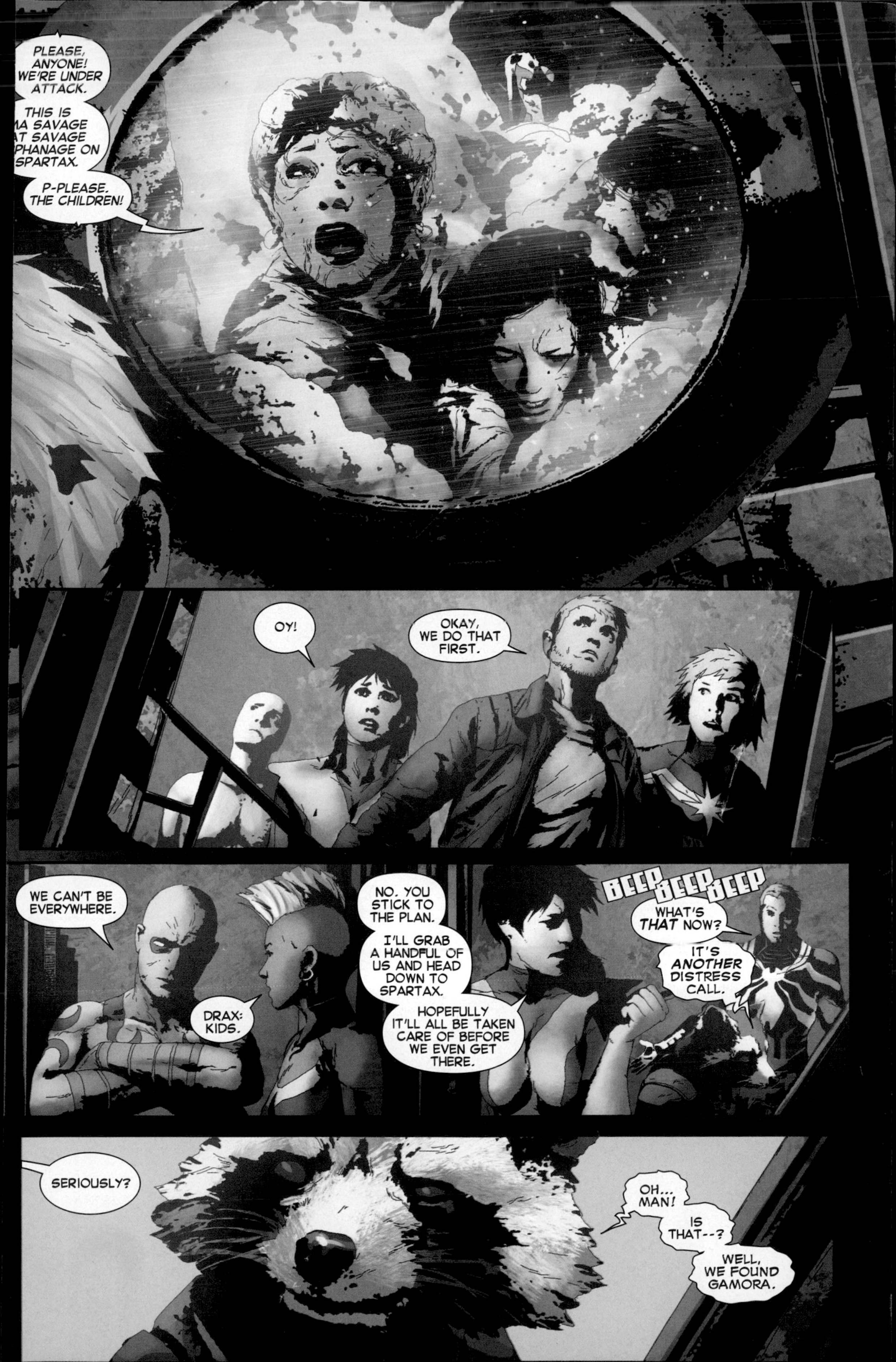

PLEASE, ANYONE! WE'RE UNDER ATTACK.
THIS IS MA SAVAGE AT SAVAGE PHANAGE ON SPARTAX.
P-PLEASE. THE CHILDREN!
OY!
OKAY, WE DO THAT FIRST.
WE CAN'T BE EVERYWHERE.
DRAX: KIDS.
NO. YOU STICK TO THE PLAN.
I'LL GRAB A HANDFUL OF US AND HEAD DOWN TO SPARTAX.
HOPEFULLY IT'LL ALL BE TAKEN CARE OF BEFORE WE EVEN GET THERE.
BEEP BEEP BEEP
WHAT'S *THAT* NOW?
IT'S *ANOTHER* DISTRESS CALL.
SERIOUSLY?
OH... MAN!
IS THAT--?
WELL, WE FOUND GAMORA.

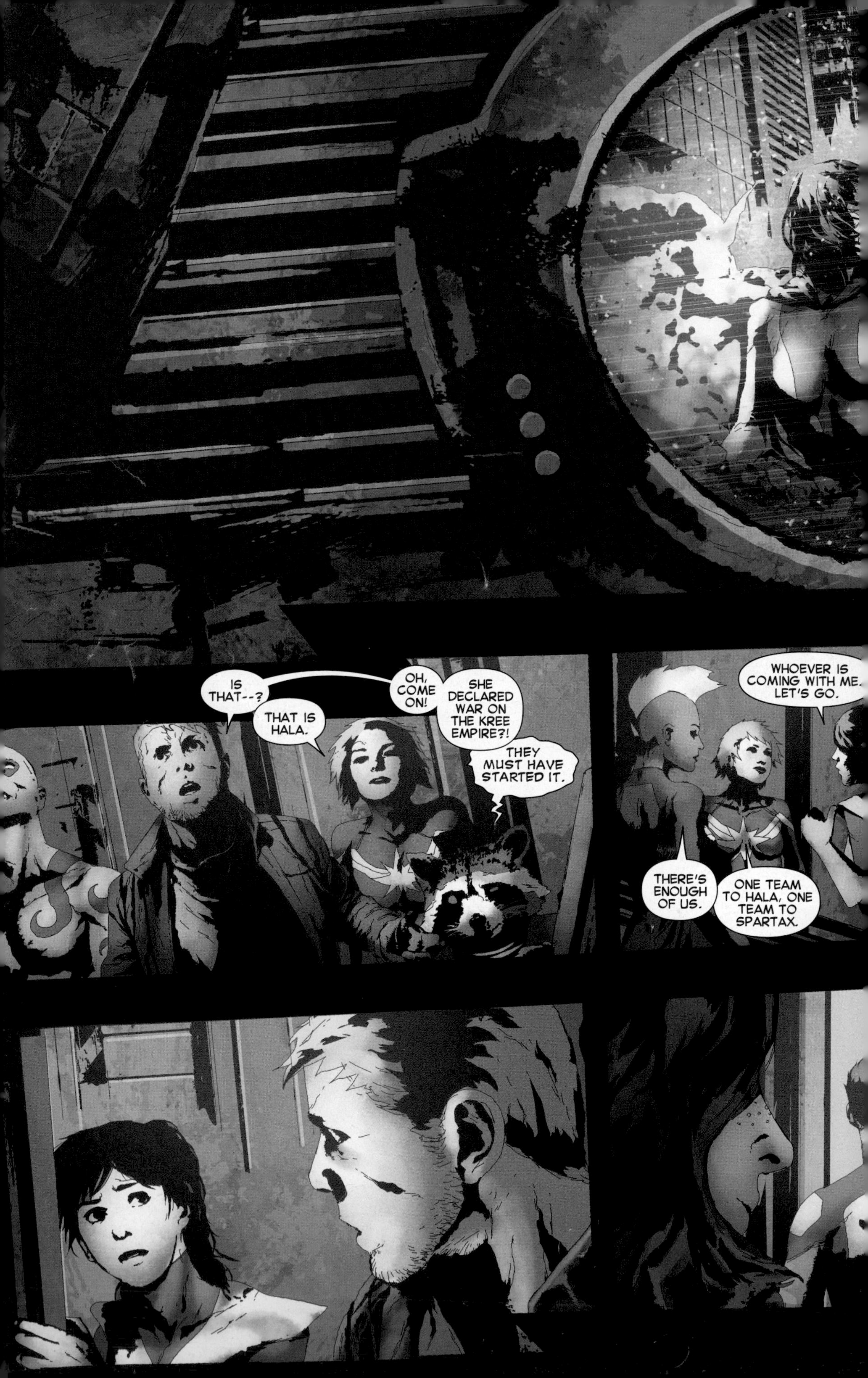
IS THAT--?
OH, COME ON!
THAT IS HALA.
SHE DECLARED WAR ON THE KREE EMPIRE?!
THEY MUST HAVE STARTED IT.
WHOEVER IS COMING WITH ME. LET'S GO.
THERE'S ENOUGH OF US.
ONE TEAM TO HALA, ONE TEAM TO SPARTAX.

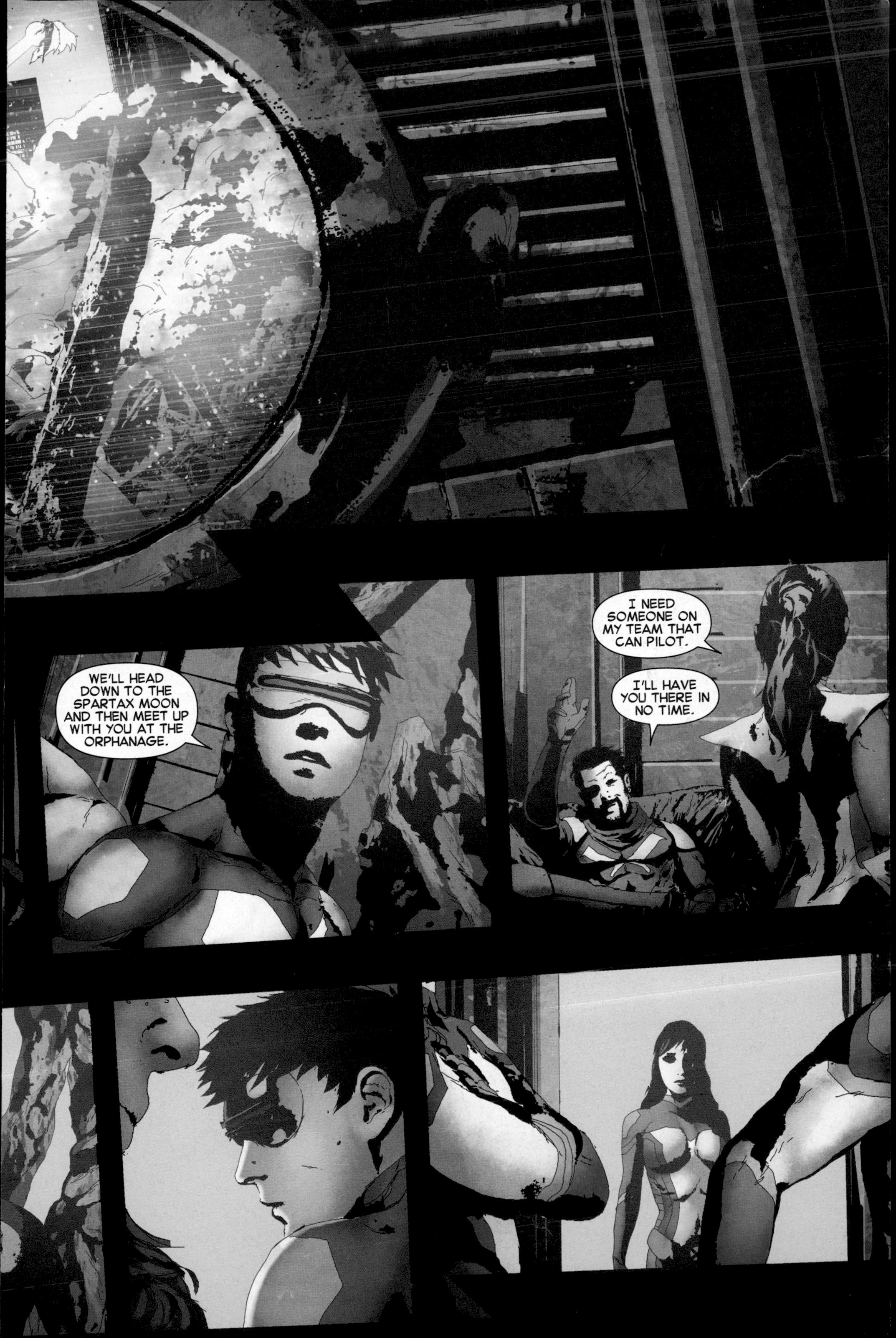
WE'LL HEAD DOWN TO THE SPARTAX MOON AND THEN MEET UP WITH YOU AT THE ORPHANAGE.
I NEED SOMEONE ON MY TEAM THAT CAN PILOT.
I'LL HAVE YOU THERE IN NO TIME.

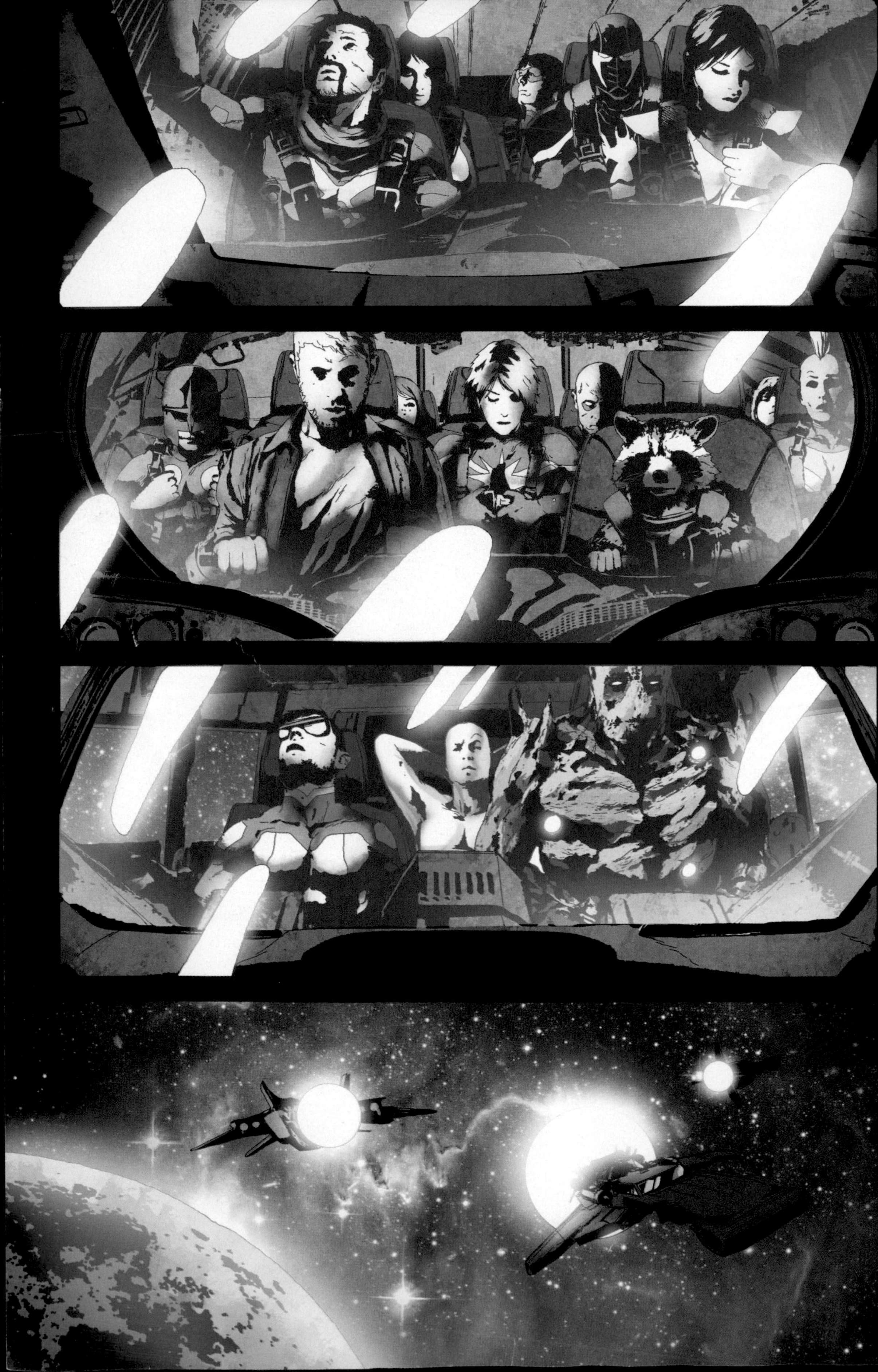

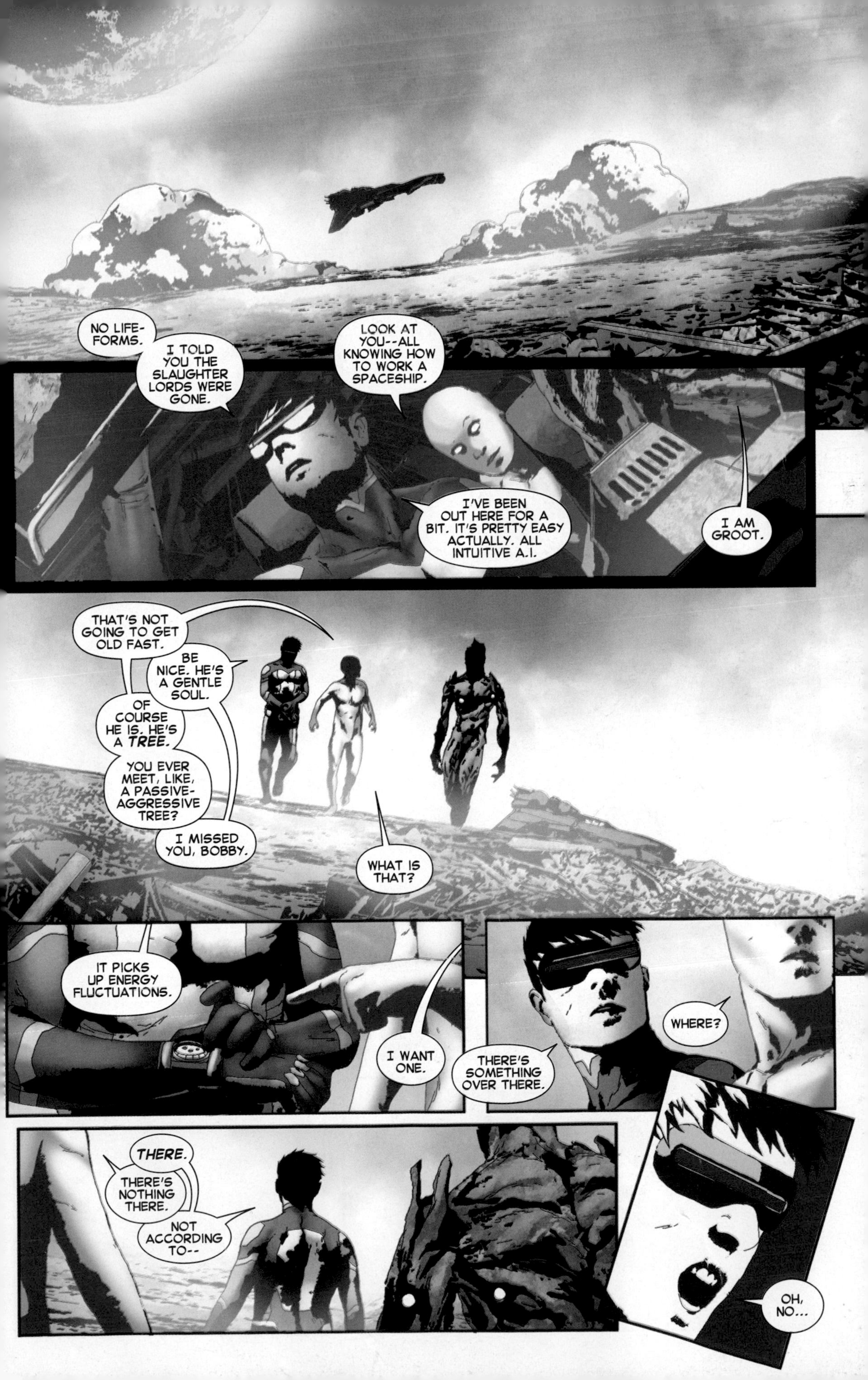
NO LIFE-FORMS.
I TOLD YOU THE SLAUGHTER LORDS WERE GONE.
LOOK AT YOU--ALL KNOWING HOW TO WORK A SPACESHIP.
I'VE BEEN OUT HERE FOR A BIT. IT'S PRETTY EASY ACTUALLY. ALL INTUITIVE A.I.
I AM GROOT.
THAT'S NOT GOING TO GET OLD FAST.
BE NICE. HE'S A GENTLE SOUL.
OF COURSE HE IS. HE'S A *TREE.*
YOU EVER MEET, LIKE, A PASSIVE-AGGRESSIVE TREE?
I MISSED YOU, BOBBY.
WHAT IS THAT?
IT PICKS UP ENERGY FLUCTUATIONS.
I WANT ONE.
THERE'S SOMETHING OVER THERE.
WHERE?
THERE.
THERE'S NOTHING THERE.
NOT ACCORDING TO--
OH, NO...

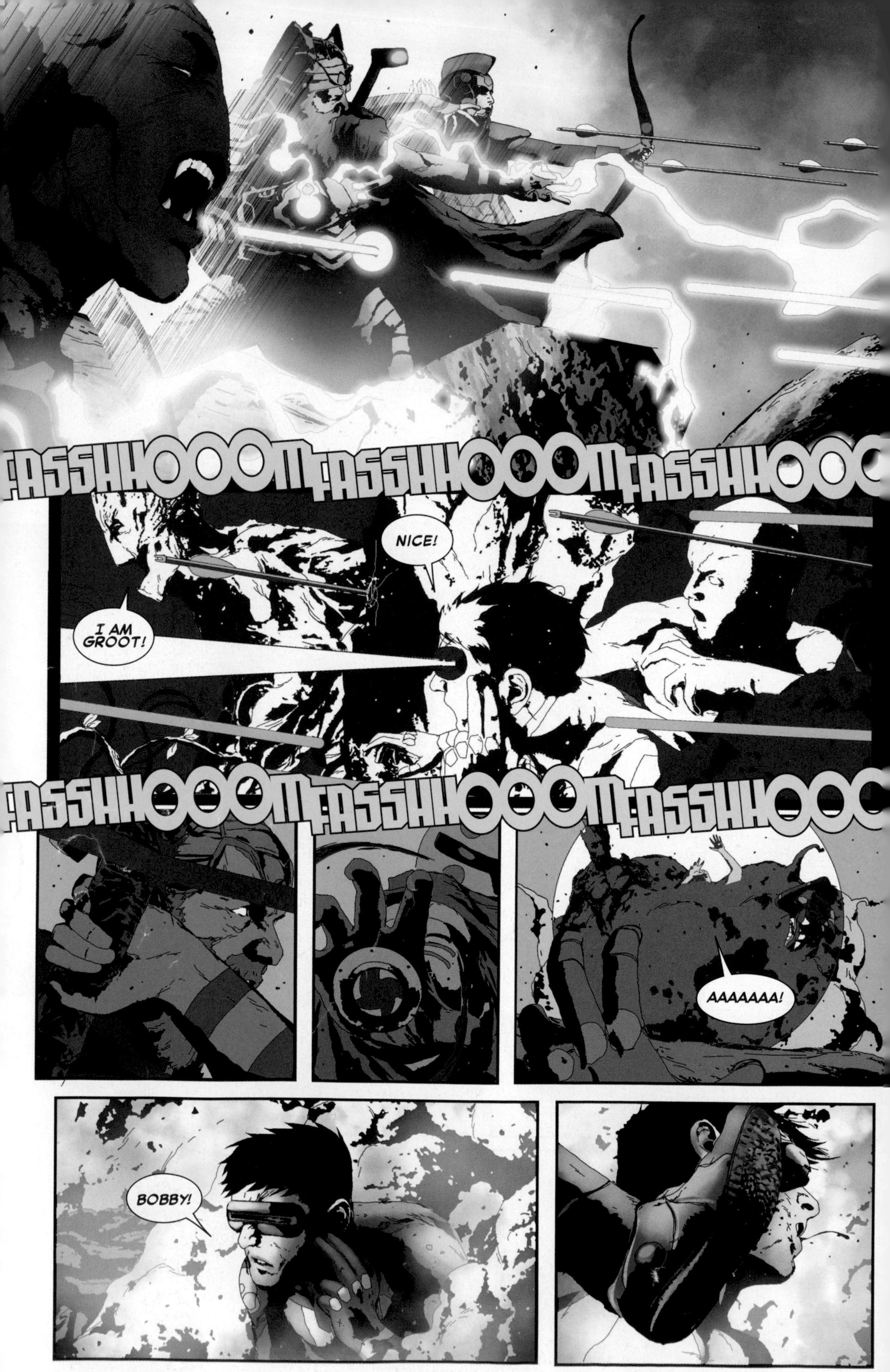
FASSHHOOOM FASSHHOOOM FASSHHOOO
NICE!
I AM GROOT!
FASSHHOOOM FASSHHOOOM FASSHHOOO
AAAAAAA!
BOBBY!

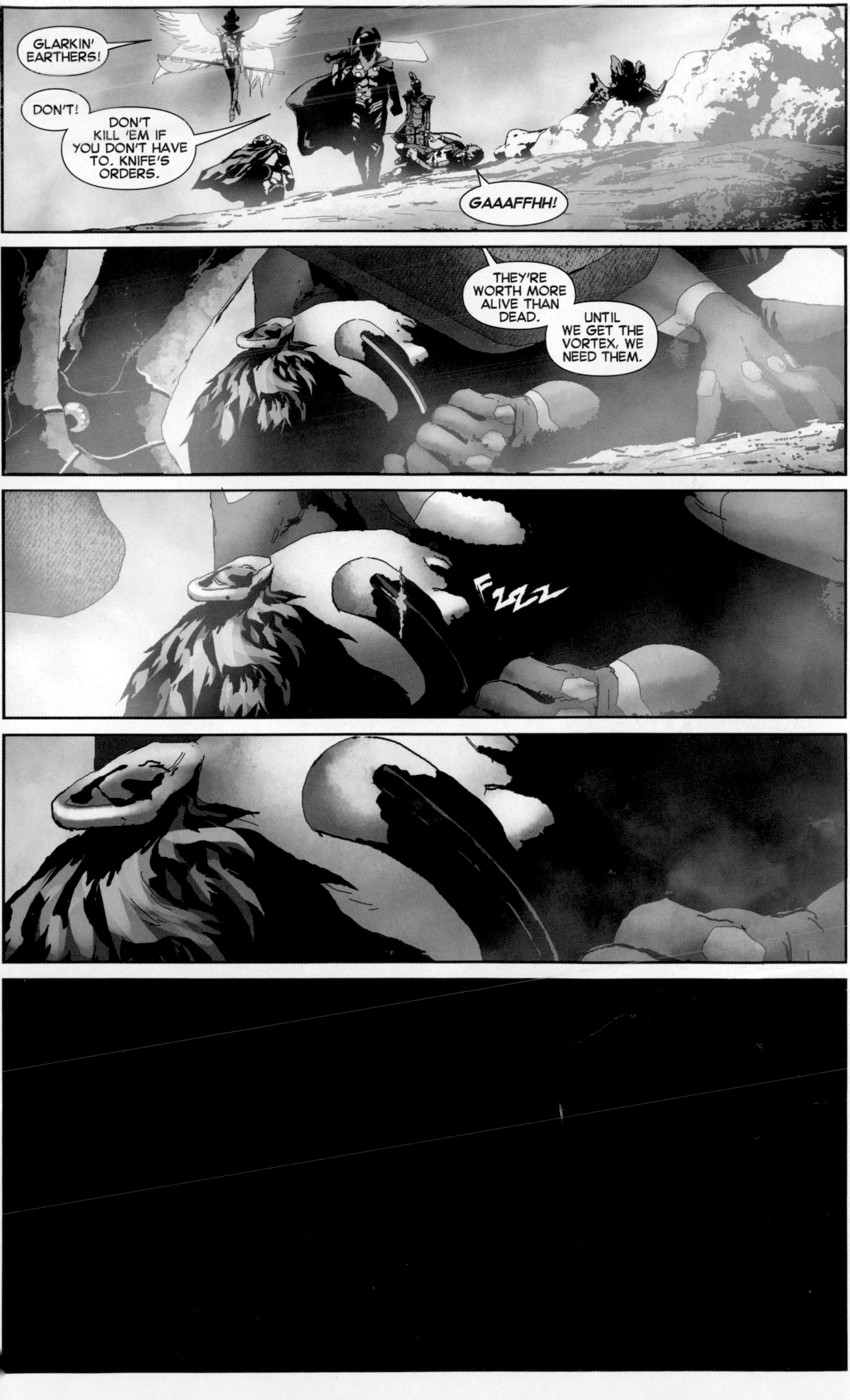
GLARKIN' EARTHERS!
DON'T!
DON'T KILL 'EM IF YOU DON'T HAVE TO. KNIFE'S ORDERS.
GAAAFFHH!
THEY'RE WORTH MORE ALIVE THAN DEAD.
UNTIL WE GET THE VORTEX, WE NEED THEM.
FZZZ

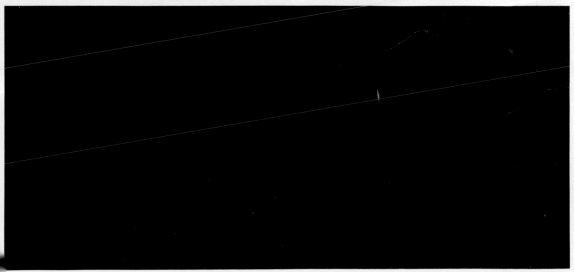

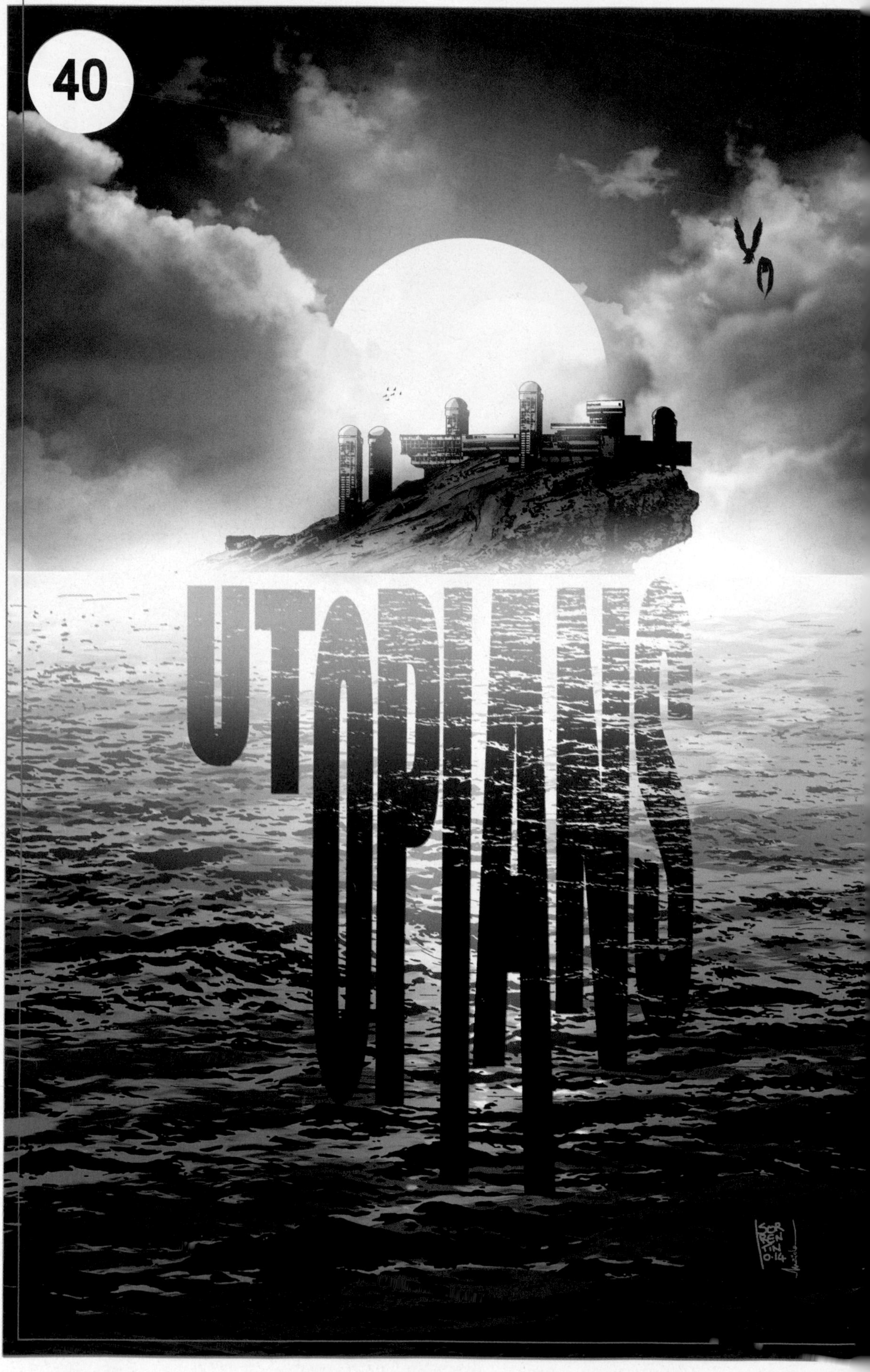
40
UTOPIANS
SOR REN TIN O·14

Since arriving in the present, the original X-Men have been hunted, jailed, divided and spurned by their own people. They have traveled the cosmos, been trapped in alternate dimensions and faced down the threat of death again and again. Despite this, they have remained strong, and it seems this "present" is finally beginning to feel like a place where they belong.

Their experience with the cosmically powered Black Vortex may have served to reunite Scott with his team, but it undoubtedly left its effects on the young teammates. Though how deeply they were each affected is still left to be seen.

It's a time of new beginnings for the All-New X-Men...and it is up to them to determine what they do with the opportunity.

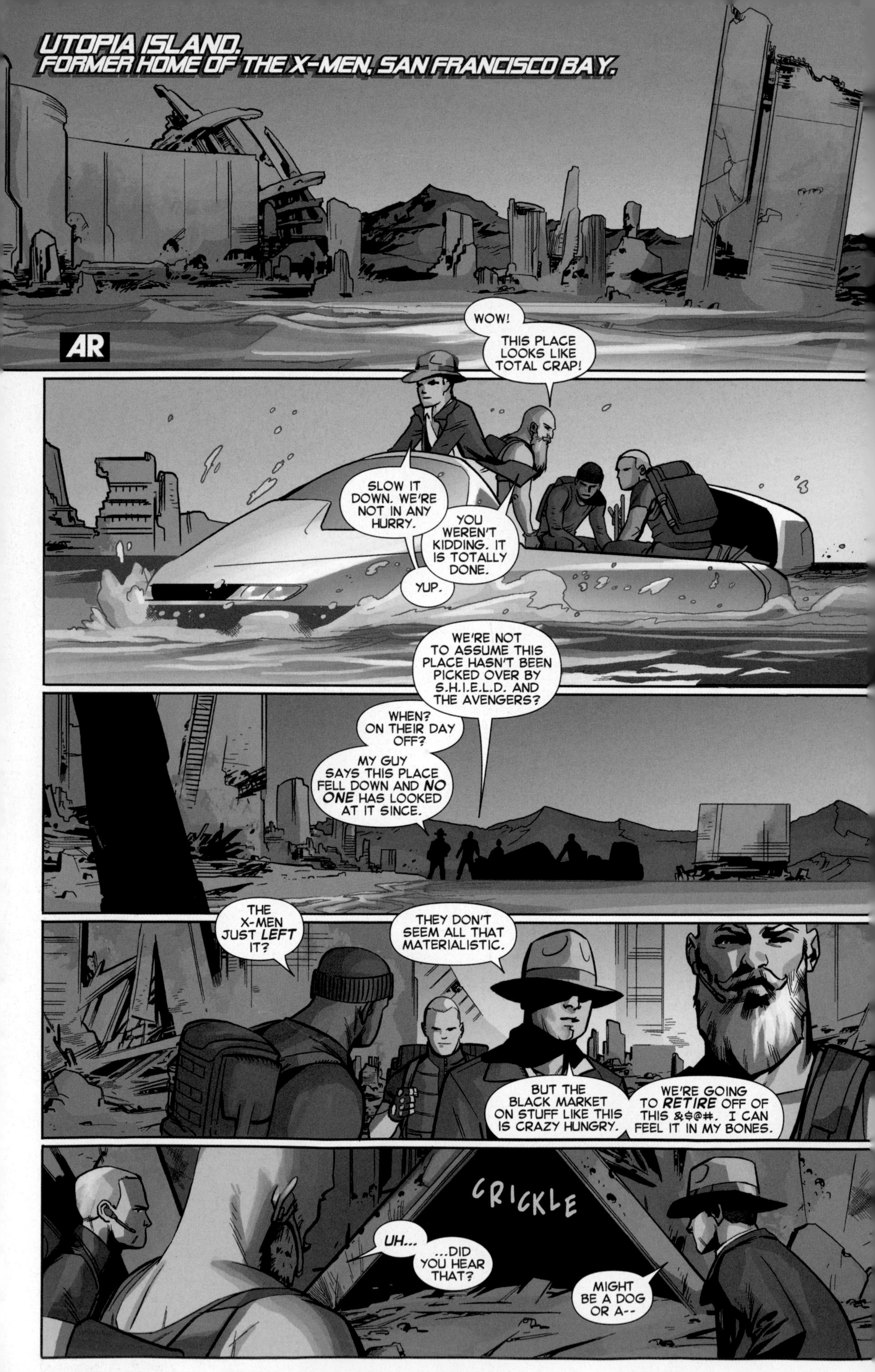
UTOPIA ISLAND.
FORMER HOME OF THE X-MEN, SAN FRANCISCO BAY.
AR
WOW!
THIS PLACE LOOKS LIKE TOTAL CRAP!
SLOW IT DOWN. WE'RE NOT IN ANY HURRY.
YOU WEREN'T KIDDING. IT IS TOTALLY DONE.
YUP.
WE'RE NOT TO ASSUME THIS PLACE HASN'T BEEN PICKED OVER BY S.H.I.E.L.D. AND THE AVENGERS?
WHEN? ON THEIR DAY OFF?
MY GUY SAYS THIS PLACE FELL DOWN AND NO ONE HAS LOOKED AT IT SINCE.
THE X-MEN JUST LEFT IT?
THEY DON'T SEEM ALL THAT MATERIALISTIC.
BUT THE BLACK MARKET ON STUFF LIKE THIS IS CRAZY HUNGRY.
WE'RE GOING TO RETIRE OFF OF THIS &$@#. I CAN FEEL IT IN MY BONES.
CRICKLE
UH...
...DID YOU HEAR THAT?
MIGHT BE A DOG OR A--

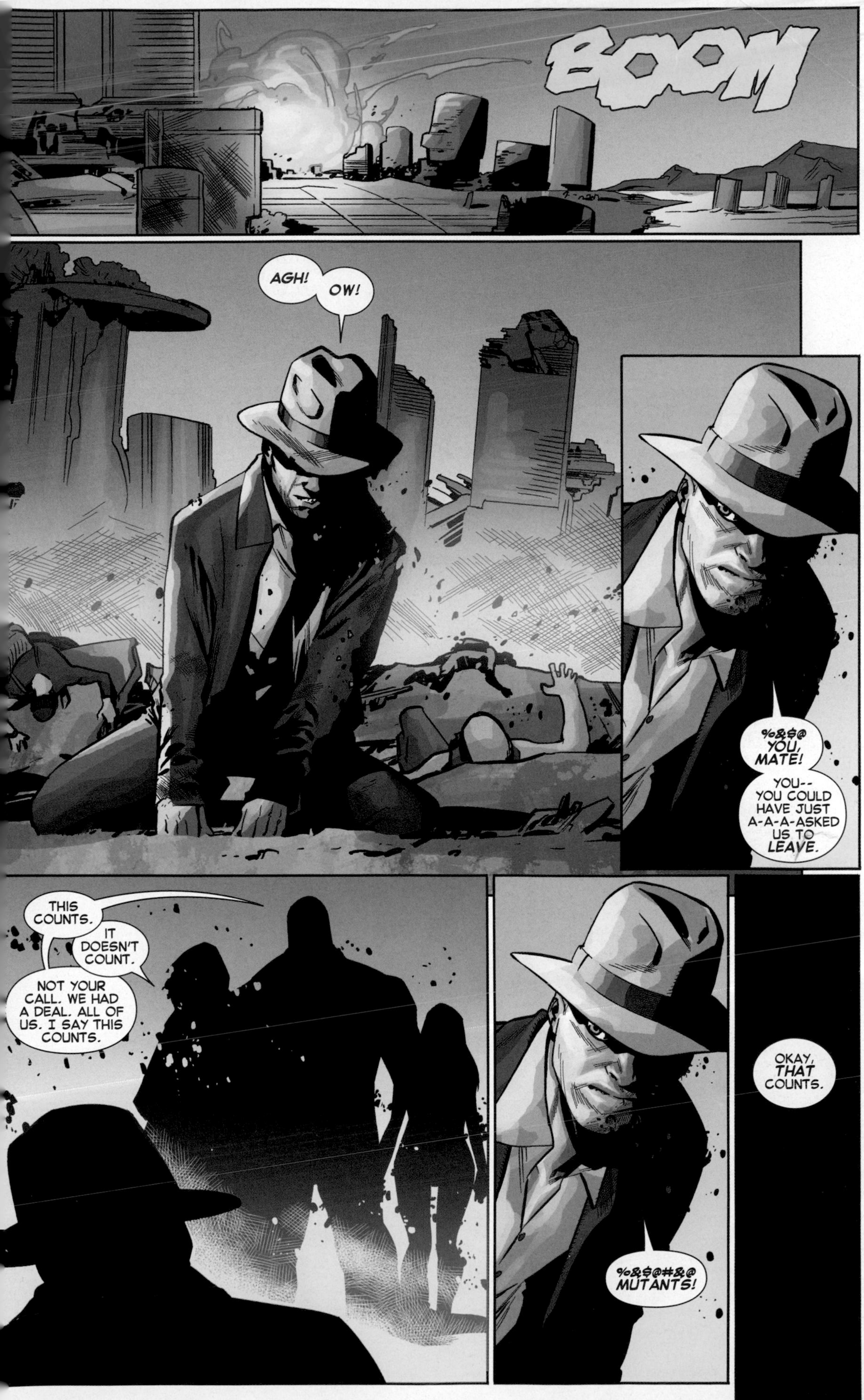
BOOM
AGH!
OW!
%&$@ YOU, MATE!
YOU-- YOU COULD HAVE JUST A-A-A-ASKED US TO LEAVE.
THIS COUNTS.
IT DOESN'T COUNT.
NOT YOUR CALL. WE HAD A DEAL. ALL OF US. I SAY THIS COUNTS.
%&$@#&@ MUTANTS!
OKAY, THAT COUNTS.

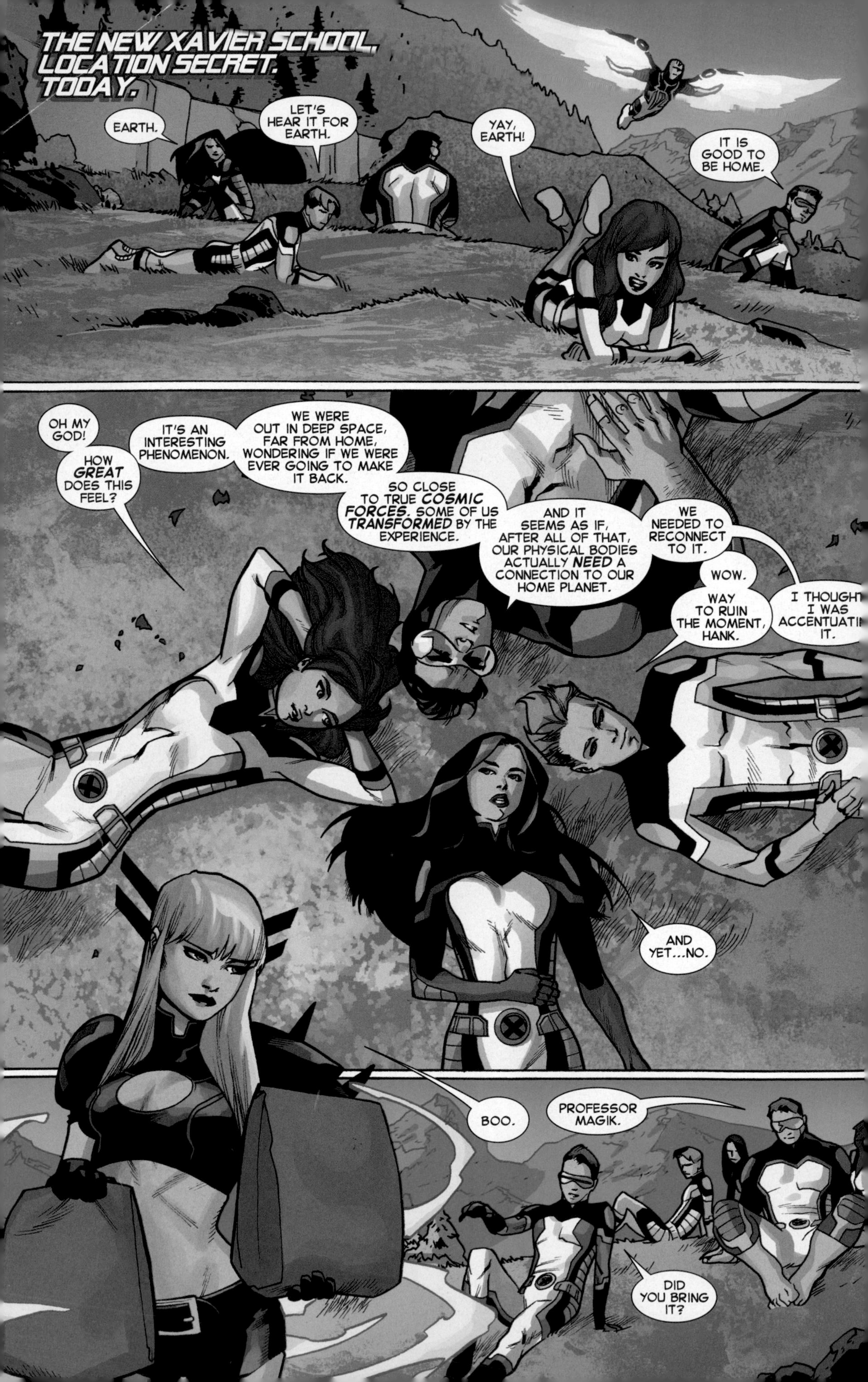
THE NEW XAVIER SCHOOL, LOCATION SECRET. TODAY.
EARTH.
LET'S HEAR IT FOR EARTH.
YAY, EARTH!
IT IS GOOD TO BE HOME.
OH MY GOD!
HOW GREAT DOES THIS FEEL?
IT'S AN INTERESTING PHENOMENON.
WE WERE OUT IN DEEP SPACE, FAR FROM HOME, WONDERING IF WE WERE EVER GOING TO MAKE IT BACK.
SO CLOSE TO TRUE COSMIC FORCES. SOME OF US TRANSFORMED BY THE EXPERIENCE.
AND IT SEEMS AS IF, AFTER ALL OF THAT, OUR PHYSICAL BODIES ACTUALLY NEED A CONNECTION TO OUR HOME PLANET.
WE NEEDED TO RECONNECT TO IT.
WOW.
WAY TO RUIN THE MOMENT, HANK.
AND YET...NO.
BOO.
PROFESSOR MAGIK.
DID YOU BRING IT?

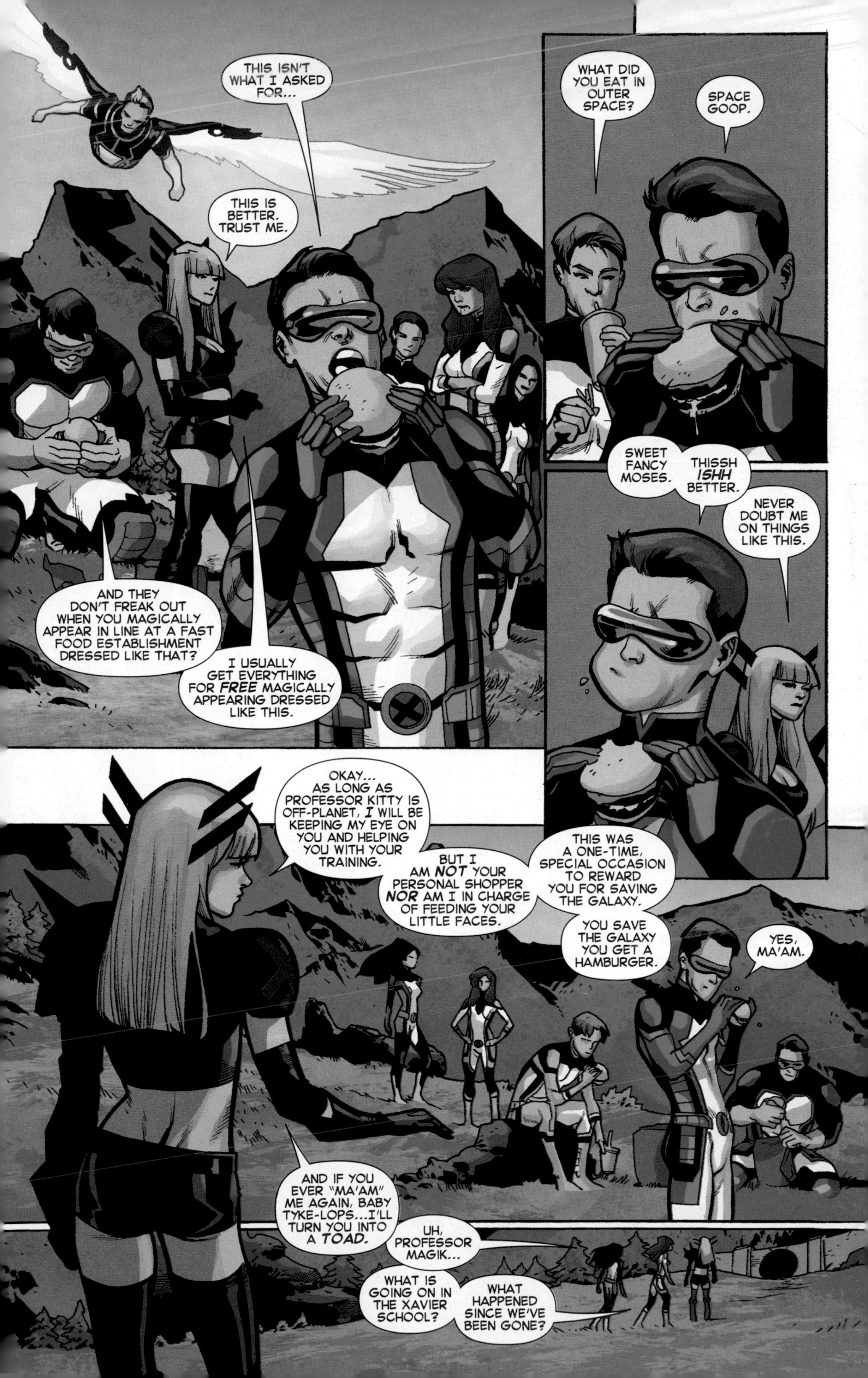
THIS ISN'T WHAT I ASKED FOR...
THIS IS BETTER. TRUST ME.
AND THEY DON'T FREAK OUT WHEN YOU MAGICALLY APPEAR IN LINE AT A FAST FOOD ESTABLISHMENT DRESSED LIKE THAT?
I USUALLY GET EVERYTHING FOR FREE MAGICALLY APPEARING DRESSED LIKE THIS.
WHAT DID YOU EAT IN OUTER SPACE?
SPACE GOOP.
SWEET FANCY MOSES.
THISSH ISHH BETTER.
NEVER DOUBT ME ON THINGS LIKE THIS.
OKAY... AS LONG AS PROFESSOR KITTY IS OFF-PLANET, I WILL BE KEEPING MY EYE ON YOU AND HELPING YOU WITH YOUR TRAINING.
BUT I AM NOT YOUR PERSONAL SHOPPER NOR AM I IN CHARGE OF FEEDING YOUR LITTLE FACES.
THIS WAS A ONE-TIME, SPECIAL OCCASION TO REWARD YOU FOR SAVING THE GALAXY.
YOU SAVE THE GALAXY YOU GET A HAMBURGER.
YES, MA'AM.
AND IF YOU EVER "MA'AM" ME AGAIN, BABY TYKE-LOPS...I'LL TURN YOU INTO A TOAD.
UH, PROFESSOR MAGIK...
WHAT IS GOING ON IN THE XAVIER SCHOOL?
WHAT HAPPENED SINCE WE'VE BEEN GONE?

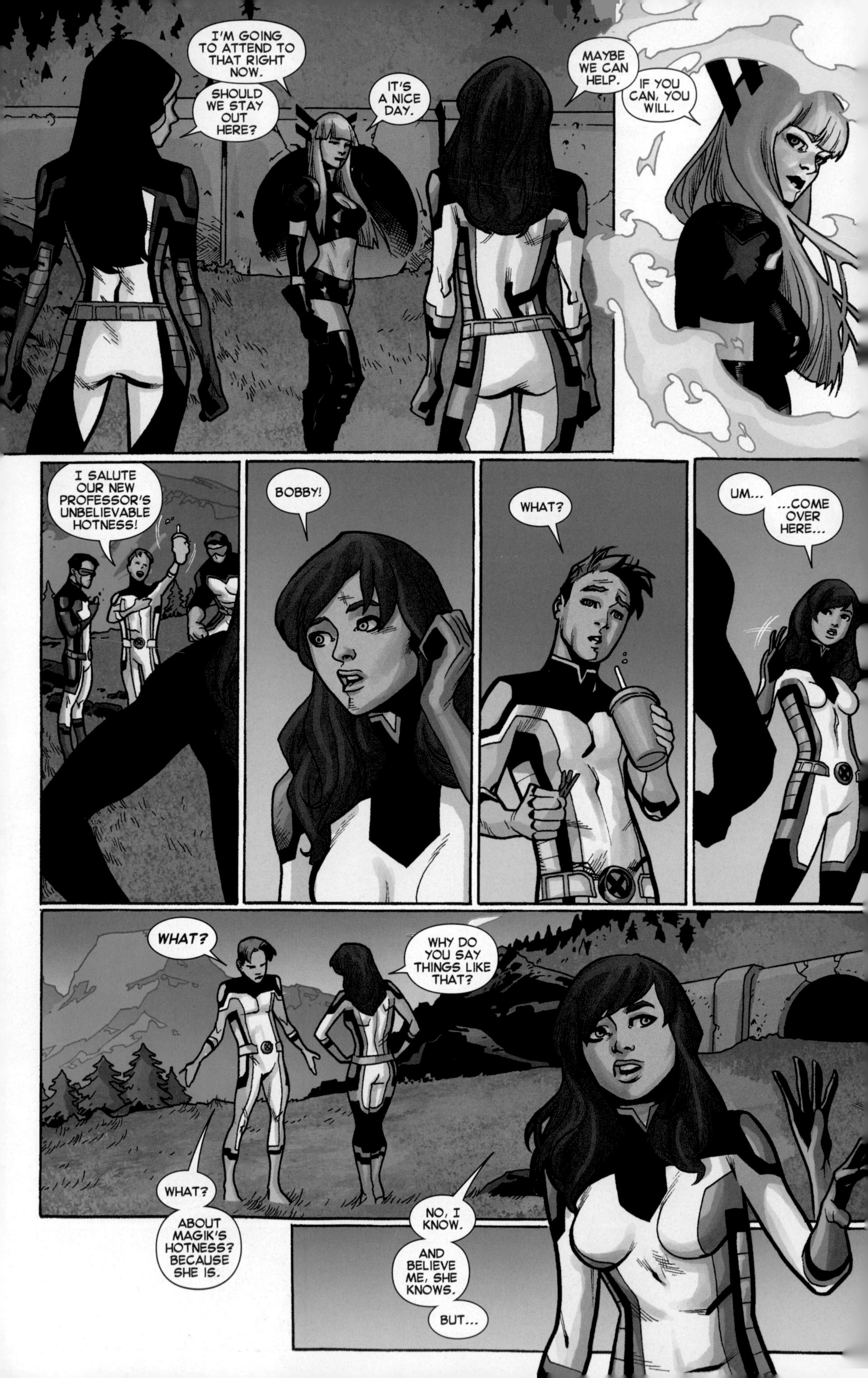
I'M GOING TO ATTEND TO THAT RIGHT NOW.
SHOULD WE STAY OUT HERE?
IT'S A NICE DAY.
MAYBE WE CAN HELP.
IF YOU CAN, YOU WILL.
I SALUTE OUR NEW PROFESSOR'S UNBELIEVABLE HOTNESS!
BOBBY!
WHAT?
UM...
...COME OVER HERE...
WHAT?
WHY DO YOU SAY THINGS LIKE THAT?
WHAT?
ABOUT MAGIK'S HOTNESS? BECAUSE SHE IS.
NO, I KNOW.
AND BELIEVE ME, SHE KNOWS.
BUT...

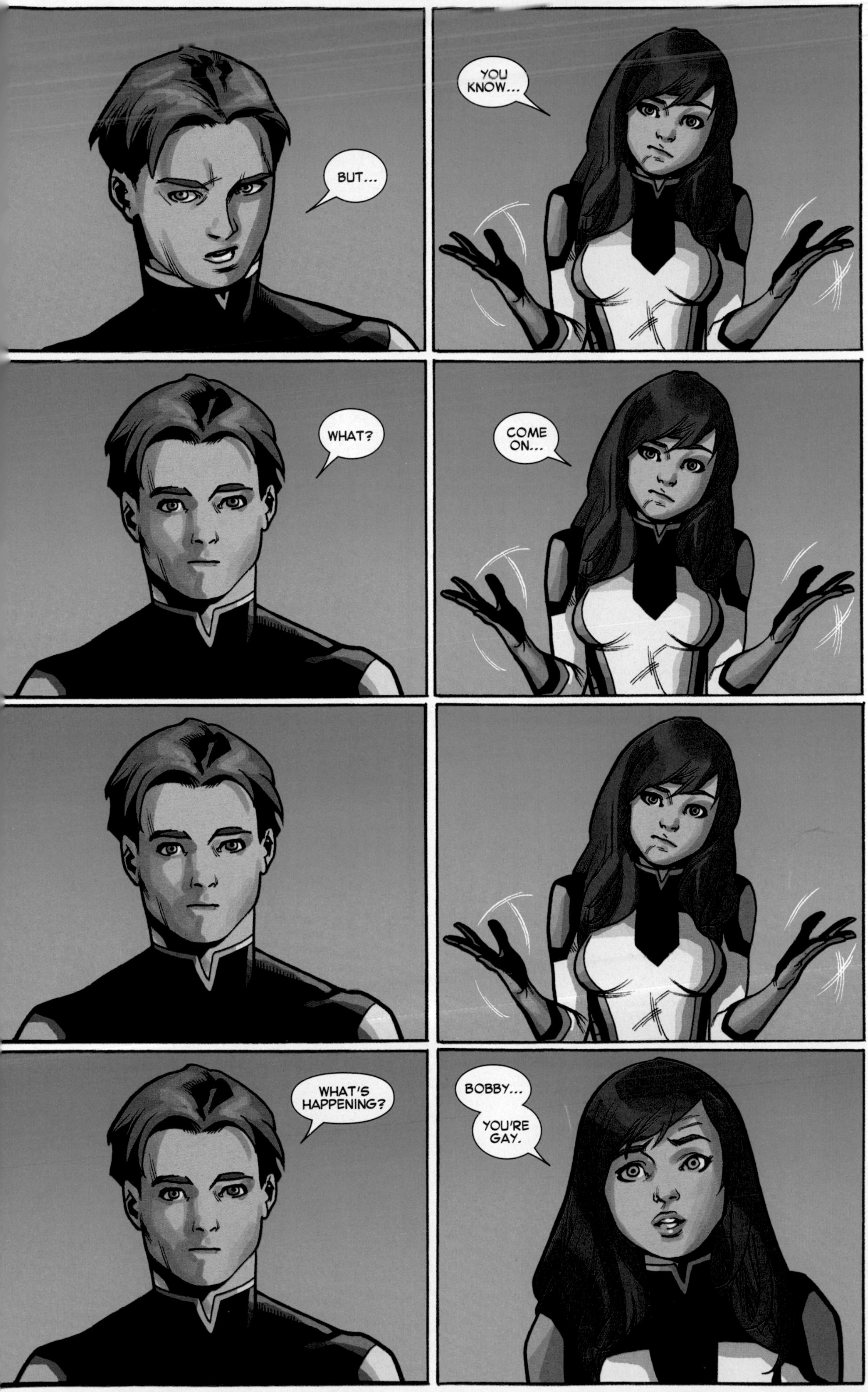
BUT...
YOU KNOW...
WHAT?
COME ON...
WHAT'S HAPPENING?
BOBBY...
YOU'RE GAY.

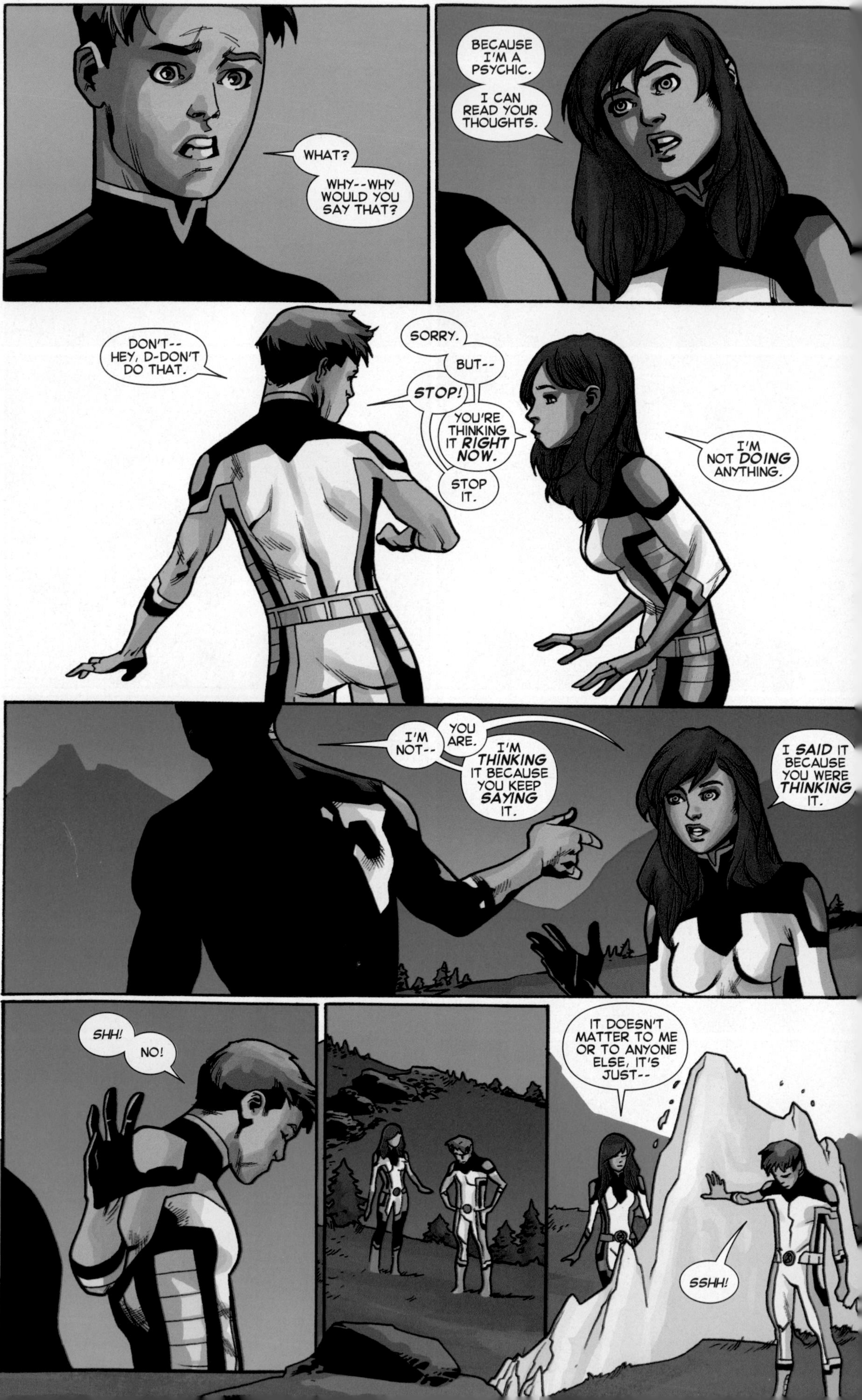
WHAT?
WHY--WHY WOULD YOU SAY THAT?
BECAUSE I'M A PSYCHIC.
I CAN READ YOUR THOUGHTS.
DON'T-- HEY, D-DON'T DO THAT.
SORRY.
BUT--
STOP!
YOU'RE THINKING IT RIGHT NOW.
STOP IT.
I'M NOT DOING ANYTHING.
I'M NOT--
YOU ARE.
I'M THINKING IT BECAUSE YOU KEEP SAYING IT.
I SAID IT BECAUSE YOU WERE THINKING IT.
SHH!
NO!
IT DOESN'T MATTER TO ME OR TO ANYONE ELSE, IT'S JUST--
SSHH!

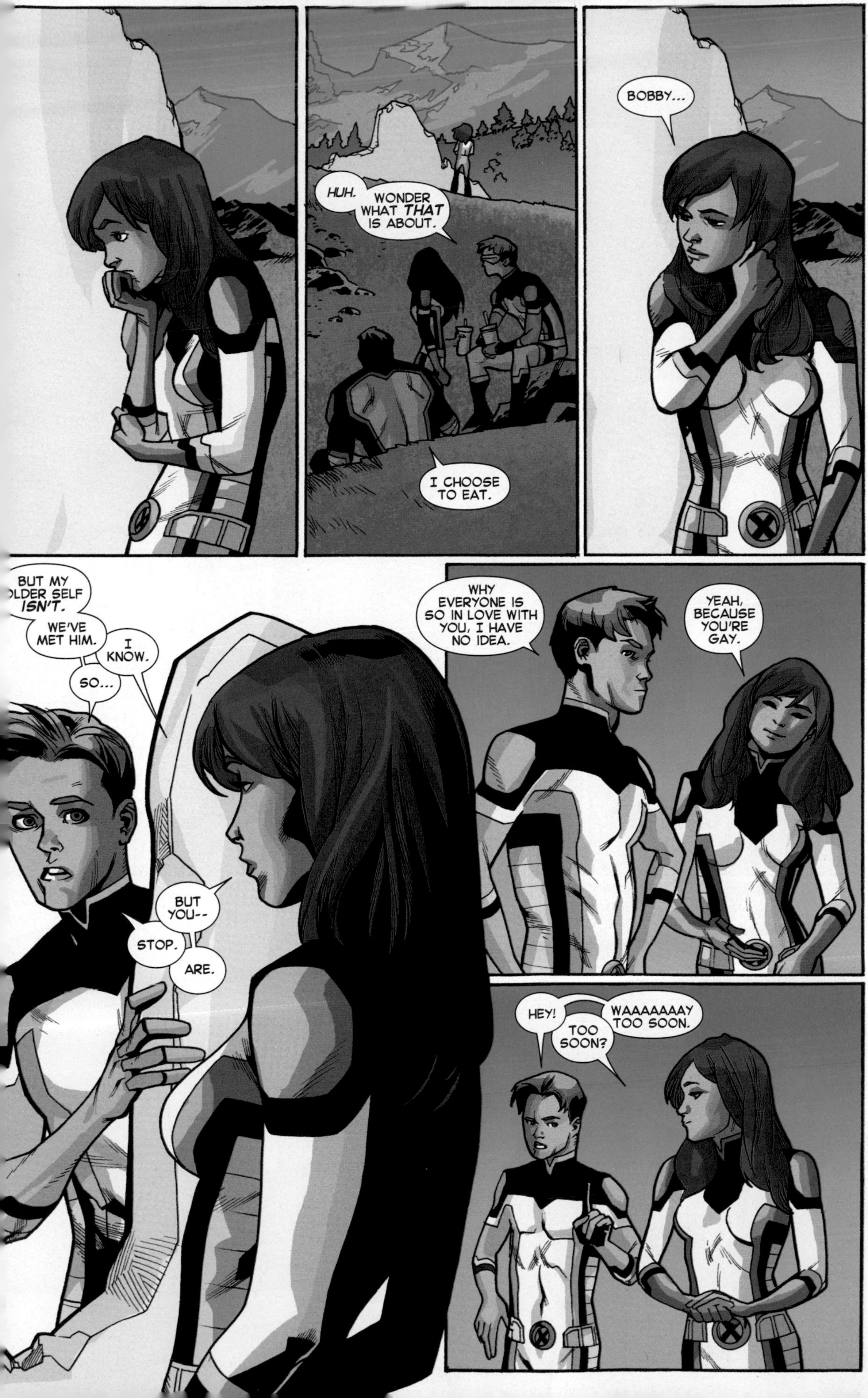
HUH.
WONDER WHAT THAT IS ABOUT.
I CHOOSE TO EAT.
BOBBY...
BUT MY OLDER SELF ISN'T.
WE'VE MET HIM.
I KNOW.
SO...
BUT YOU--
STOP.
ARE.
WHY EVERYONE IS SO IN LOVE WITH YOU, I HAVE NO IDEA.
YEAH, BECAUSE YOU'RE GAY.
HEY!
TOO SOON?
WAAAAAAAY TOO SOON.

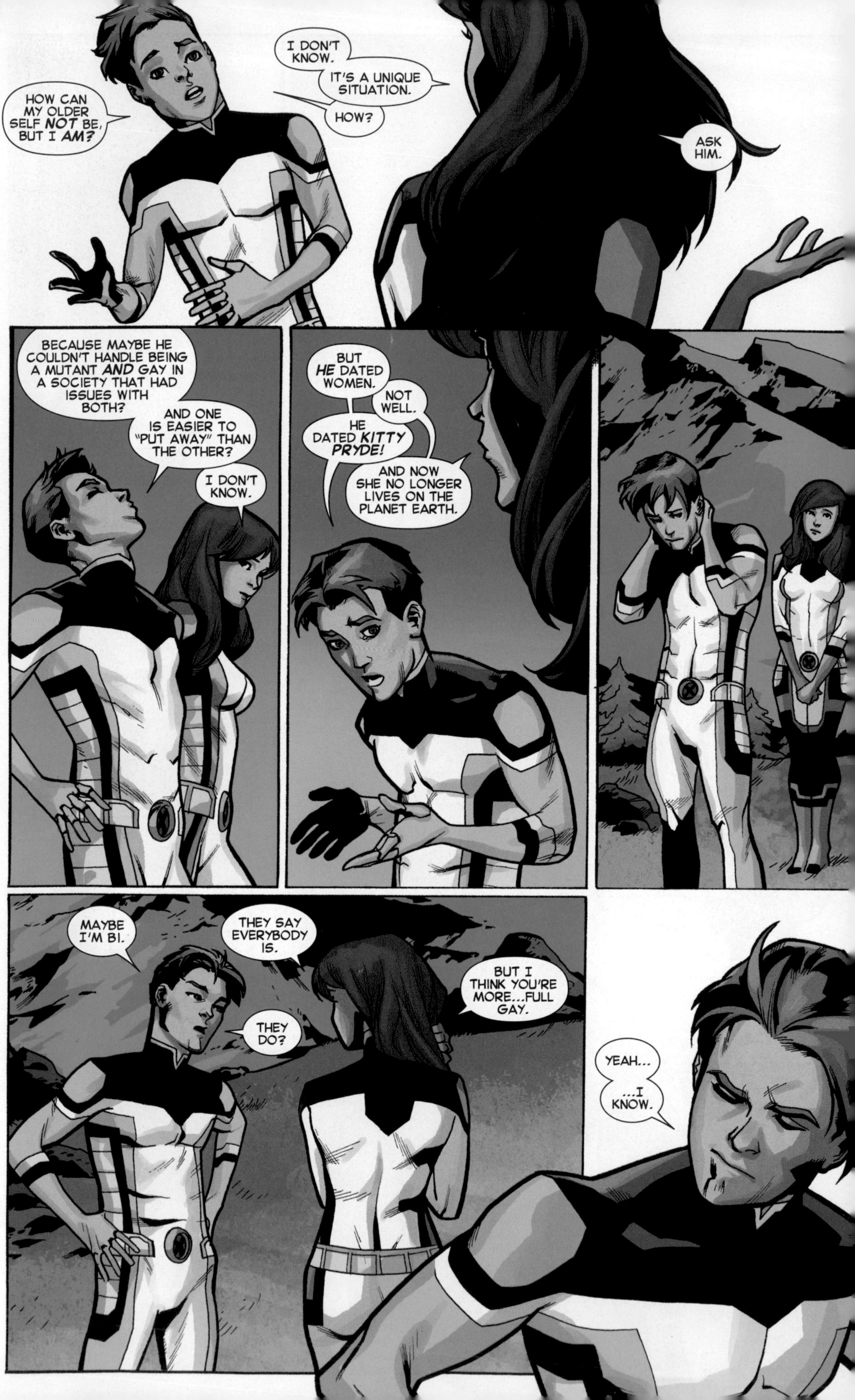
HOW CAN MY OLDER SELF NOT BE, BUT I AM?
I DON'T KNOW.
IT'S A UNIQUE SITUATION.
HOW?
ASK HIM.
BECAUSE MAYBE HE COULDN'T HANDLE BEING A MUTANT AND GAY IN A SOCIETY THAT HAD ISSUES WITH BOTH?
AND ONE IS EASIER TO "PUT AWAY" THAN THE OTHER?
I DON'T KNOW.
BUT HE DATED WOMEN.
NOT WELL.
HE DATED KITTY PRYDE!
AND NOW SHE NO LONGER LIVES ON THE PLANET EARTH.
MAYBE I'M BI.
THEY SAY EVERYBODY IS.
THEY DO?
BUT I THINK YOU'RE MORE...FULL GAY.
YEAH...
...I KNOW.

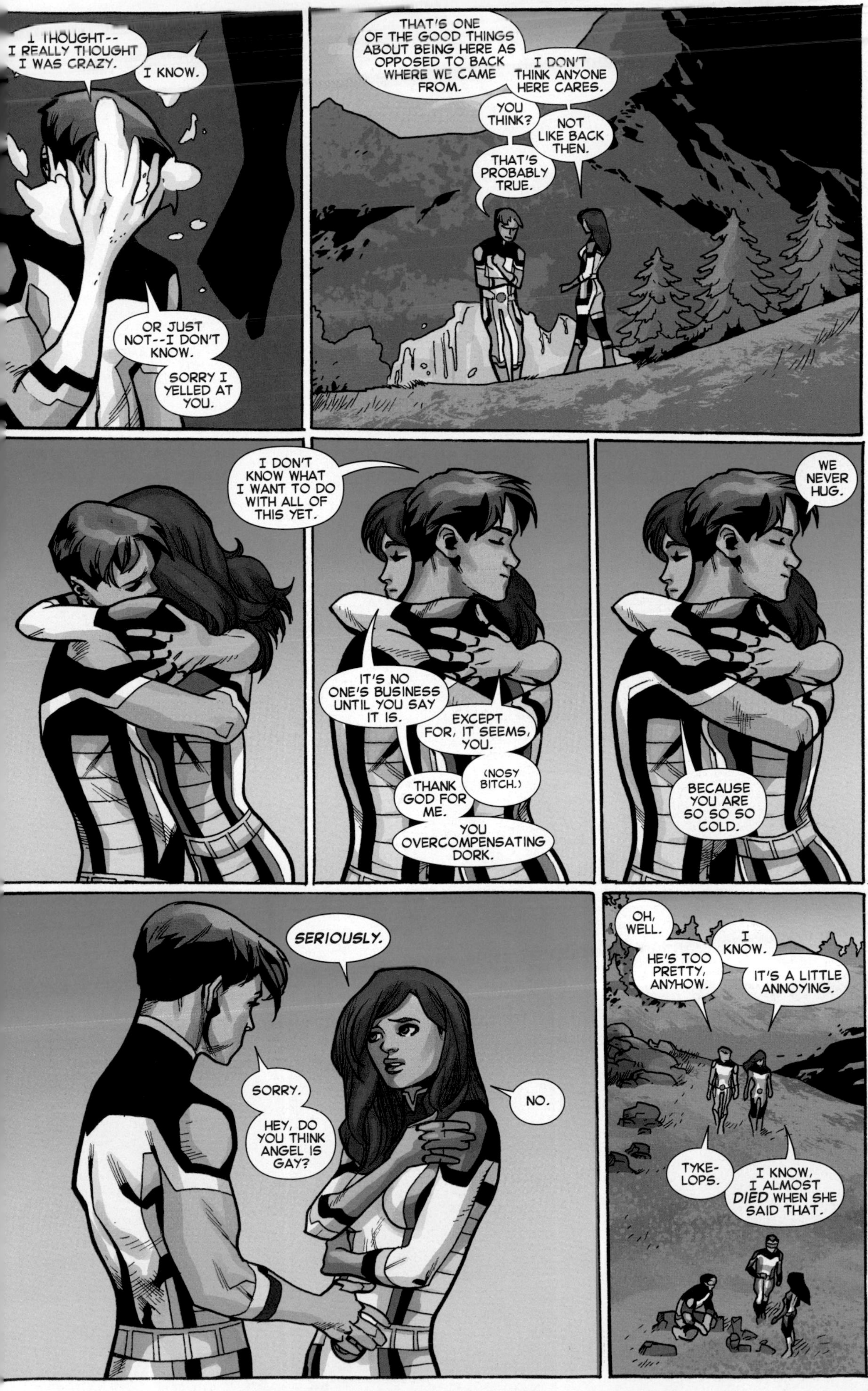

I THOUGHT-- I REALLY THOUGHT I WAS CRAZY.
I KNOW.
OR JUST NOT--I DON'T KNOW.
SORRY I YELLED AT YOU.
THAT'S ONE OF THE GOOD THINGS ABOUT BEING HERE AS OPPOSED TO BACK WHERE WE CAME FROM.
I DON'T THINK ANYONE HERE CARES.
YOU THINK?
NOT LIKE BACK THEN.
THAT'S PROBABLY TRUE.
I DON'T KNOW WHAT I WANT TO DO WITH ALL OF THIS YET.
IT'S NO ONE'S BUSINESS UNTIL YOU SAY IT IS.
EXCEPT FOR, IT SEEMS, YOU.
(NOSY BITCH.)
THANK GOD FOR ME.
YOU OVERCOMPENSATING DORK.
WE NEVER HUG.
BECAUSE YOU ARE SO SO SO COLD.
SERIOUSLY.
SORRY.
HEY, DO YOU THINK ANGEL IS GAY?
NO.
OH, WELL.
HE'S TOO PRETTY, ANYHOW.
I KNOW.
IT'S A LITTLE ANNOYING.
TYKE-LOPS.
I KNOW, I ALMOST DIED WHEN SHE SAID THAT.

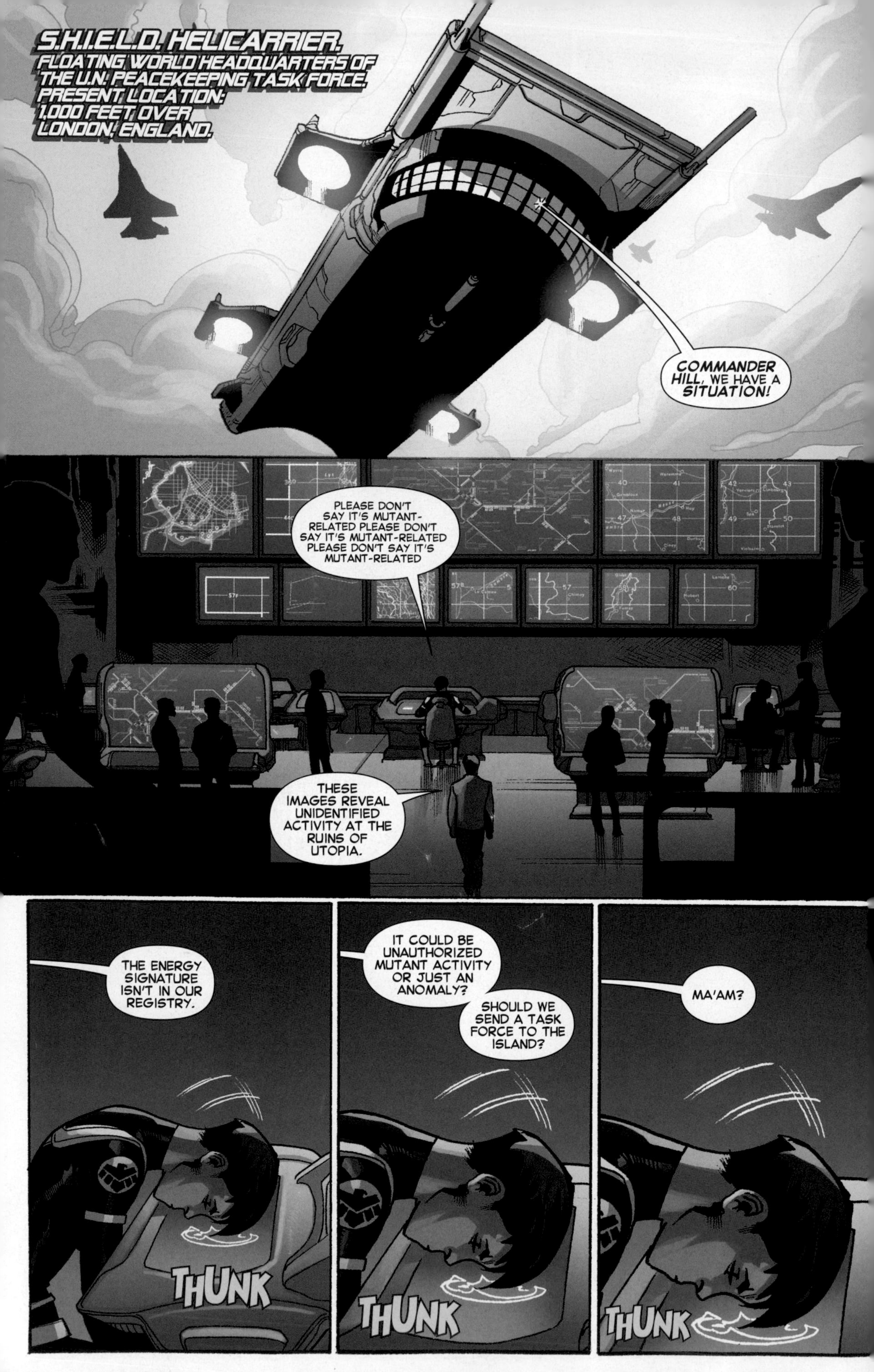
S.H.I.E.L.D. HELICARRIER.
FLOATING WORLD HEADQUARTERS OF THE U.N. PEACEKEEPING TASK FORCE. PRESENT LOCATION: 1,000 FEET OVER LONDON, ENGLAND.
COMMANDER HILL, WE HAVE A SITUATION!
PLEASE DON'T SAY IT'S MUTANT-RELATED PLEASE DON'T SAY IT'S MUTANT-RELATED PLEASE DON'T SAY IT'S MUTANT-RELATED
THESE IMAGES REVEAL UNIDENTIFIED ACTIVITY AT THE RUINS OF UTOPIA.
THE ENERGY SIGNATURE ISN'T IN OUR REGISTRY.
THUNK
IT COULD BE UNAUTHORIZED MUTANT ACTIVITY OR JUST AN ANOMALY?
SHOULD WE SEND A TASK FORCE TO THE ISLAND?
THUNK
MA'AM?
THUNK

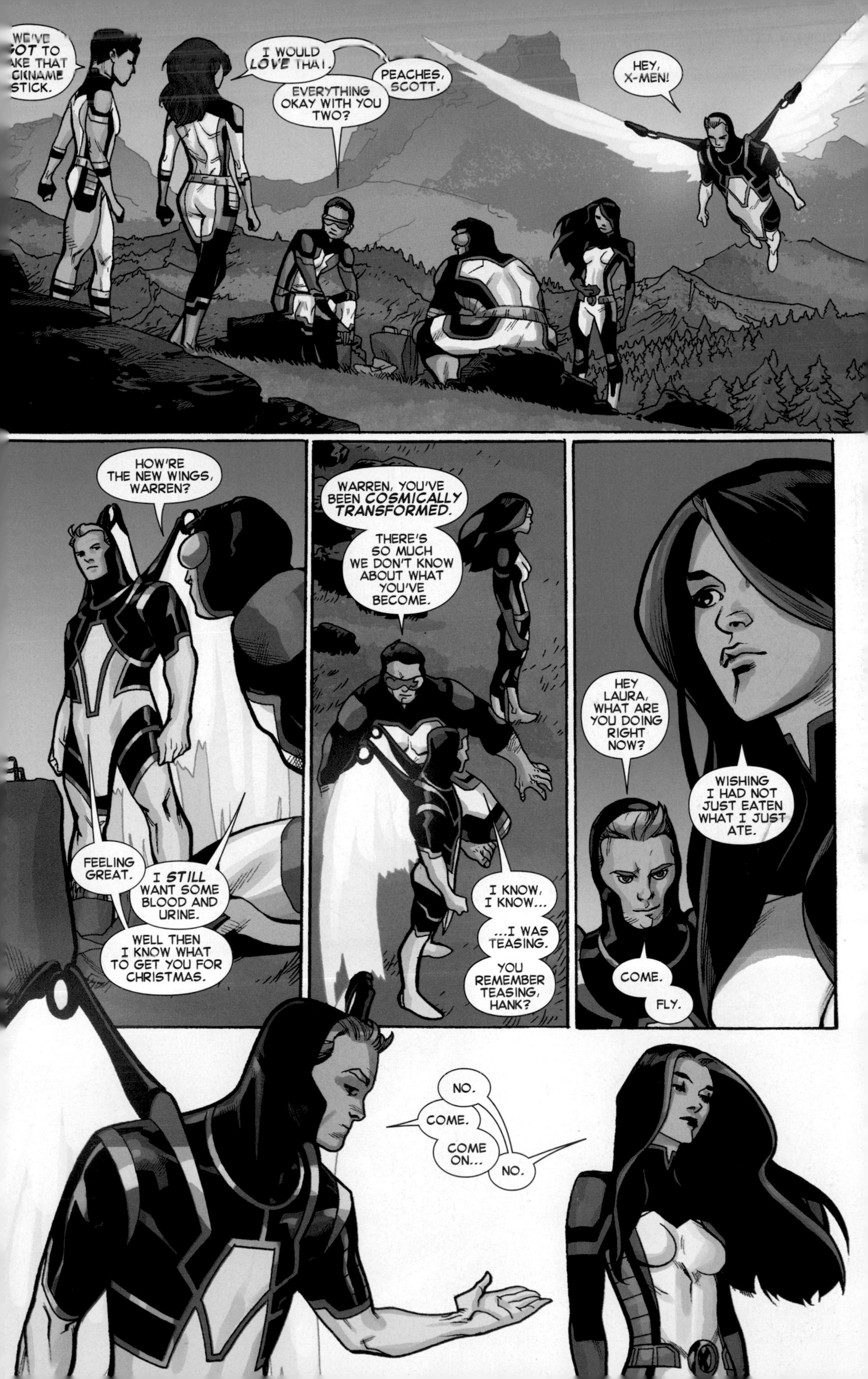
WE'VE GOT TO MAKE THAT NICKNAME STICK.
I WOULD LOVE THAT.
PEACHES, SCOTT.
EVERYTHING OKAY WITH YOU TWO?
HEY, X-MEN!
HOW'RE THE NEW WINGS, WARREN?
FEELING GREAT.
I STILL WANT SOME BLOOD AND URINE.
WELL THEN I KNOW WHAT TO GET YOU FOR CHRISTMAS.
WARREN, YOU'VE BEEN COSMICALLY TRANSFORMED.
THERE'S SO MUCH WE DON'T KNOW ABOUT WHAT YOU'VE BECOME.
I KNOW, I KNOW...
...I WAS TEASING.
YOU REMEMBER TEASING, HANK?
HEY LAURA, WHAT ARE YOU DOING RIGHT NOW?
WISHING I HAD NOT JUST EATEN WHAT I JUST ATE.
COME.
FLY.
NO.
COME.
COME ON...
NO.

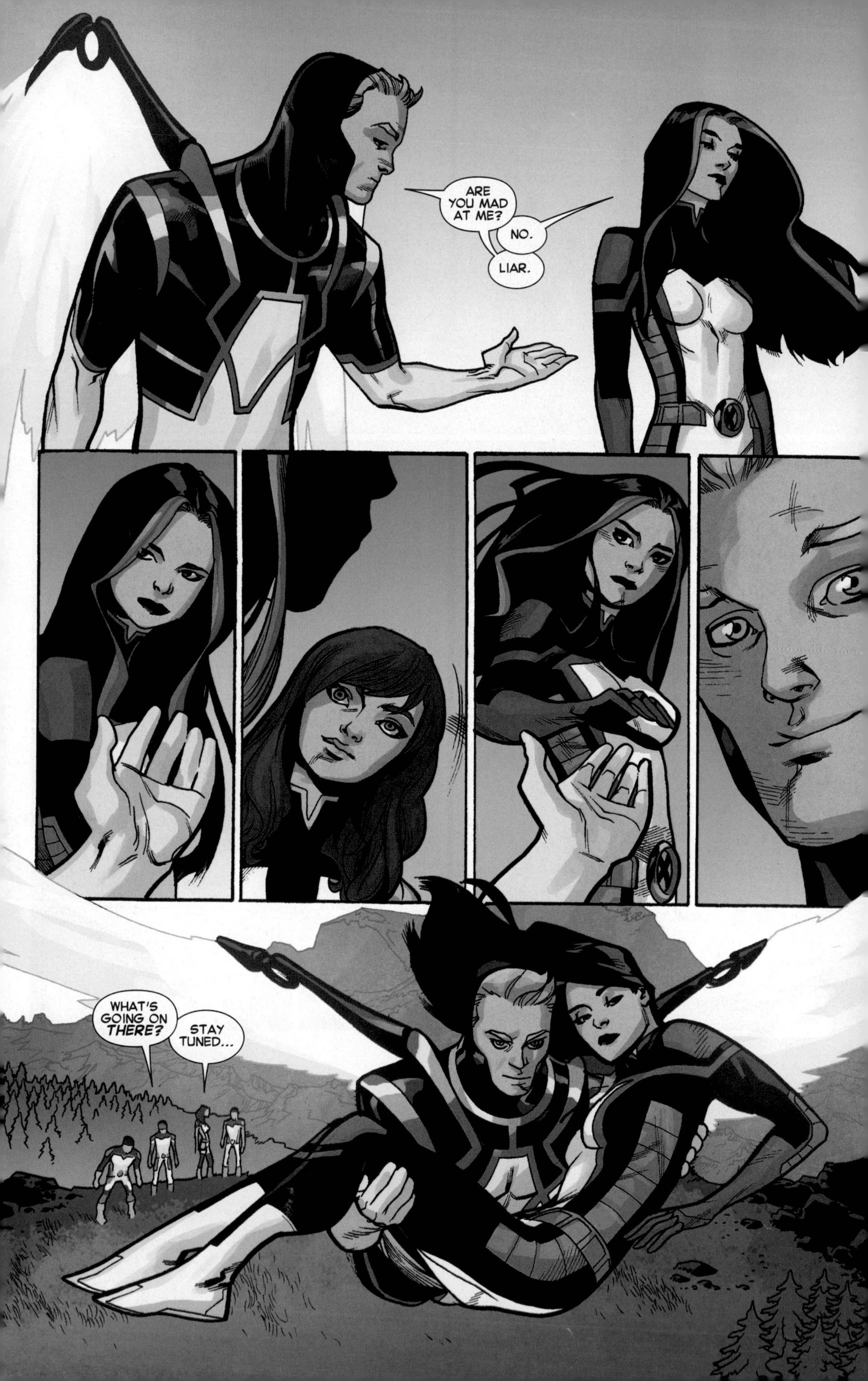
ARE YOU MAD AT ME?
NO.
LIAR.
WHAT'S GOING ON *THERE?*
STAY TUNED...

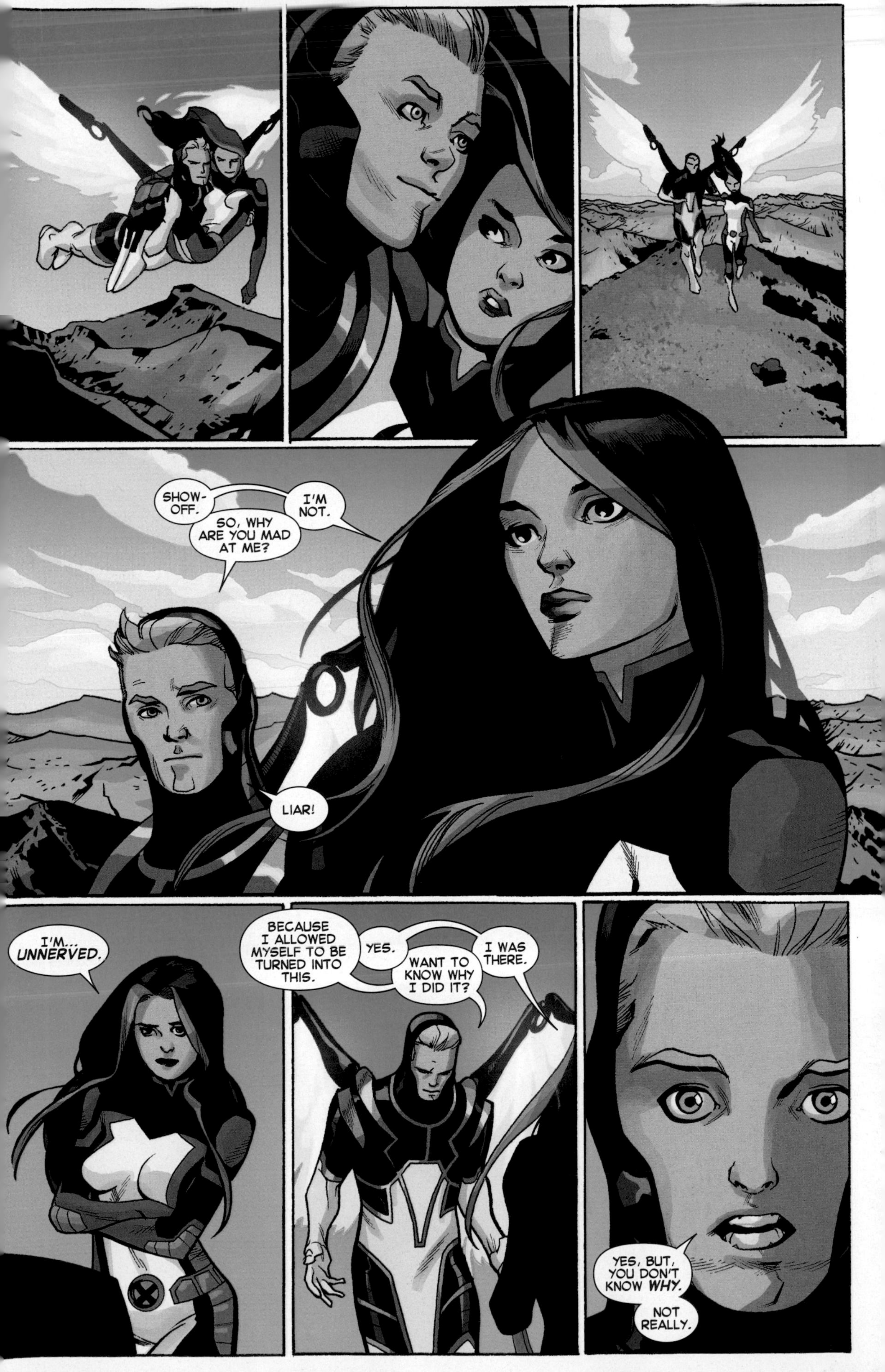
SHOW-OFF.
I'M NOT.
SO, WHY ARE YOU MAD AT ME?
LIAR!
I'M... UNNERVED.
BECAUSE I ALLOWED MYSELF TO BE TURNED INTO THIS.
YES.
I WAS THERE.
WANT TO KNOW WHY I DID IT?
YES, BUT, YOU DON'T KNOW WHY.
NOT REALLY.

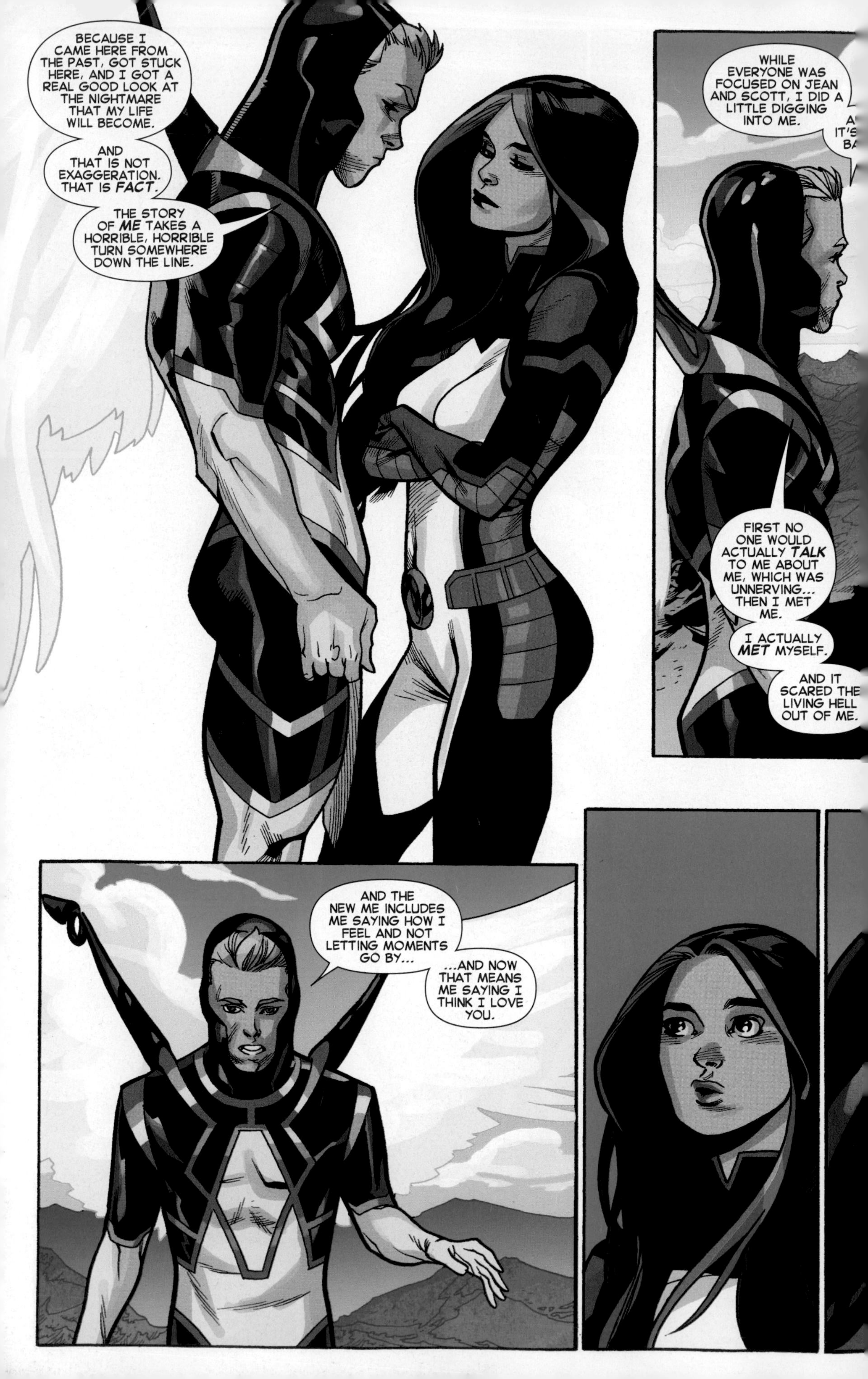
BECAUSE I CAME HERE FROM THE PAST, GOT STUCK HERE, AND I GOT A REAL GOOD LOOK AT THE NIGHTMARE THAT MY LIFE WILL BECOME.
AND THAT IS NOT EXAGGERATION. THAT IS FACT.
THE STORY OF ME TAKES A HORRIBLE, HORRIBLE TURN SOMEWHERE DOWN THE LINE.
WHILE EVERYONE WAS FOCUSED ON JEAN AND SCOTT, I DID A LITTLE DIGGING INTO ME.
FIRST NO ONE WOULD ACTUALLY TALK TO ME ABOUT ME, WHICH WAS UNNERVING... THEN I MET ME.
I ACTUALLY MET MYSELF.
AND IT SCARED THE LIVING HELL OUT OF ME.
AND THE NEW ME INCLUDES ME SAYING HOW I FEEL AND NOT LETTING MOMENTS GO BY...
...AND NOW THAT MEANS ME SAYING I THINK I LOVE YOU.

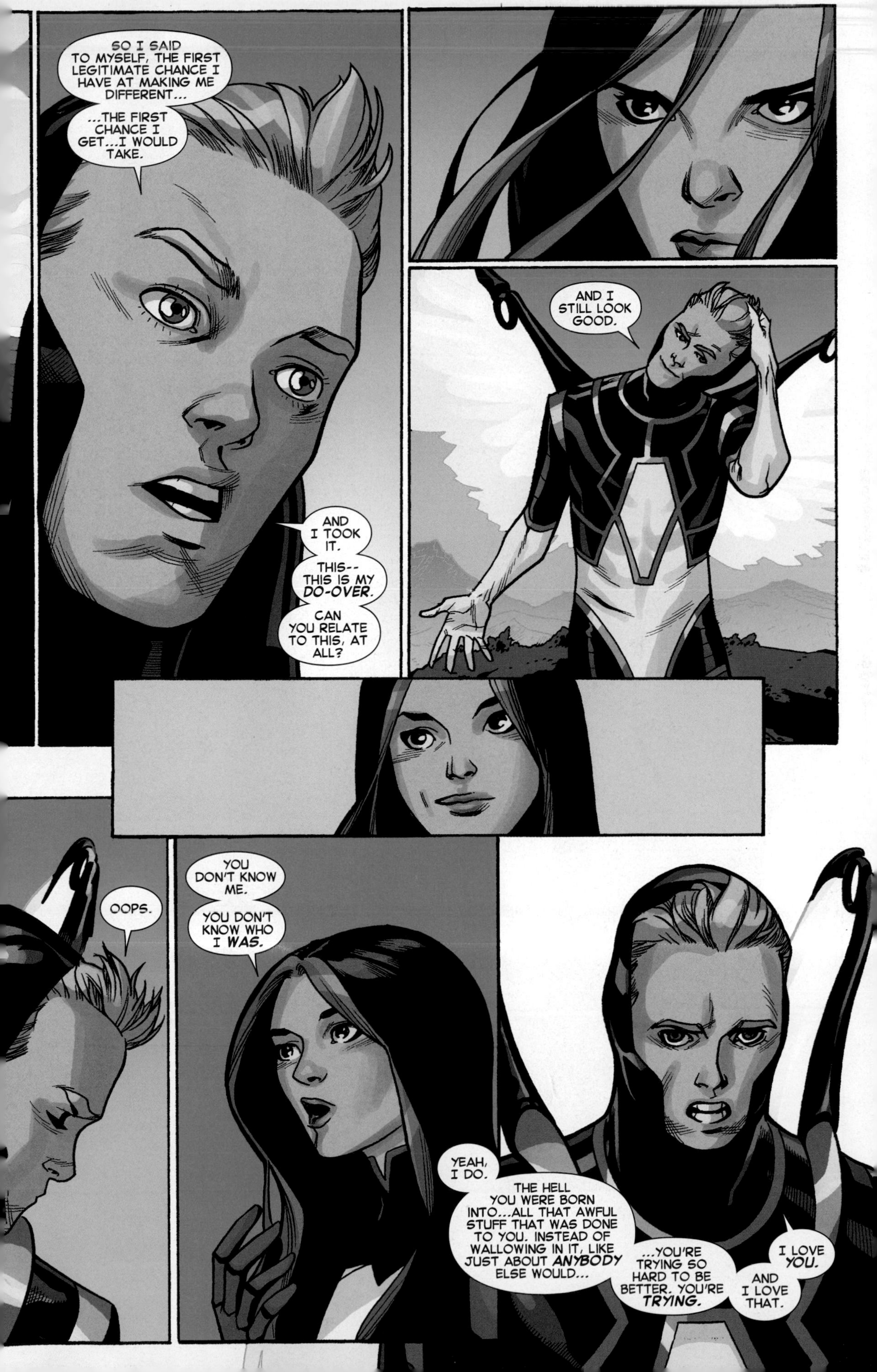
SO I SAID TO MYSELF, THE FIRST LEGITIMATE CHANCE I HAVE AT MAKING ME DIFFERENT...
...THE FIRST CHANCE I GET...I WOULD TAKE.
AND I TOOK IT.
THIS-- THIS IS MY DO-OVER.
CAN YOU RELATE TO THIS, AT ALL?
AND I STILL LOOK GOOD.
OOPS.
YOU DON'T KNOW ME.
YOU DON'T KNOW WHO I WAS.
YEAH, I DO.
THE HELL YOU WERE BORN INTO...ALL THAT AWFUL STUFF THAT WAS DONE TO YOU. INSTEAD OF WALLOWING IN IT, LIKE JUST ABOUT ANYBODY ELSE WOULD...
...YOU'RE TRYING SO HARD TO BE BETTER. YOU'RE TRYING.
I LOVE YOU.
AND I LOVE THAT.

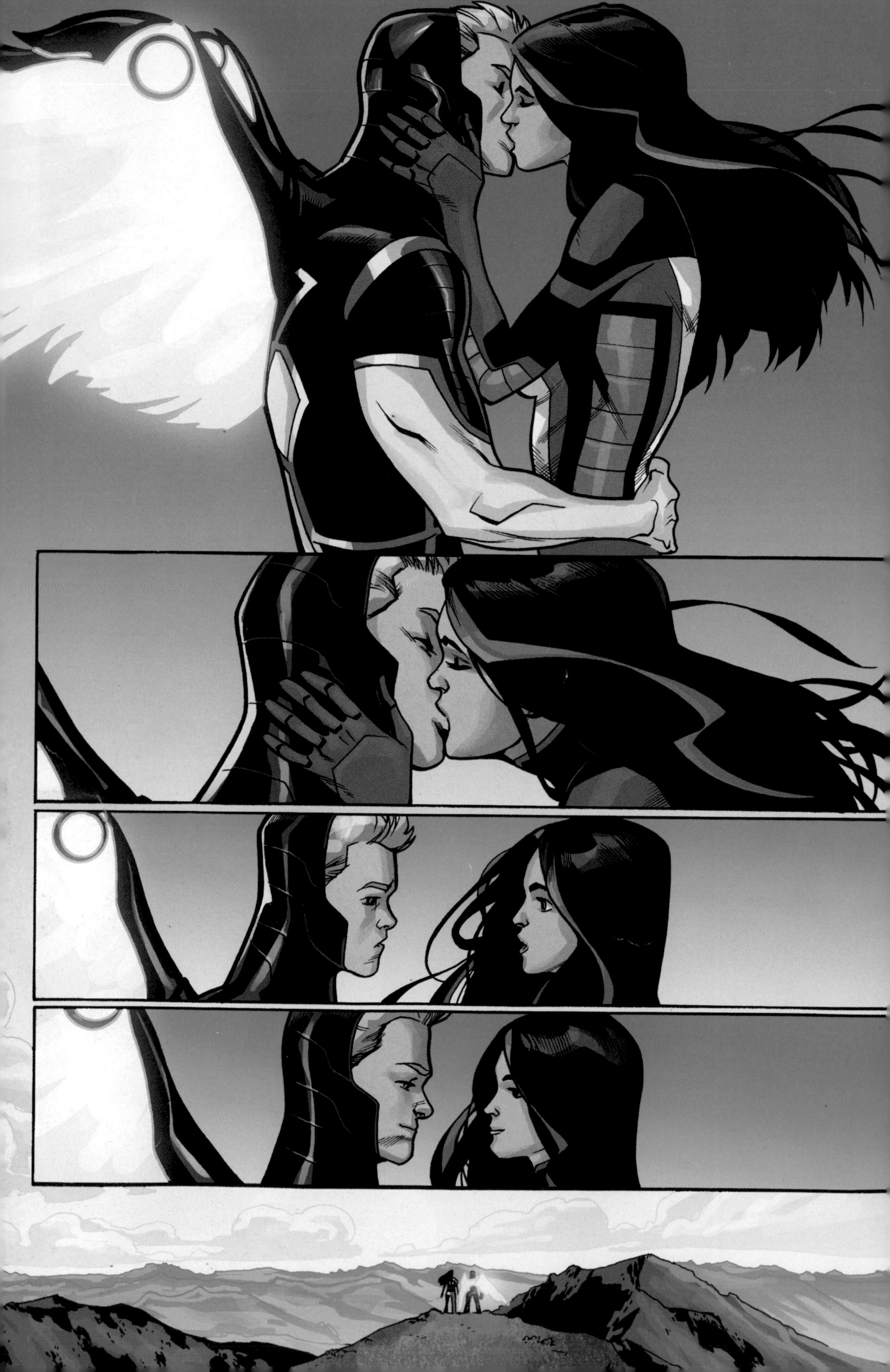

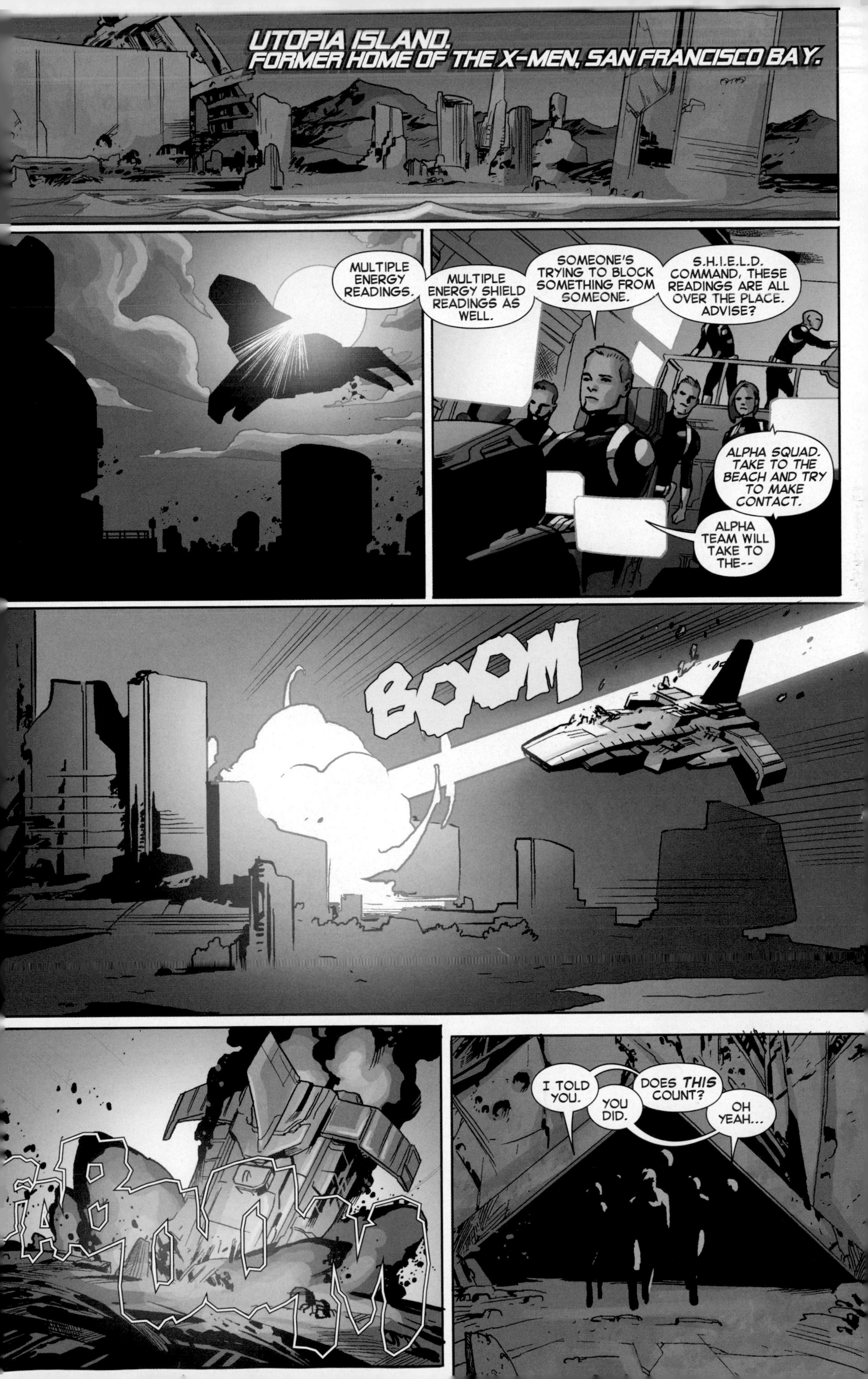
UTOPIA ISLAND.
FORMER HOME OF THE X-MEN, SAN FRANCISCO BAY.
MULTIPLE ENERGY READINGS.
MULTIPLE ENERGY SHIELD READINGS AS WELL.
SOMEONE'S TRYING TO BLOCK SOMETHING FROM SOMEONE.
S.H.I.E.L.D. COMMAND, THESE READINGS ARE ALL OVER THE PLACE. ADVISE?
ALPHA SQUAD. TAKE TO THE BEACH AND TRY TO MAKE CONTACT.
ALPHA TEAM WILL TAKE TO THE--
BOOM
I TOLD YOU.
DOES THIS COUNT?
YOU DID.
OH YEAH...

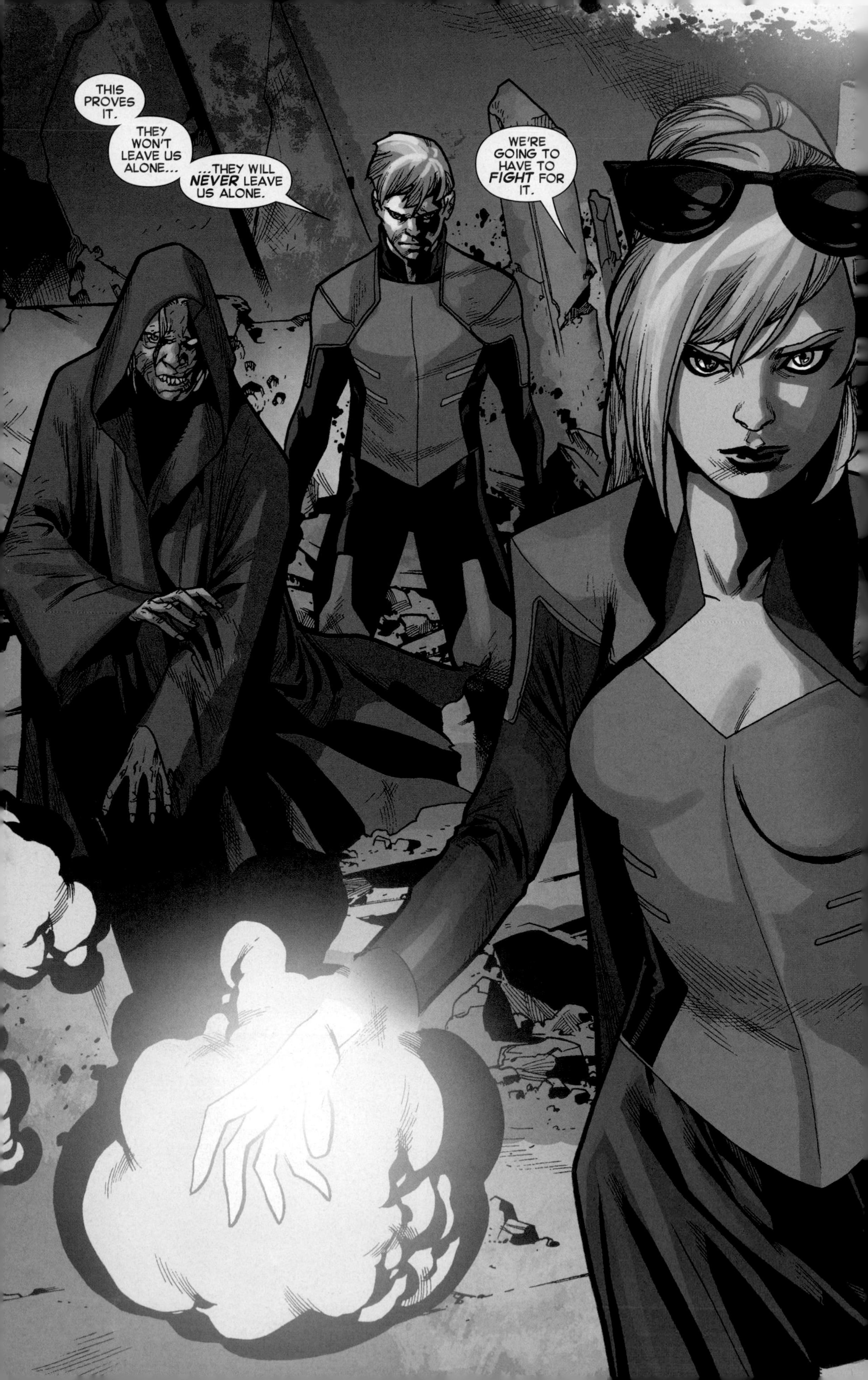
THIS PROVES IT.
THEY WON'T LEAVE US ALONE...
...THEY WILL NEVER LEAVE US ALONE.
WE'RE GOING TO HAVE TO FIGHT FOR IT.

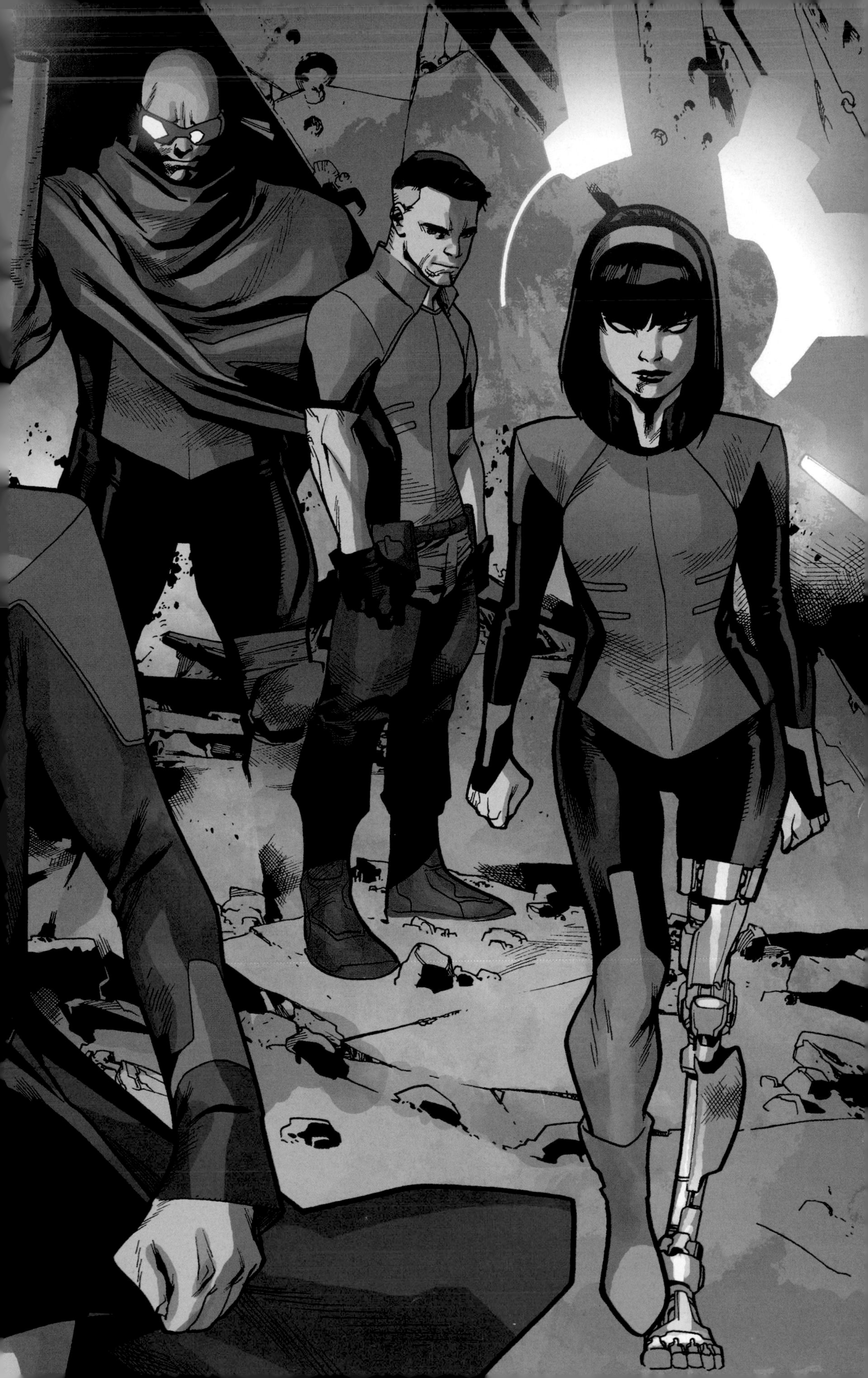

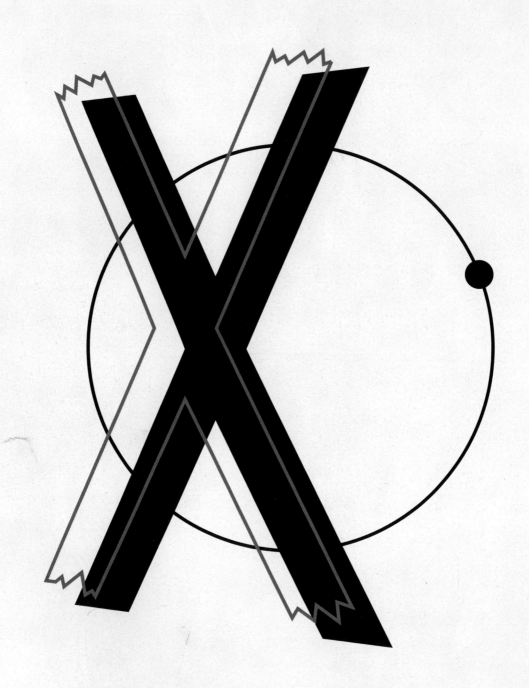

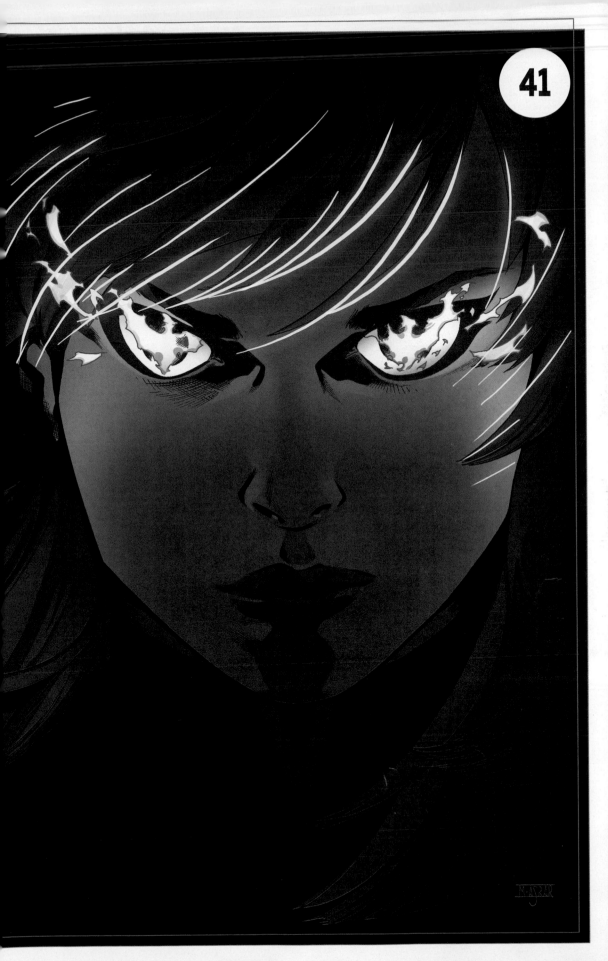

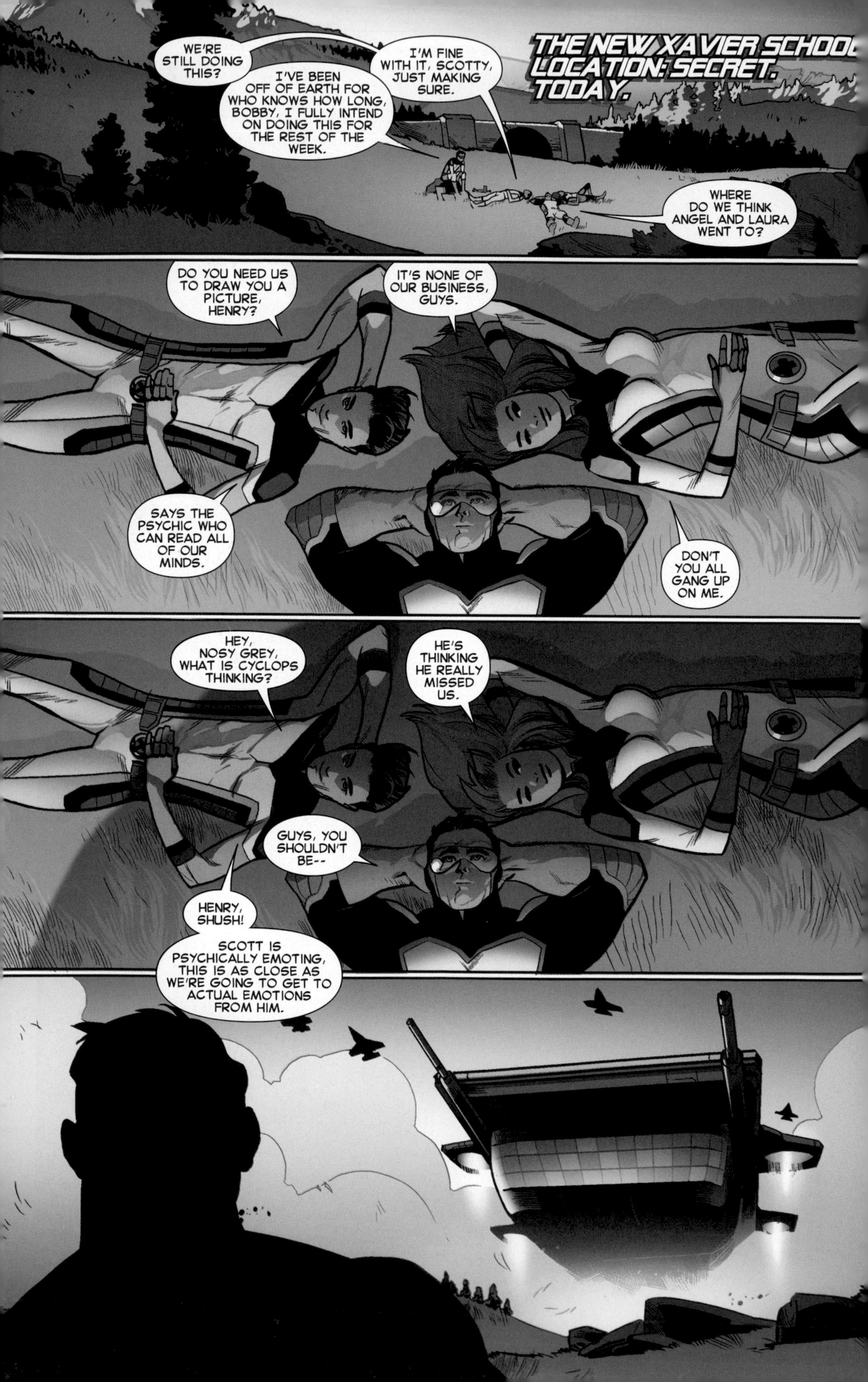
THE NEW XAVIER SCHOOL
LOCATION: SECRET.
TODAY.
WE'RE STILL DOING THIS?
I'VE BEEN OFF OF EARTH FOR WHO KNOWS HOW LONG, BOBBY, I FULLY INTEND ON DOING THIS FOR THE REST OF THE WEEK.
I'M FINE WITH IT, SCOTTY, JUST MAKING SURE.
WHERE DO WE THINK ANGEL AND LAURA WENT TO?
DO YOU NEED US TO DRAW YOU A PICTURE, HENRY?
IT'S NONE OF OUR BUSINESS, GUYS.
SAYS THE PSYCHIC WHO CAN READ ALL OF OUR MINDS.
DON'T YOU ALL GANG UP ON ME.
HEY, NOSY GREY, WHAT IS CYCLOPS THINKING?
HE'S THINKING HE REALLY MISSED US.
GUYS, YOU SHOULDN'T BE--
HENRY, SHUSH!
SCOTT IS PSYCHICALLY EMOTING, THIS IS AS CLOSE AS WE'RE GOING TO GET TO ACTUAL EMOTIONS FROM HIM.

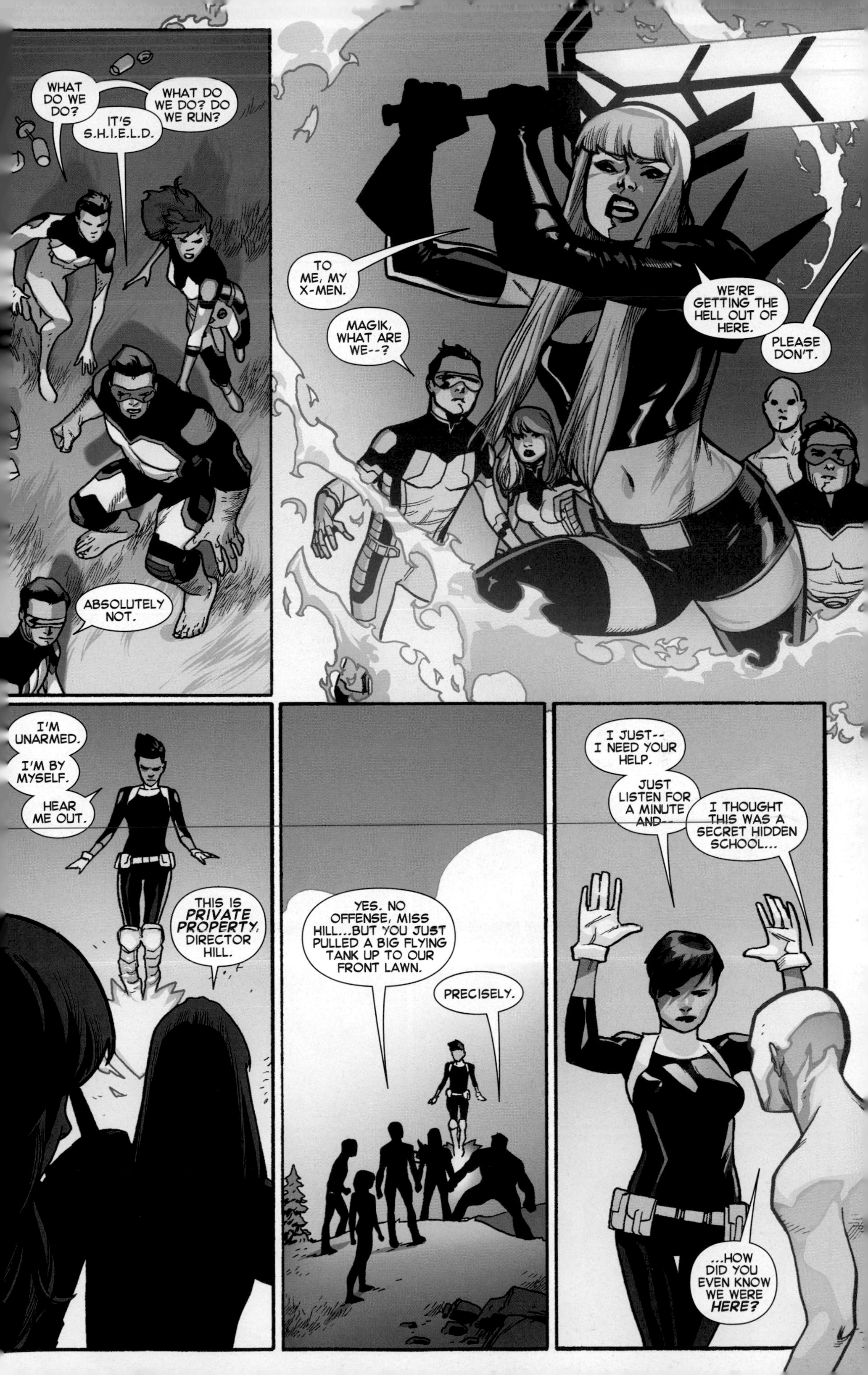
WHAT DO WE DO?
IT'S S.H.I.E.L.D.
WHAT DO WE DO? DO WE RUN?
ABSOLUTELY NOT.
TO ME, MY X-MEN.
MAGIK, WHAT ARE WE--?
WE'RE GETTING THE HELL OUT OF HERE.
PLEASE DON'T.
I'M UNARMED.
I'M BY MYSELF.
HEAR ME OUT.
THIS IS PRIVATE PROPERTY, DIRECTOR HILL.
YES. NO OFFENSE, MISS HILL...BUT YOU JUST PULLED A BIG FLYING TANK UP TO OUR FRONT LAWN.
PRECISELY.
I JUST-- I NEED YOUR HELP.
JUST LISTEN FOR A MINUTE AND--
I THOUGHT THIS WAS A SECRET HIDDEN SCHOOL...
...HOW DID YOU EVEN KNOW WE WERE HERE?

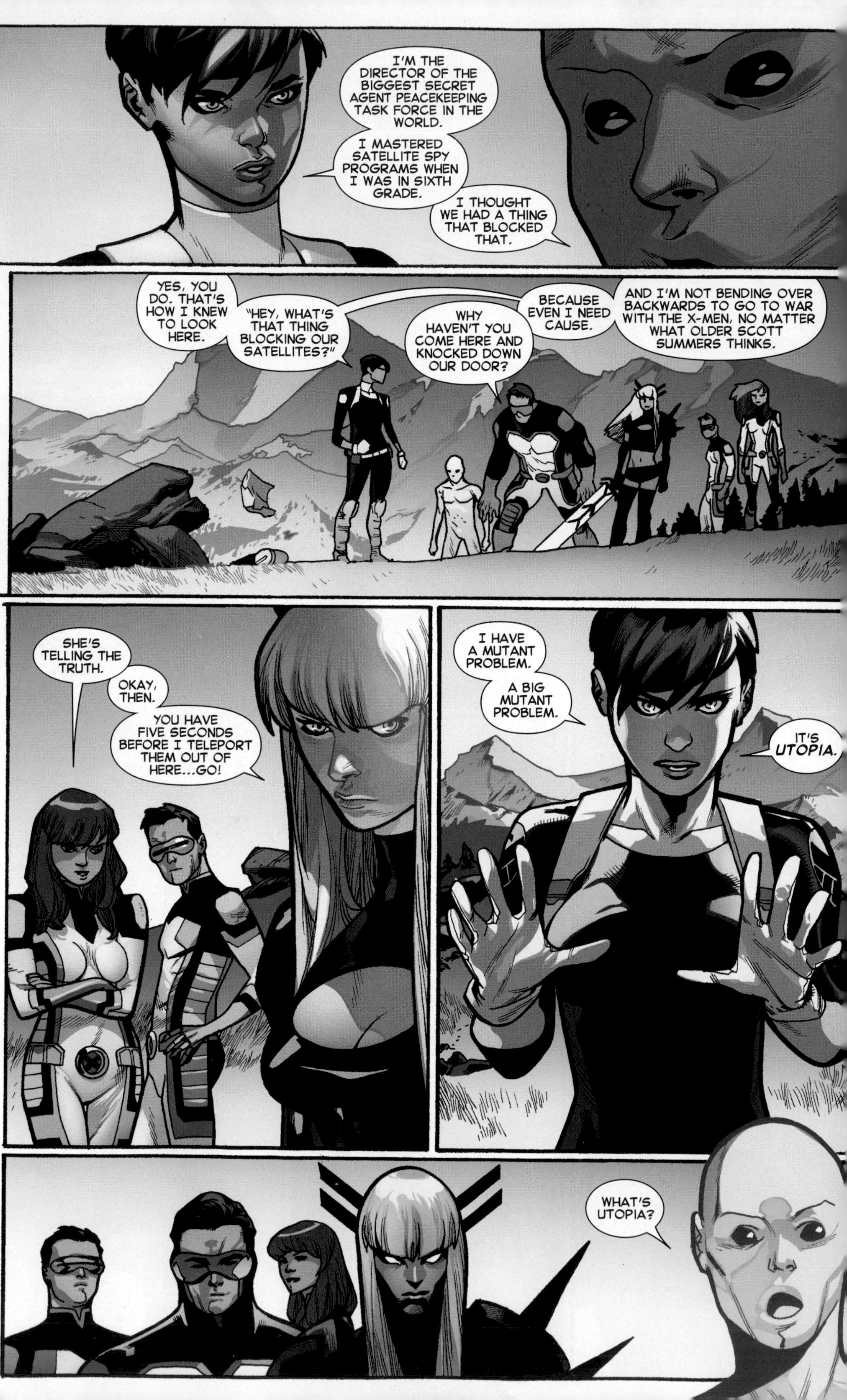
I'M THE DIRECTOR OF THE BIGGEST SECRET AGENT PEACEKEEPING TASK FORCE IN THE WORLD.
I MASTERED SATELLITE SPY PROGRAMS WHEN I WAS IN SIXTH GRADE.
I THOUGHT WE HAD A THING THAT BLOCKED THAT.
YES, YOU DO. THAT'S HOW I KNEW TO LOOK HERE.
"HEY, WHAT'S THAT THING BLOCKING OUR SATELLITES?"
WHY HAVEN'T YOU COME HERE AND KNOCKED DOWN OUR DOOR?
BECAUSE EVEN I NEED CAUSE.
AND I'M NOT BENDING OVER BACKWARDS TO GO TO WAR WITH THE X-MEN, NO MATTER WHAT OLDER SCOTT SUMMERS THINKS.
SHE'S TELLING THE TRUTH.
OKAY, THEN.
YOU HAVE FIVE SECONDS BEFORE I TELEPORT THEM OUT OF HERE...GO!
I HAVE A MUTANT PROBLEM.
A BIG MUTANT PROBLEM.
IT'S *UTOPIA*.
WHAT'S UTOPIA?

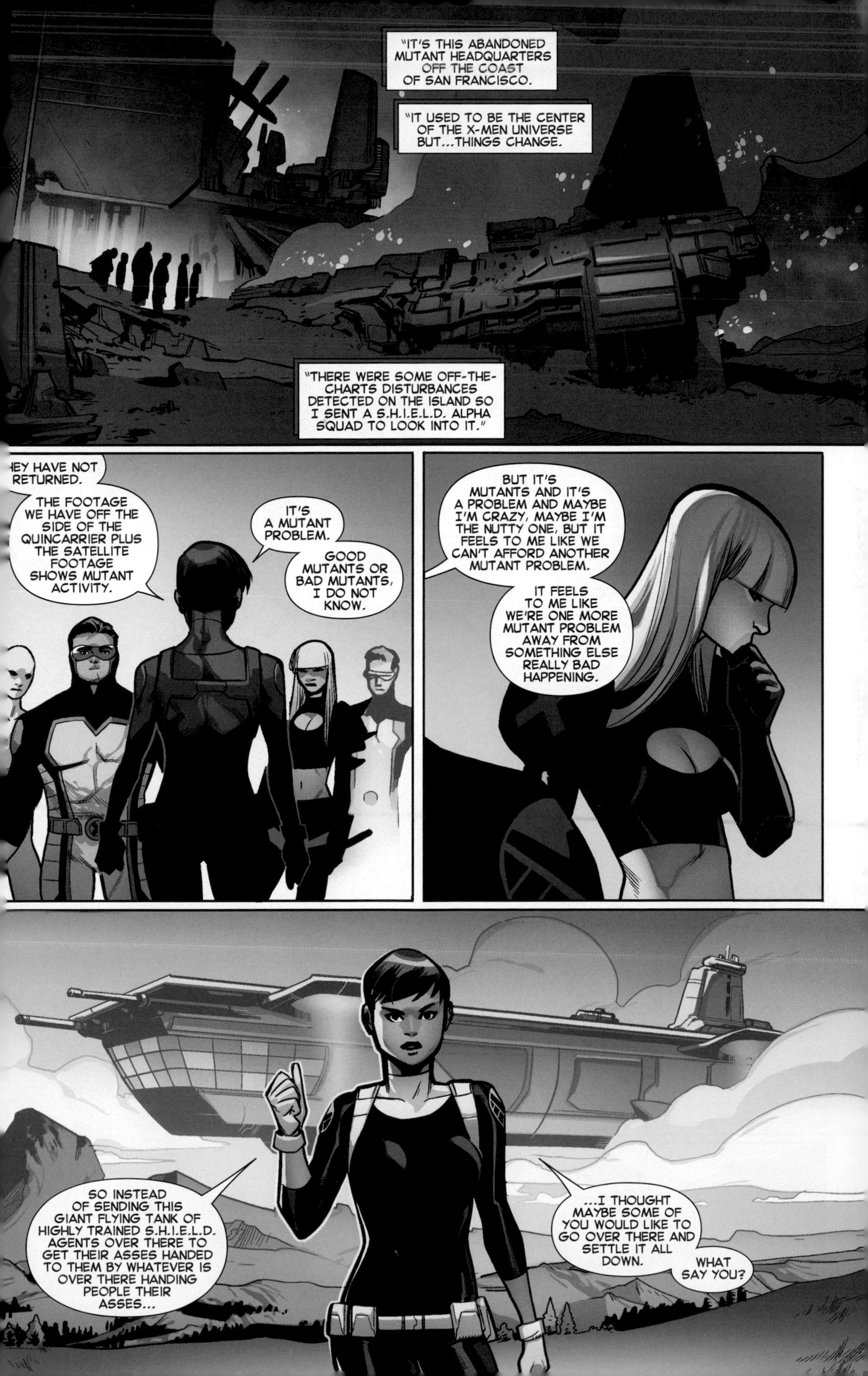
"IT'S THIS ABANDONED MUTANT HEADQUARTERS OFF THE COAST OF SAN FRANCISCO.
"IT USED TO BE THE CENTER OF THE X-MEN UNIVERSE BUT...THINGS CHANGE.
"THERE WERE SOME OFF-THE-CHARTS DISTURBANCES DETECTED ON THE ISLAND SO I SENT A S.H.I.E.L.D. ALPHA SQUAD TO LOOK INTO IT."
HEY HAVE NOT RETURNED.
THE FOOTAGE WE HAVE OFF THE SIDE OF THE QUINCARRIER PLUS THE SATELLITE FOOTAGE SHOWS MUTANT ACTIVITY.
IT'S A MUTANT PROBLEM.
GOOD MUTANTS OR BAD MUTANTS, I DO NOT KNOW.
BUT IT'S MUTANTS AND IT'S A PROBLEM AND MAYBE I'M CRAZY, MAYBE I'M THE NUTTY ONE, BUT IT FEELS TO ME LIKE WE CAN'T AFFORD ANOTHER MUTANT PROBLEM.
IT FEELS TO ME LIKE WE'RE ONE MORE MUTANT PROBLEM AWAY FROM SOMETHING ELSE REALLY BAD HAPPENING.
SO INSTEAD OF SENDING THIS GIANT FLYING TANK OF HIGHLY TRAINED S.H.I.E.L.D. AGENTS OVER THERE TO GET THEIR ASSES HANDED TO THEM BY WHATEVER IS OVER THERE HANDING PEOPLE THEIR ASSES...
...I THOUGHT MAYBE SOME OF YOU WOULD LIKE TO GO OVER THERE AND SETTLE IT ALL DOWN.
WHAT SAY YOU?

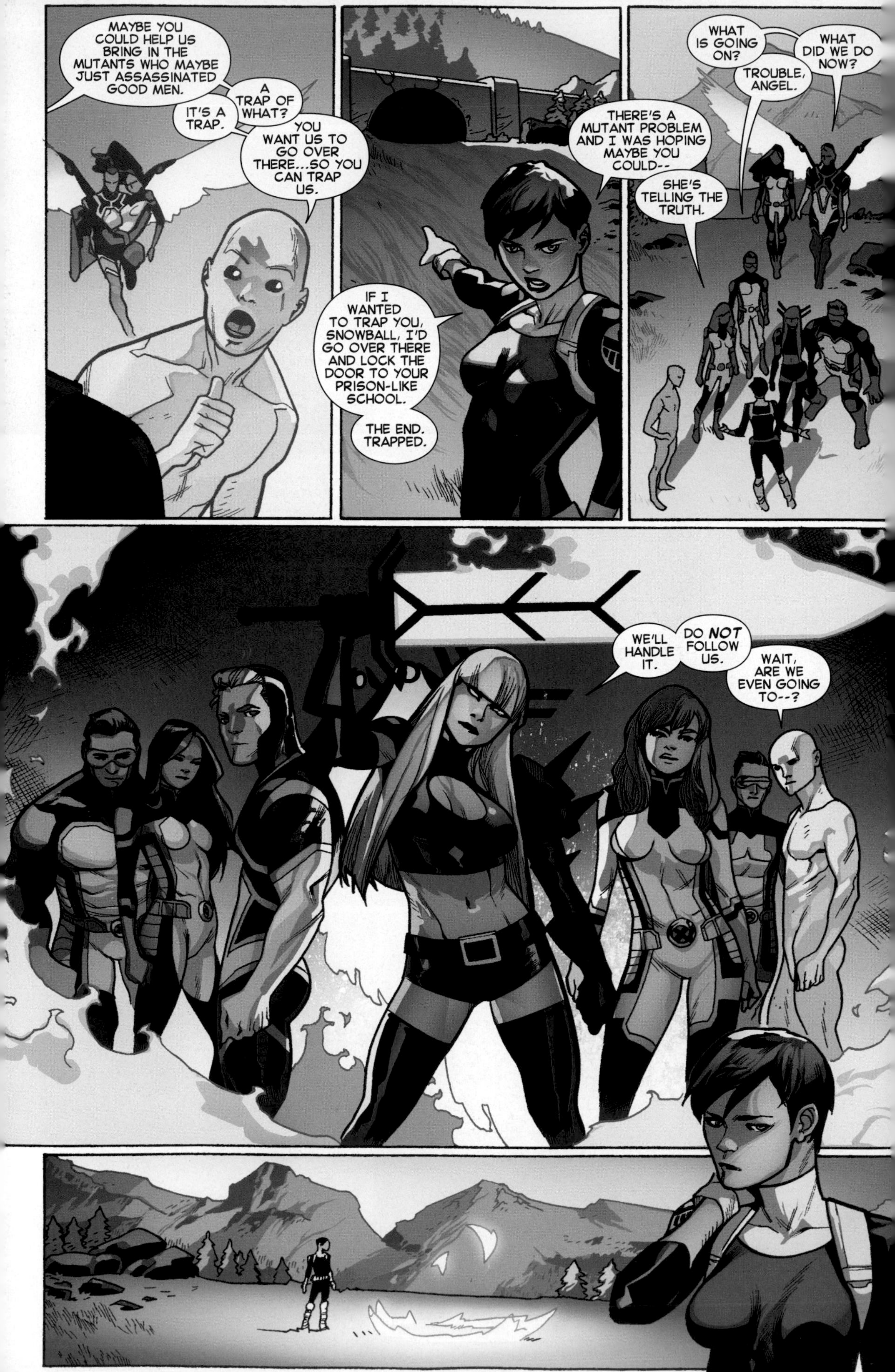
MAYBE YOU COULD HELP US BRING IN THE MUTANTS WHO MAYBE JUST ASSASSINATED GOOD MEN.
IT'S A TRAP.
A TRAP OF WHAT?
YOU WANT US TO GO OVER THERE...SO YOU CAN TRAP US.
IF I WANTED TO TRAP YOU, SNOWBALL, I'D GO OVER THERE AND LOCK THE DOOR TO YOUR PRISON-LIKE SCHOOL.
THE END. TRAPPED.
WHAT IS GOING ON?
WHAT DID WE DO NOW?
TROUBLE, ANGEL.
THERE'S A MUTANT PROBLEM AND I WAS HOPING MAYBE YOU COULD--
SHE'S TELLING THE TRUTH.
WE'LL HANDLE IT.
DO **NOT** FOLLOW US.
WAIT, ARE WE EVEN GOING TO--?

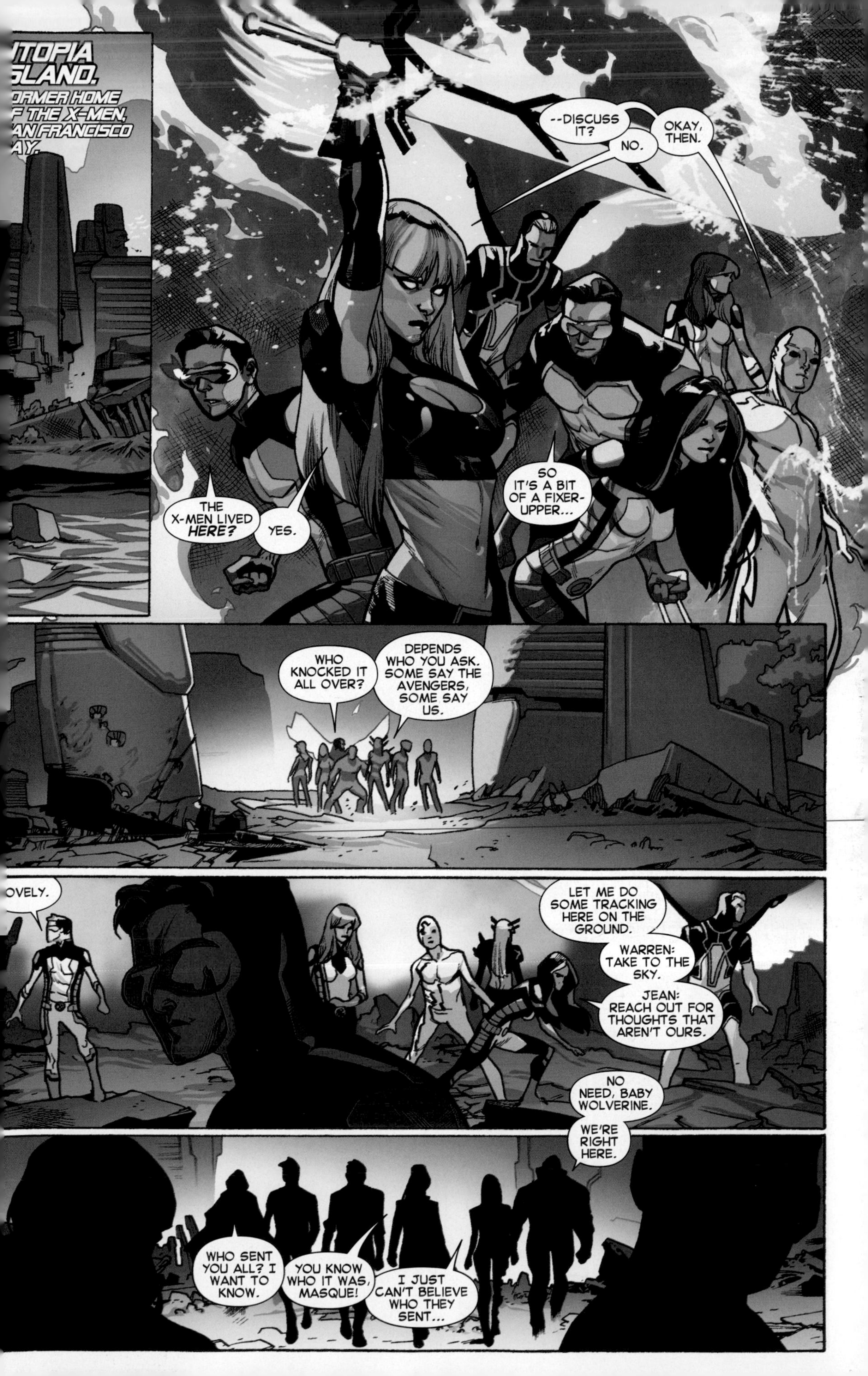
UTOPIA ISLAND.
FORMER HOME OF THE X-MEN, SAN FRANCISCO BAY.
--DISCUSS IT?
NO.
OKAY, THEN.
THE X-MEN LIVED HERE?
YES.
SO IT'S A BIT OF A FIXER-UPPER...
WHO KNOCKED IT ALL OVER?
DEPENDS WHO YOU ASK. SOME SAY THE AVENGERS, SOME SAY US.
LOVELY.
LET ME DO SOME TRACKING HERE ON THE GROUND.
WARREN: TAKE TO THE SKY.
JEAN: REACH OUT FOR THOUGHTS THAT AREN'T OURS.
NO NEED, BABY WOLVERINE.
WE'RE RIGHT HERE.
WHO SENT YOU ALL? I WANT TO KNOW.
YOU KNOW WHO IT WAS, MASQUE!
I JUST CAN'T BELIEVE WHO THEY SENT...

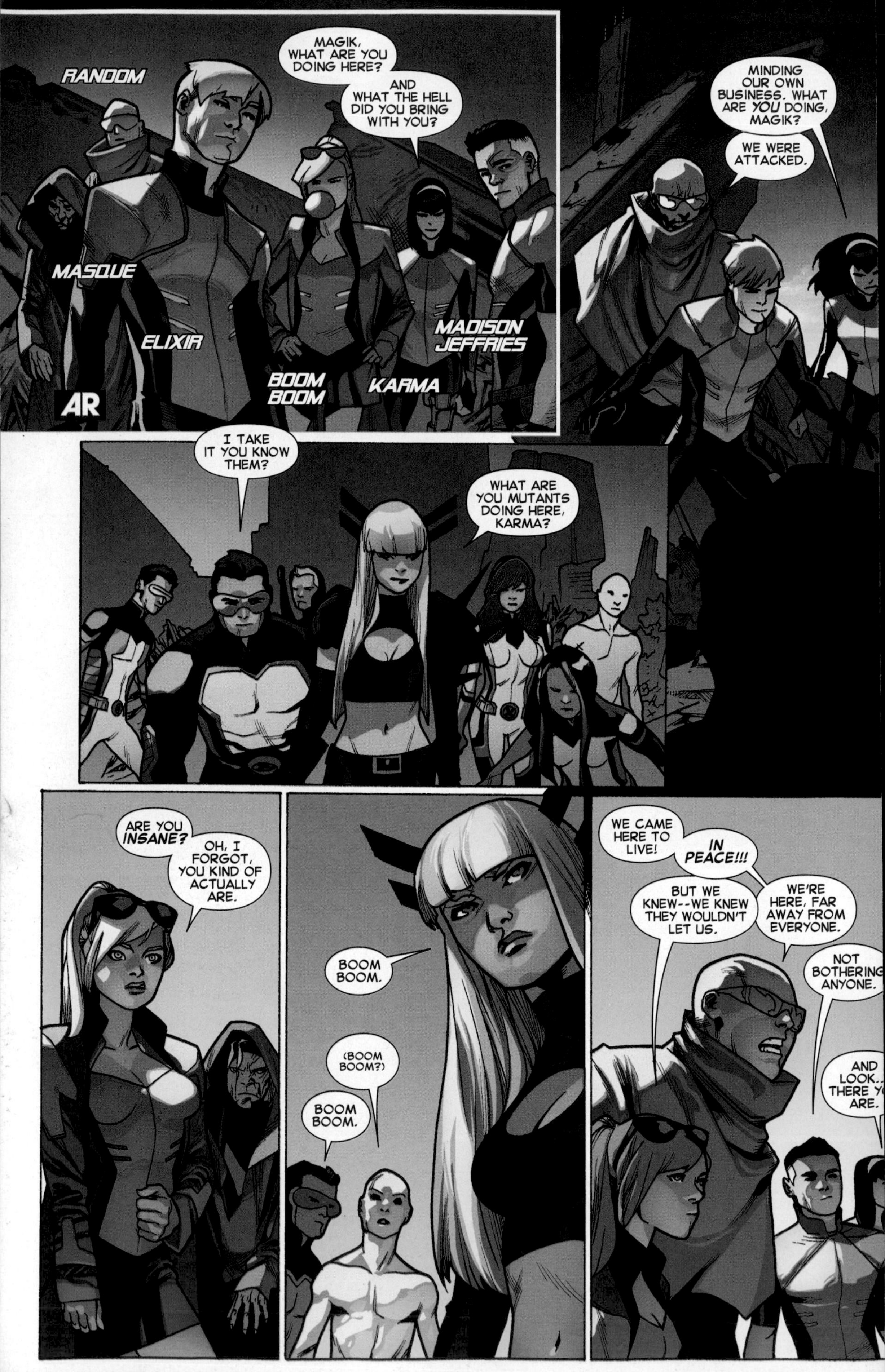
RANDOM
MASQUE
ELIXIR
BOOM BOOM
KARMA
MADISON JEFFRIES
MAGIK, WHAT ARE YOU DOING HERE?
AND WHAT THE HELL DID YOU BRING WITH YOU?
MINDING OUR OWN BUSINESS. WHAT ARE YOU DOING, MAGIK?
WE WERE ATTACKED.
I TAKE IT YOU KNOW THEM?
WHAT ARE YOU MUTANTS DOING HERE, KARMA?
ARE YOU INSANE?
OH, I FORGOT, YOU KIND OF ACTUALLY ARE.
BOOM BOOM.
(BOOM BOOM?)
BOOM BOOM.
WE CAME HERE TO LIVE!
IN PEACE!!!
BUT WE KNEW--WE KNEW THEY WOULDN'T LET US.
WE'RE HERE, FAR AWAY FROM EVERYONE.
NOT BOTHERING ANYONE.
AND LOOK.. THERE Y ARE.

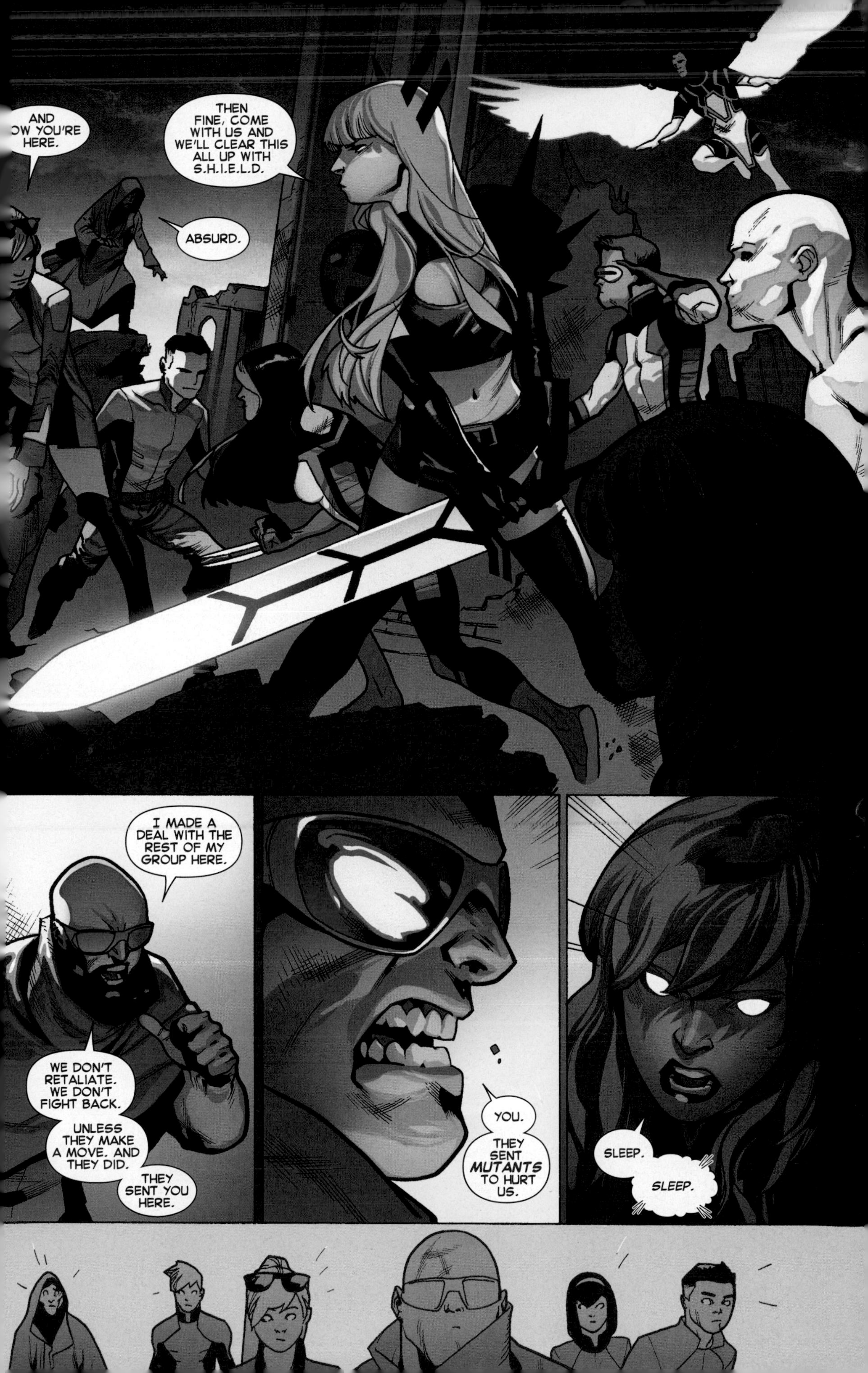
AND
OW YOU'RE
HERE.
THEN FINE, COME WITH US AND WE'LL CLEAR THIS ALL UP WITH S.H.I.E.L.D.
ABSURD.
I MADE A DEAL WITH THE REST OF MY GROUP HERE.
WE DON'T RETALIATE. WE DON'T FIGHT BACK.
UNLESS THEY MAKE A MOVE. AND THEY DID.
THEY SENT YOU HERE.
YOU.
THEY SENT MUTANTS TO HURT US.
SLEEP.
SLEEP.

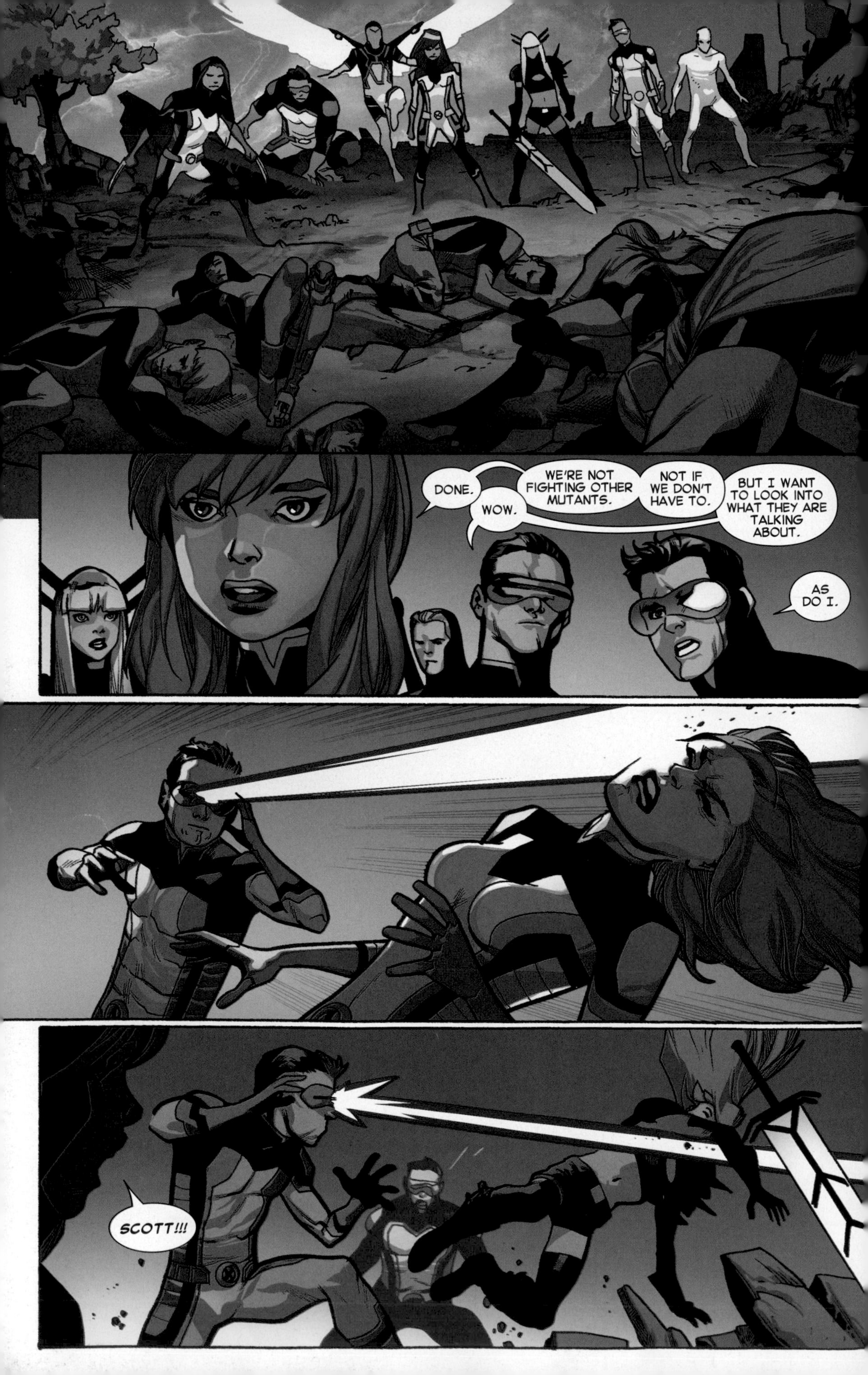
DONE.
WOW.
WE'RE NOT FIGHTING OTHER MUTANTS.
NOT IF WE DON'T HAVE TO.
BUT I WANT TO LOOK INTO WHAT THEY ARE TALKING ABOUT.
AS DO I.
SCOTT!!!

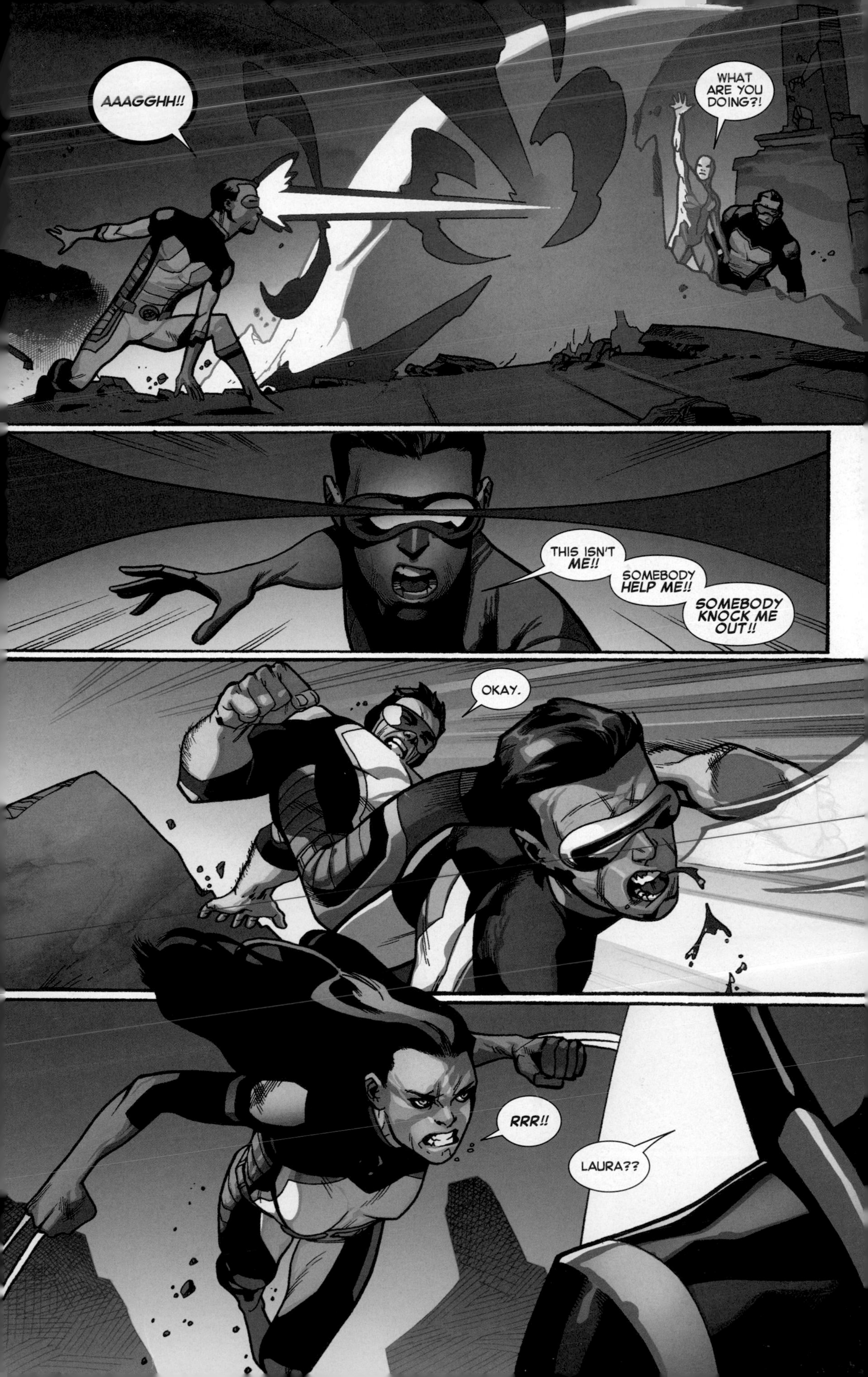
AAAGGHH!!
WHAT ARE YOU DOING?!
THIS ISN'T ME!!
SOMEBODY HELP ME!!
SOMEBODY KNOCK ME OUT!!
OKAY.
RRR!!
LAURA??

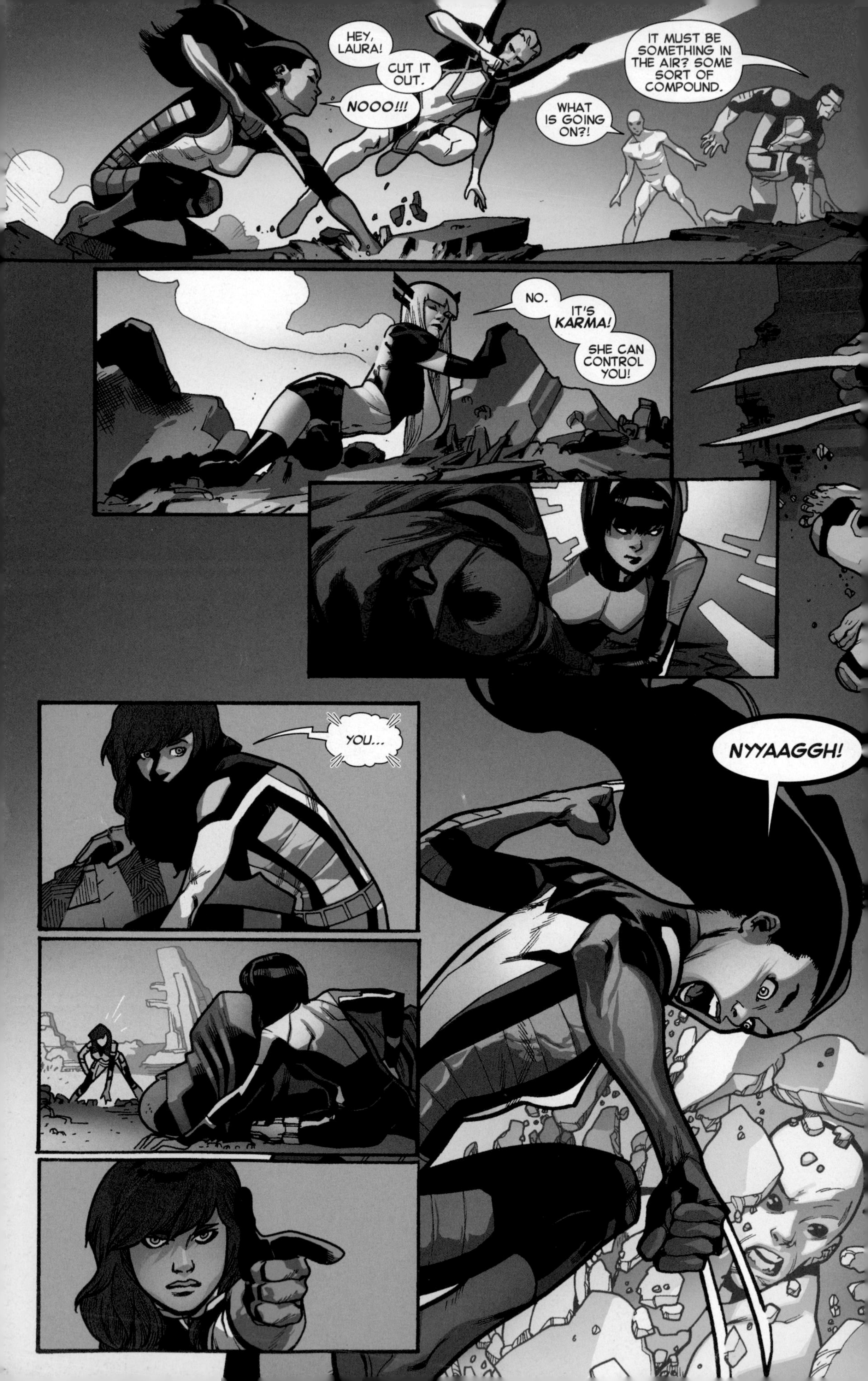
HEY, LAURA!
CUT IT OUT.
NOOO!!!
IT MUST BE SOMETHING IN THE AIR? SOME SORT OF COMPOUND.
WHAT IS GOING ON?!
NO.
IT'S KARMA!
SHE CAN CONTROL YOU!
YOU...
NYYAAGGH!

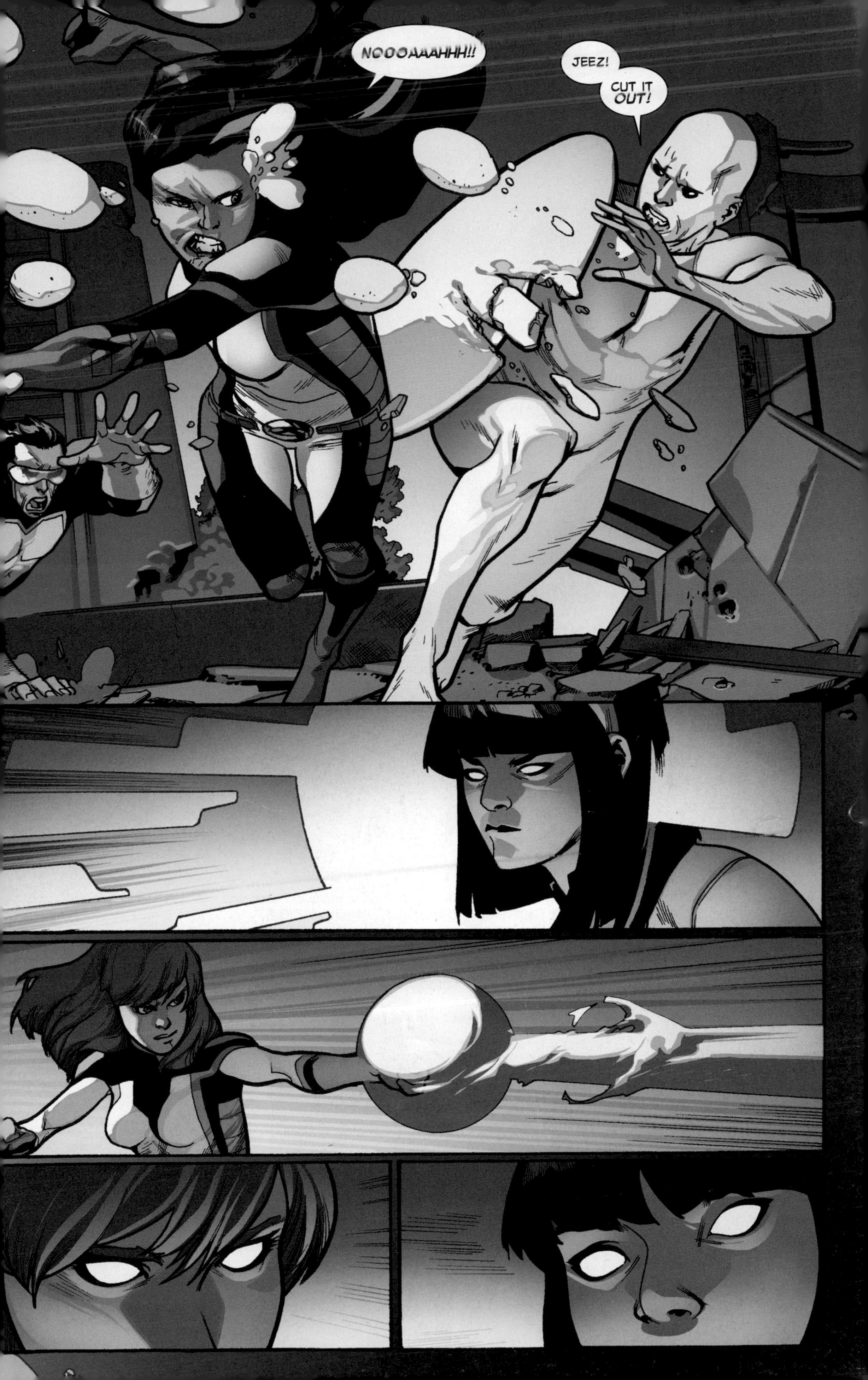
NOOOAAAHHH!!
JEEZ!
CUT IT OUT!

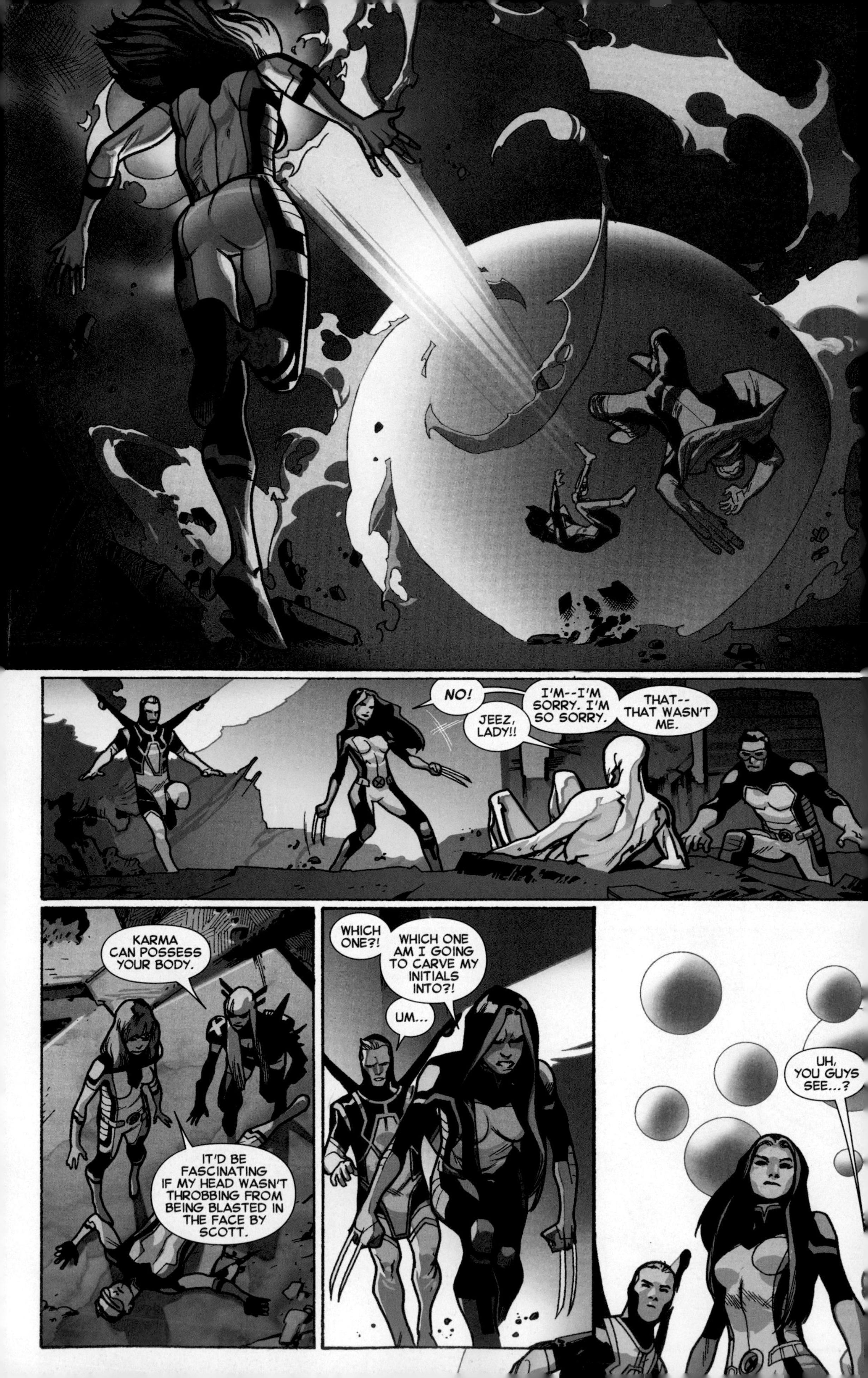
NO!
I'M--I'M SORRY. I'M SO SORRY.
THAT--THAT WASN'T ME.
JEEZ, LADY!!
KARMA CAN POSSESS YOUR BODY.
IT'D BE FASCINATING IF MY HEAD WASN'T THROBBING FROM BEING BLASTED IN THE FACE BY SCOTT.
WHICH ONE?!
WHICH ONE AM I GOING TO CARVE MY INITIALS INTO?!
UM...
UH, YOU GUYS SEE...?

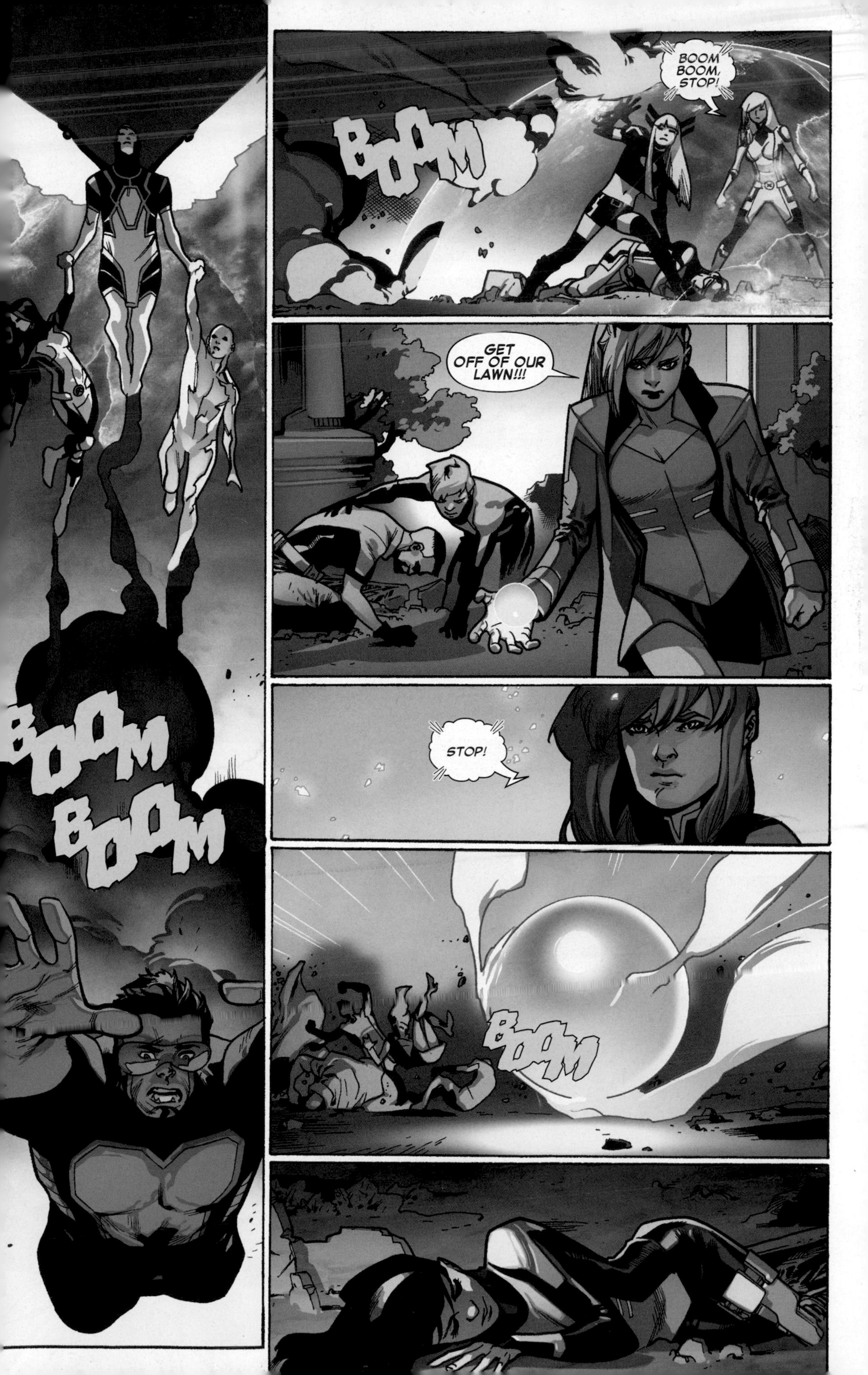

BOOM
BOOM
BOOM BOOM, STOP!
BOOM
GET OFF OF OUR LAWN!!!
STOP!
BOOM

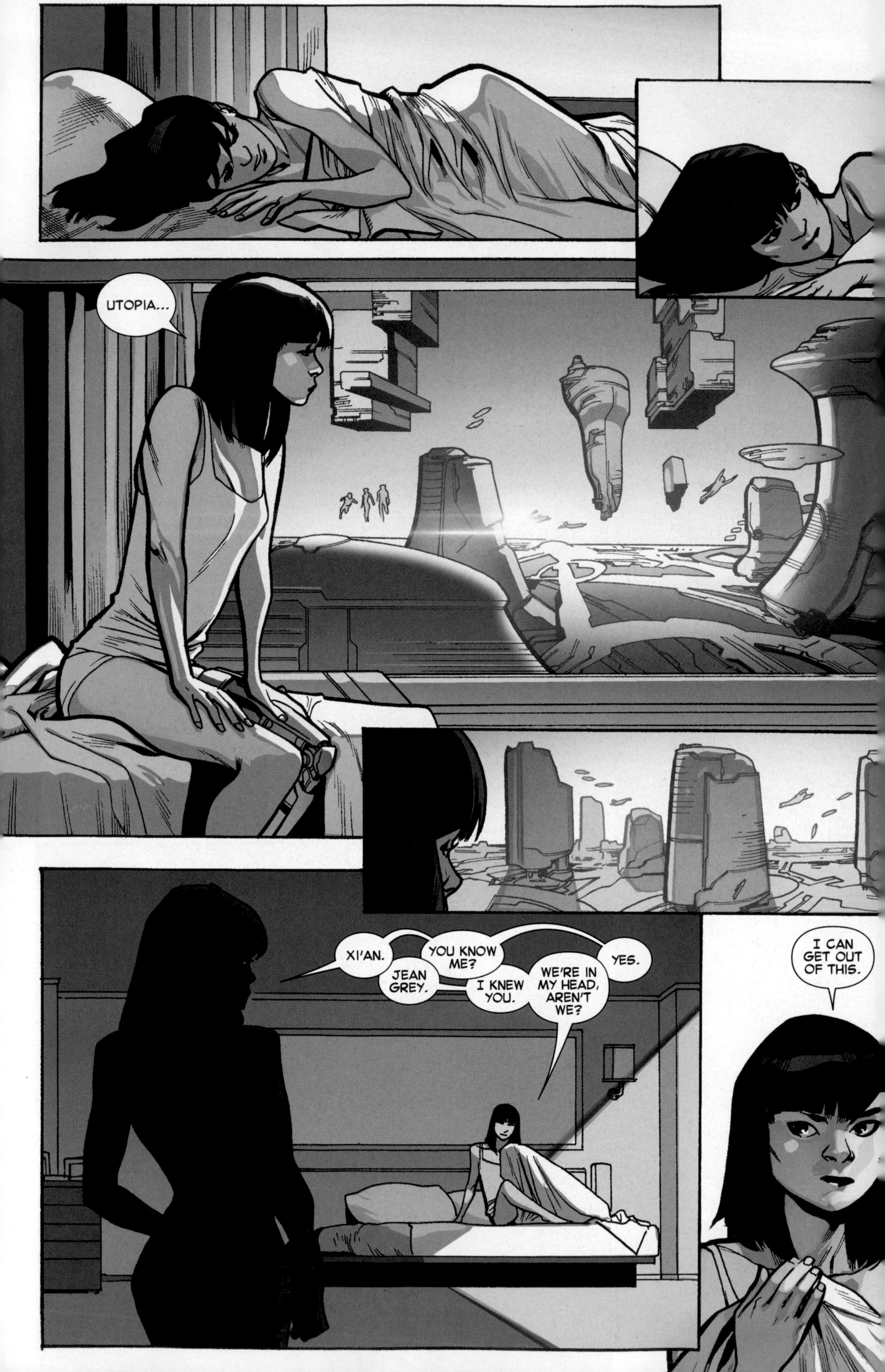
UTOPIA...
XI'AN.
YOU KNOW ME?
JEAN GREY.
I KNEW YOU.
YES.
WE'RE IN MY HEAD, AREN'T WE?
I CAN GET OUT OF THIS.

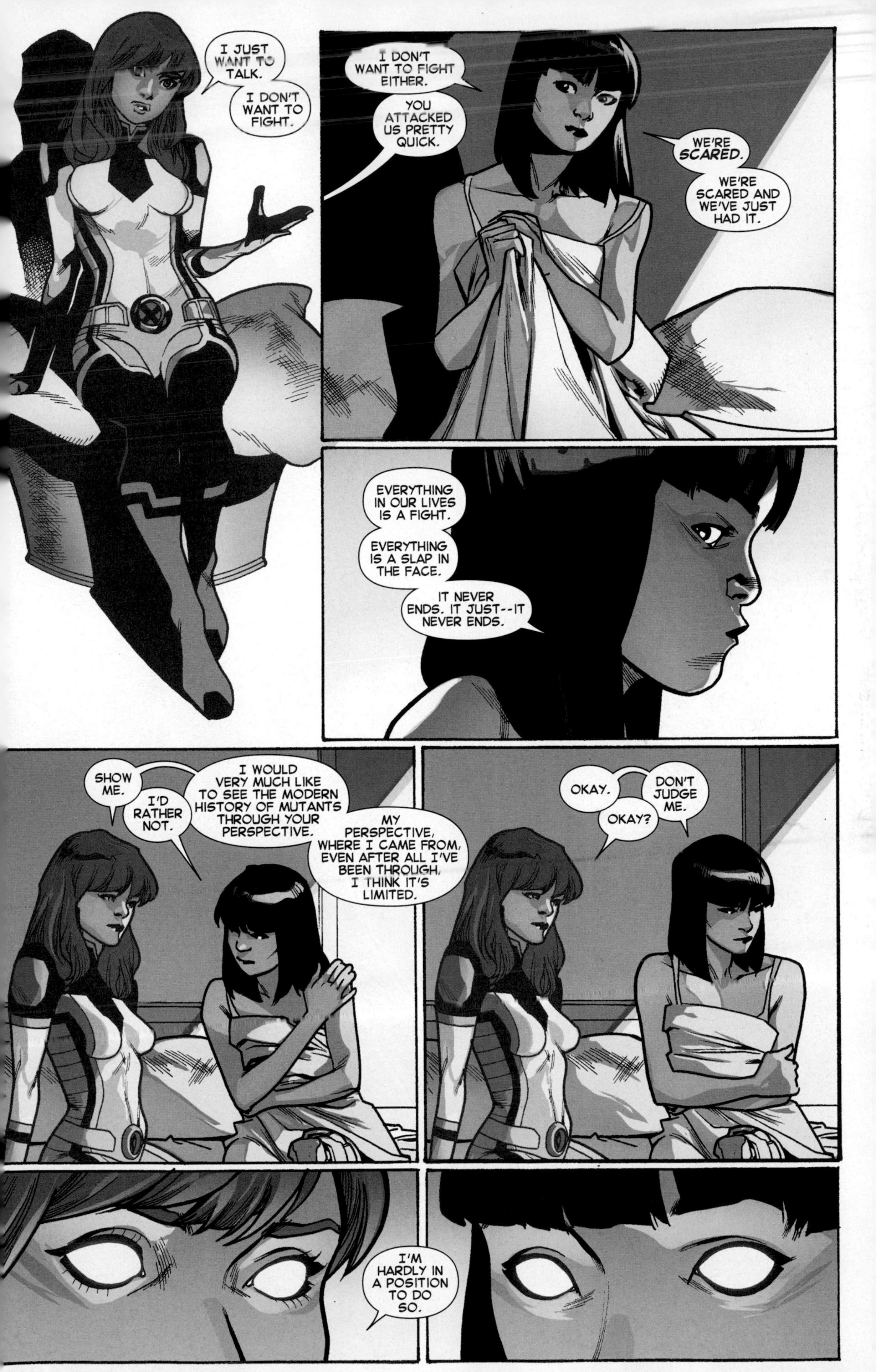
I JUST WANT TO TALK.
I DON'T WANT TO FIGHT.
I DON'T WANT TO FIGHT EITHER.
YOU ATTACKED US PRETTY QUICK.
WE'RE SCARED.
WE'RE SCARED AND WE'VE JUST HAD IT.
EVERYTHING IN OUR LIVES IS A FIGHT.
EVERYTHING IS A SLAP IN THE FACE.
IT NEVER ENDS. IT JUST--IT NEVER ENDS.
SHOW ME.
I'D RATHER NOT.
I WOULD VERY MUCH LIKE TO SEE THE MODERN HISTORY OF MUTANTS THROUGH YOUR PERSPECTIVE.
MY PERSPECTIVE, WHERE I CAME FROM, EVEN AFTER ALL I'VE BEEN THROUGH, I THINK IT'S LIMITED.
OKAY.
DON'T JUDGE ME.
OKAY?
I'M HARDLY IN A POSITION TO DO SO.

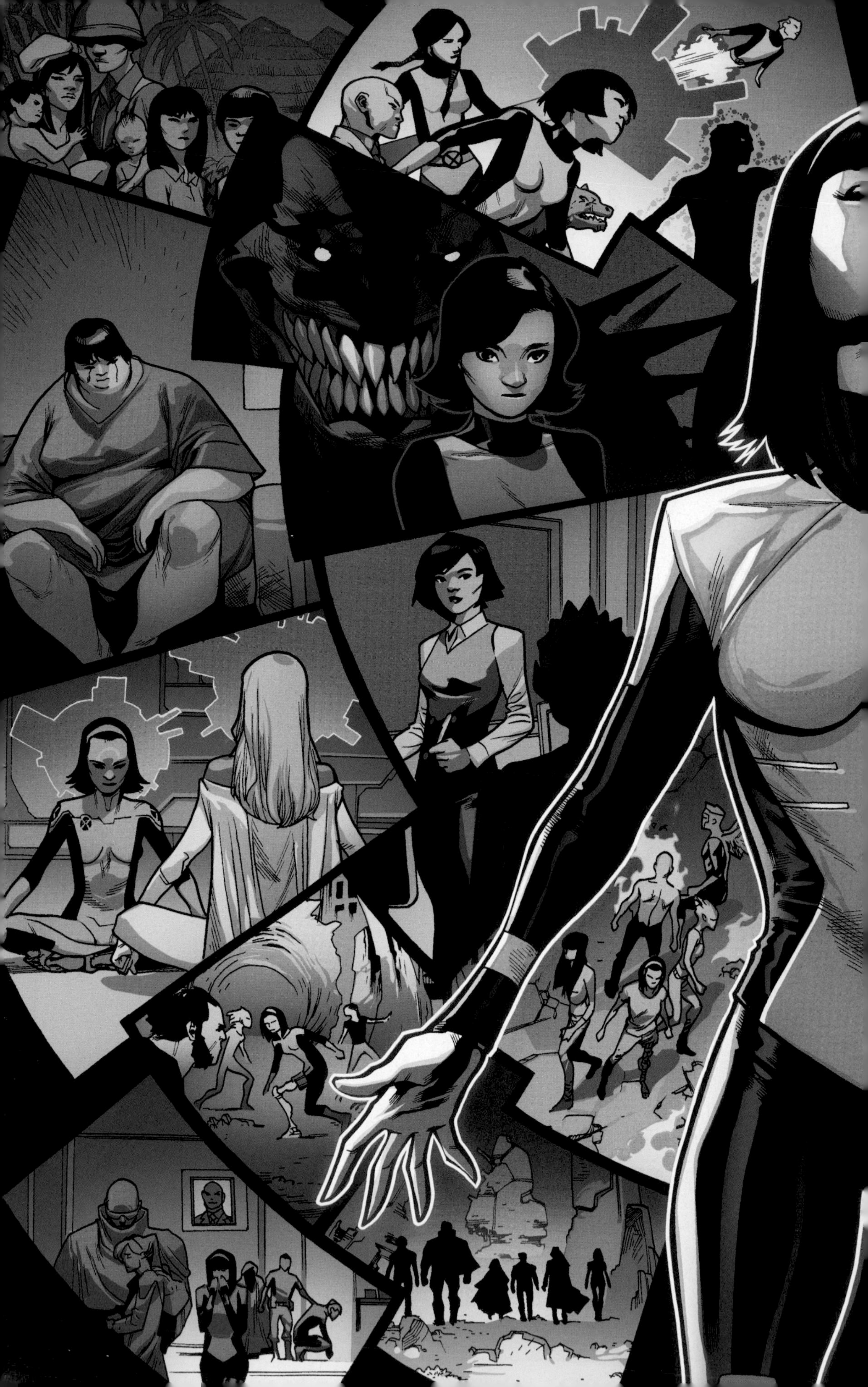

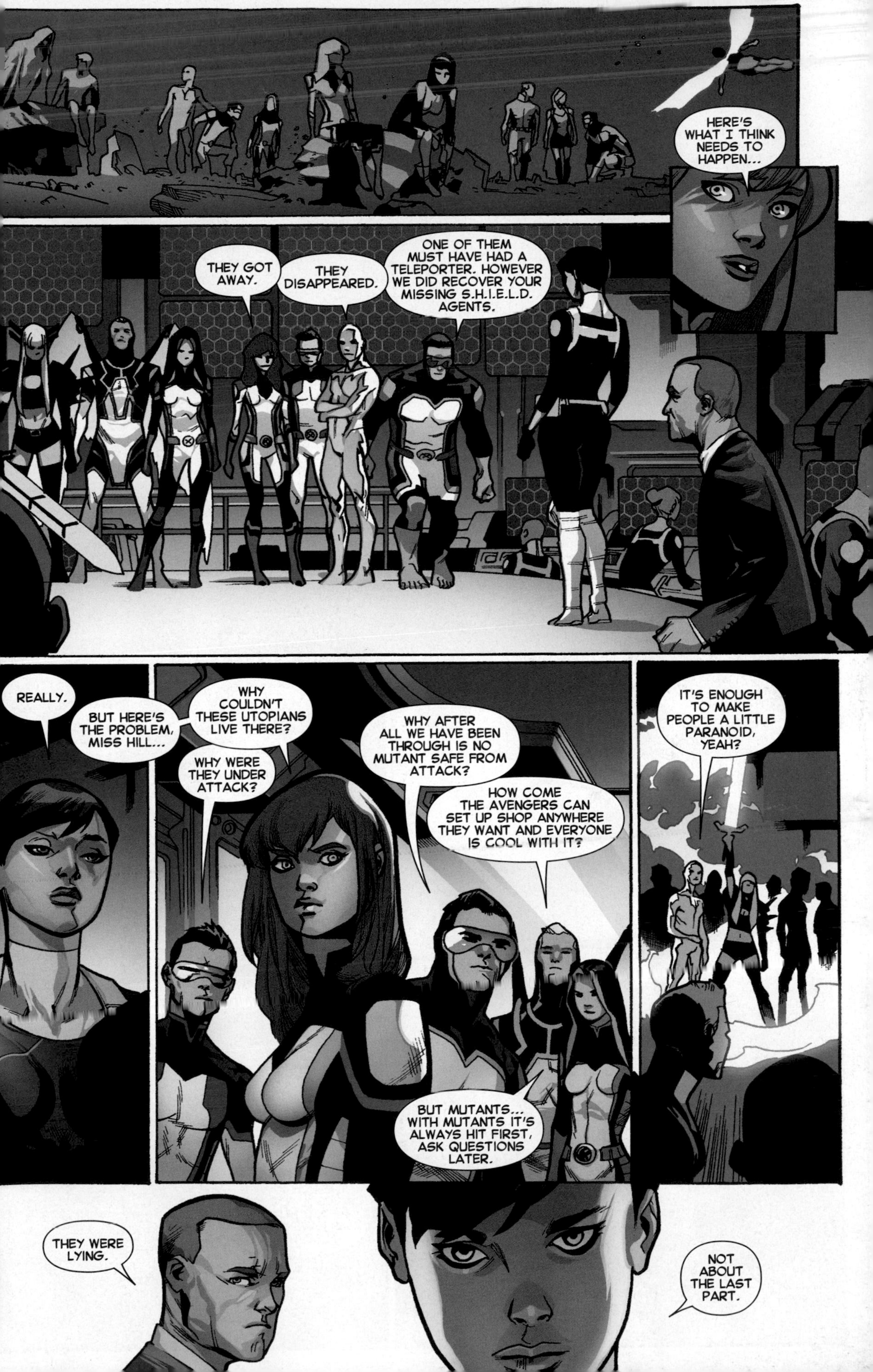
HERE'S WHAT I THINK NEEDS TO HAPPEN...
THEY GOT AWAY.
THEY DISAPPEARED.
ONE OF THEM MUST HAVE HAD A TELEPORTER. HOWEVER WE DID RECOVER YOUR MISSING S.H.I.E.L.D. AGENTS.
REALLY.
BUT HERE'S THE PROBLEM, MISS HILL...
WHY COULDN'T THESE UTOPIANS LIVE THERE?
WHY WERE THEY UNDER ATTACK?
WHY AFTER ALL WE HAVE BEEN THROUGH IS NO MUTANT SAFE FROM ATTACK?
HOW COME THE AVENGERS CAN SET UP SHOP ANYWHERE THEY WANT AND EVERYONE IS COOL WITH IT?
BUT MUTANTS... WITH MUTANTS IT'S ALWAYS HIT FIRST, ASK QUESTIONS LATER.
IT'S ENOUGH TO MAKE PEOPLE A LITTLE PARANOID, YEAH?
THEY WERE LYING.
NOT ABOUT THE LAST PART.

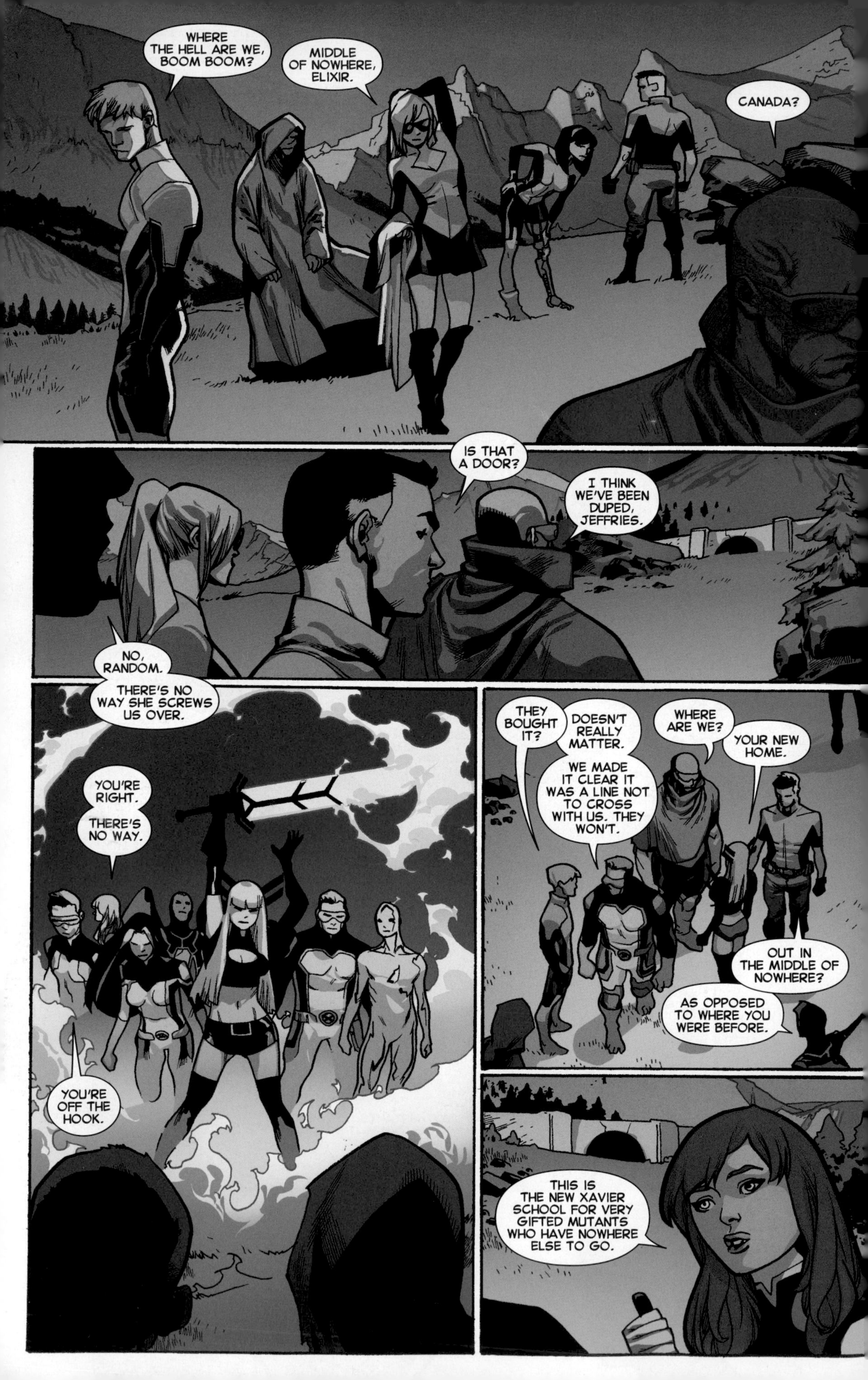
WHERE THE HELL ARE WE, BOOM BOOM?
MIDDLE OF NOWHERE, ELIXIR.
CANADA?
IS THAT A DOOR?
I THINK WE'VE BEEN DUPED, JEFFRIES.
NO, RANDOM.
THERE'S NO WAY SHE SCREWS US OVER.
YOU'RE RIGHT.
THERE'S NO WAY.
YOU'RE OFF THE HOOK.
THEY BOUGHT IT?
DOESN'T REALLY MATTER.
WE MADE IT CLEAR IT WAS A LINE NOT TO CROSS WITH US. THEY WON'T.
WHERE ARE WE?
YOUR NEW HOME.
OUT IN THE MIDDLE OF NOWHERE?
AS OPPOSED TO WHERE YOU WERE BEFORE.
THIS IS THE NEW XAVIER SCHOOL FOR VERY GIFTED MUTANTS WHO HAVE NOWHERE ELSE TO GO.

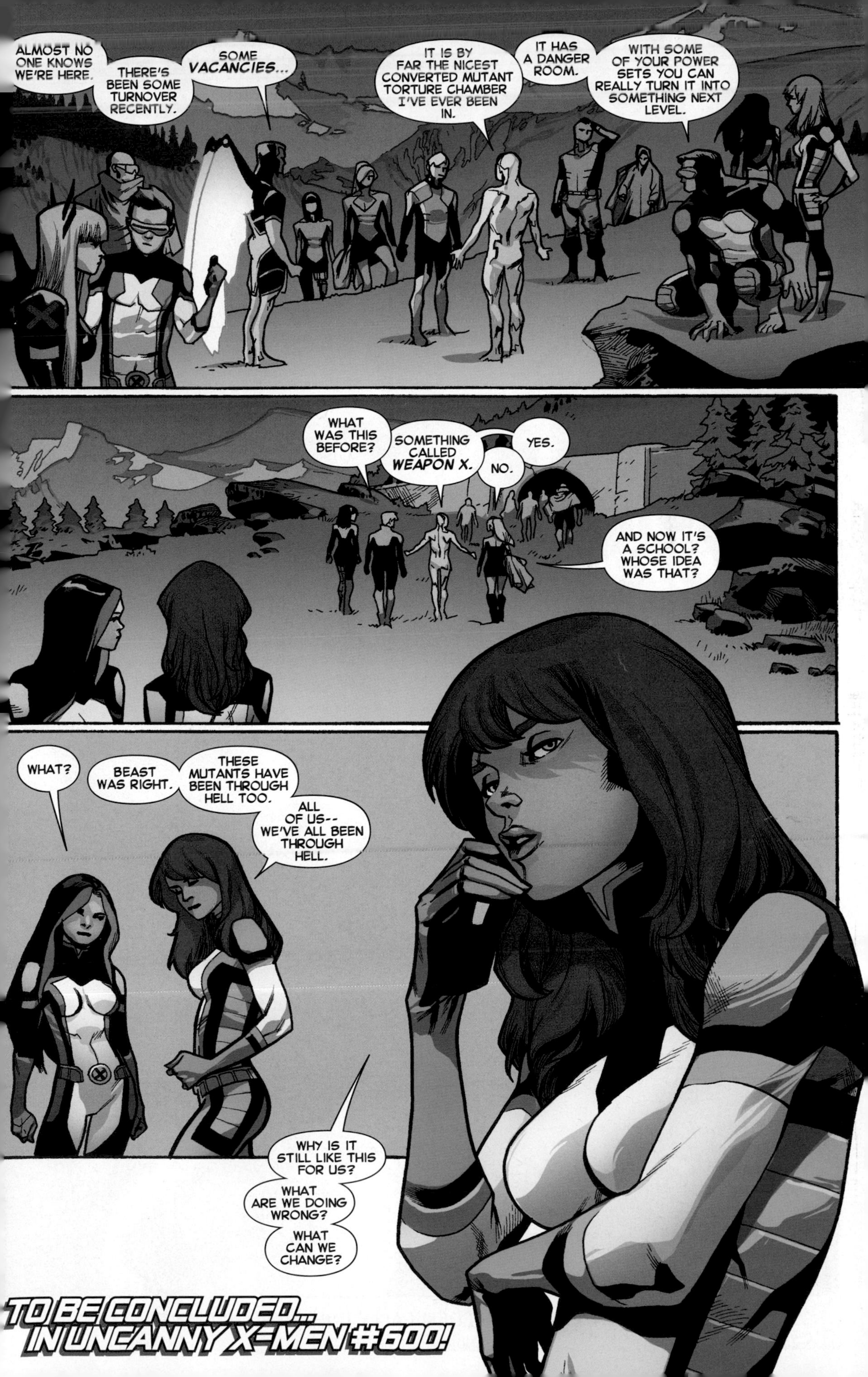
ALMOST NO ONE KNOWS WE'RE HERE.
THERE'S BEEN SOME TURNOVER RECENTLY.
SOME VACANCIES...
IT IS BY FAR THE NICEST CONVERTED MUTANT TORTURE CHAMBER I'VE EVER BEEN IN.
IT HAS A DANGER ROOM.
WITH SOME OF YOUR POWER SETS YOU CAN REALLY TURN IT INTO SOMETHING NEXT LEVEL.
WHAT WAS THIS BEFORE?
SOMETHING CALLED WEAPON X.
YES.
NO.
AND NOW IT'S A SCHOOL? WHOSE IDEA WAS THAT?
WHAT?
BEAST WAS RIGHT.
THESE MUTANTS HAVE BEEN THROUGH HELL TOO.
ALL OF US-- WE'VE ALL BEEN THROUGH HELL.
WHY IS IT STILL LIKE THIS FOR US?
WHAT ARE WE DOING WRONG?
WHAT CAN WE CHANGE?
TO BE CONCLUDED... IN UNCANNY X-MEN #600!

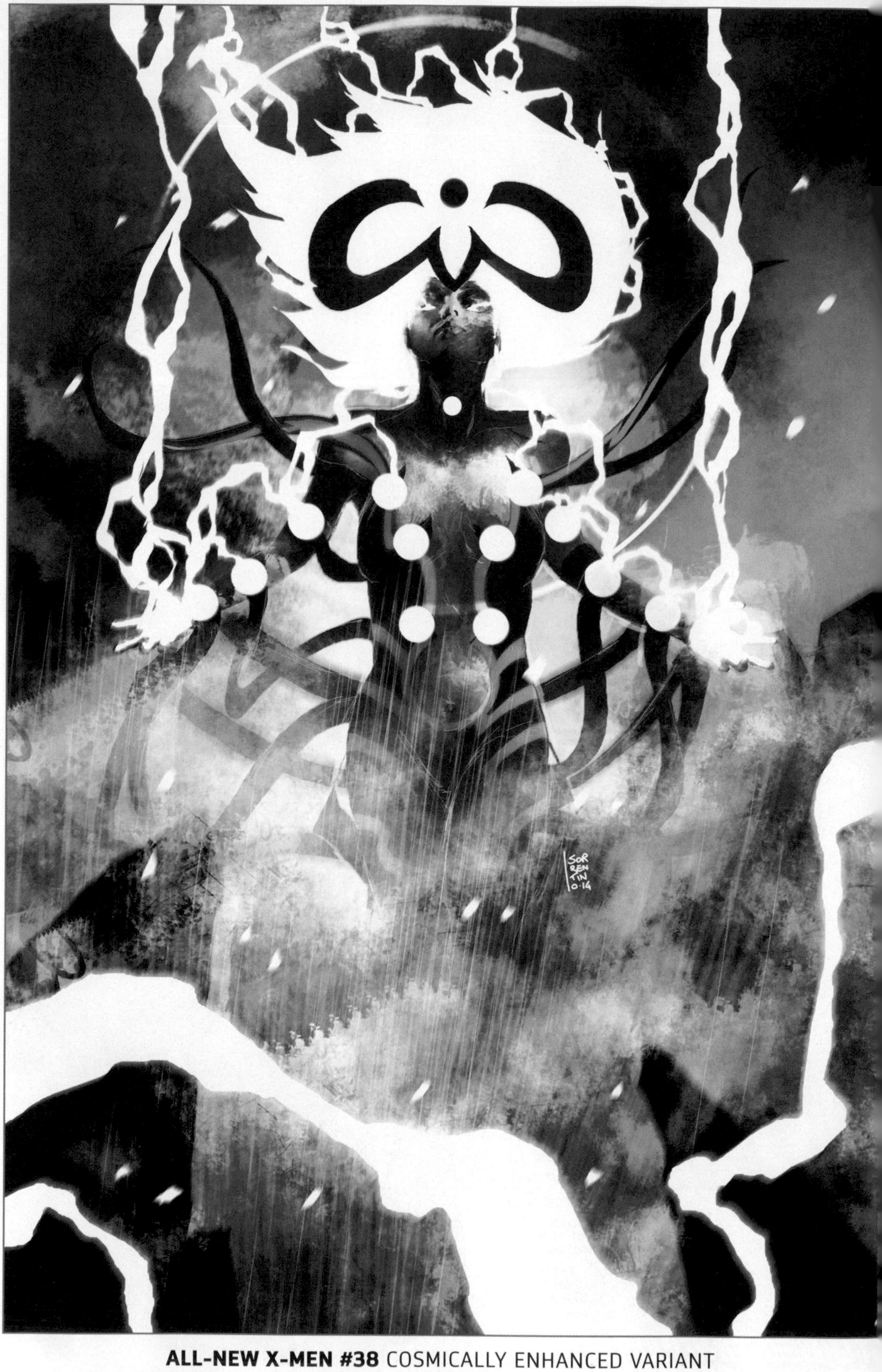

ALL-NEW X-MEN #38 COSMICALLY ENHANCED VARIANT
BY ANDREA SORRENTINO

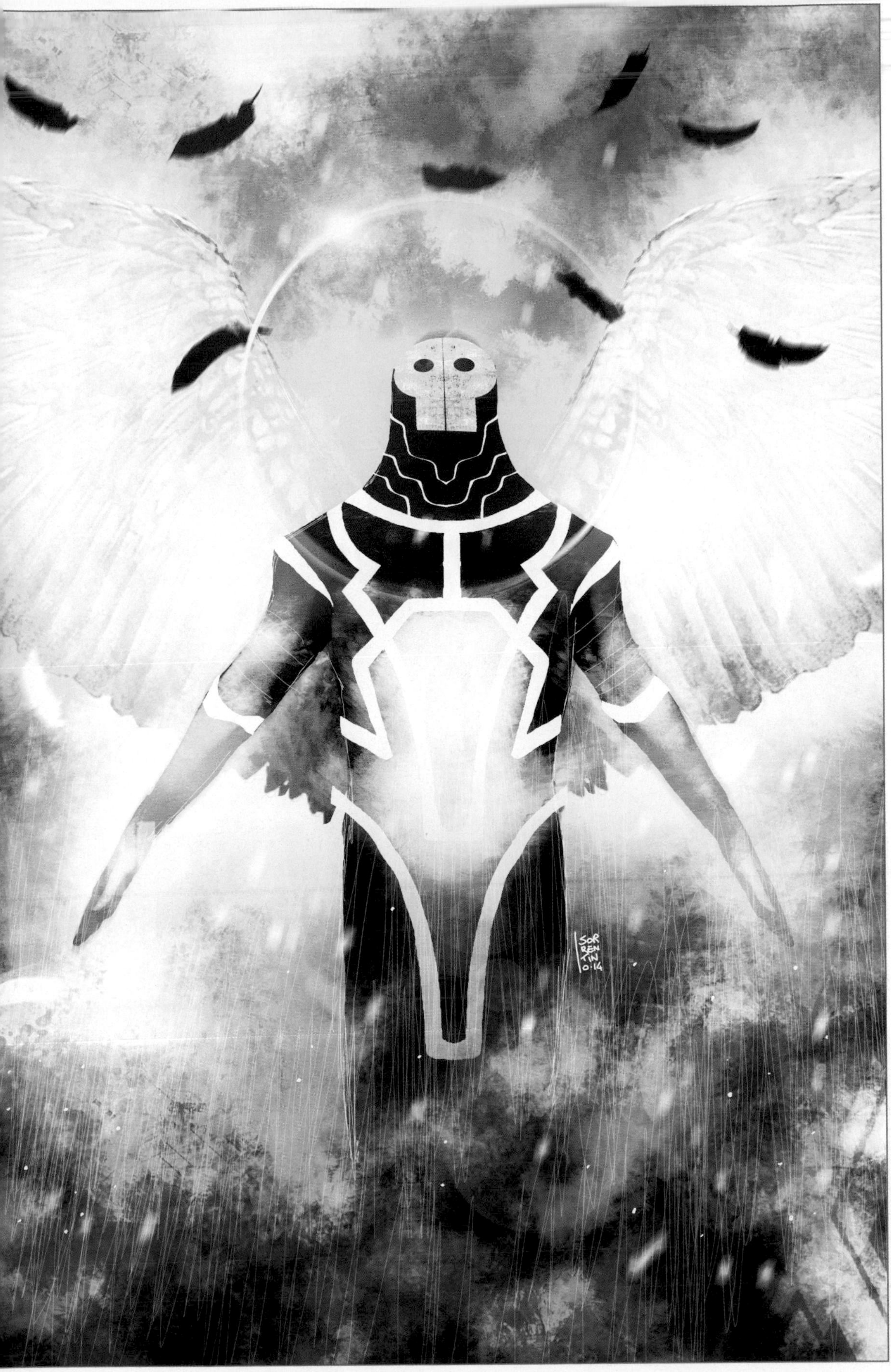

ALL-NEW X-MEN #39 COSMICALLY ENHANCED VARIANT
BY ANDREA SORRENTINO

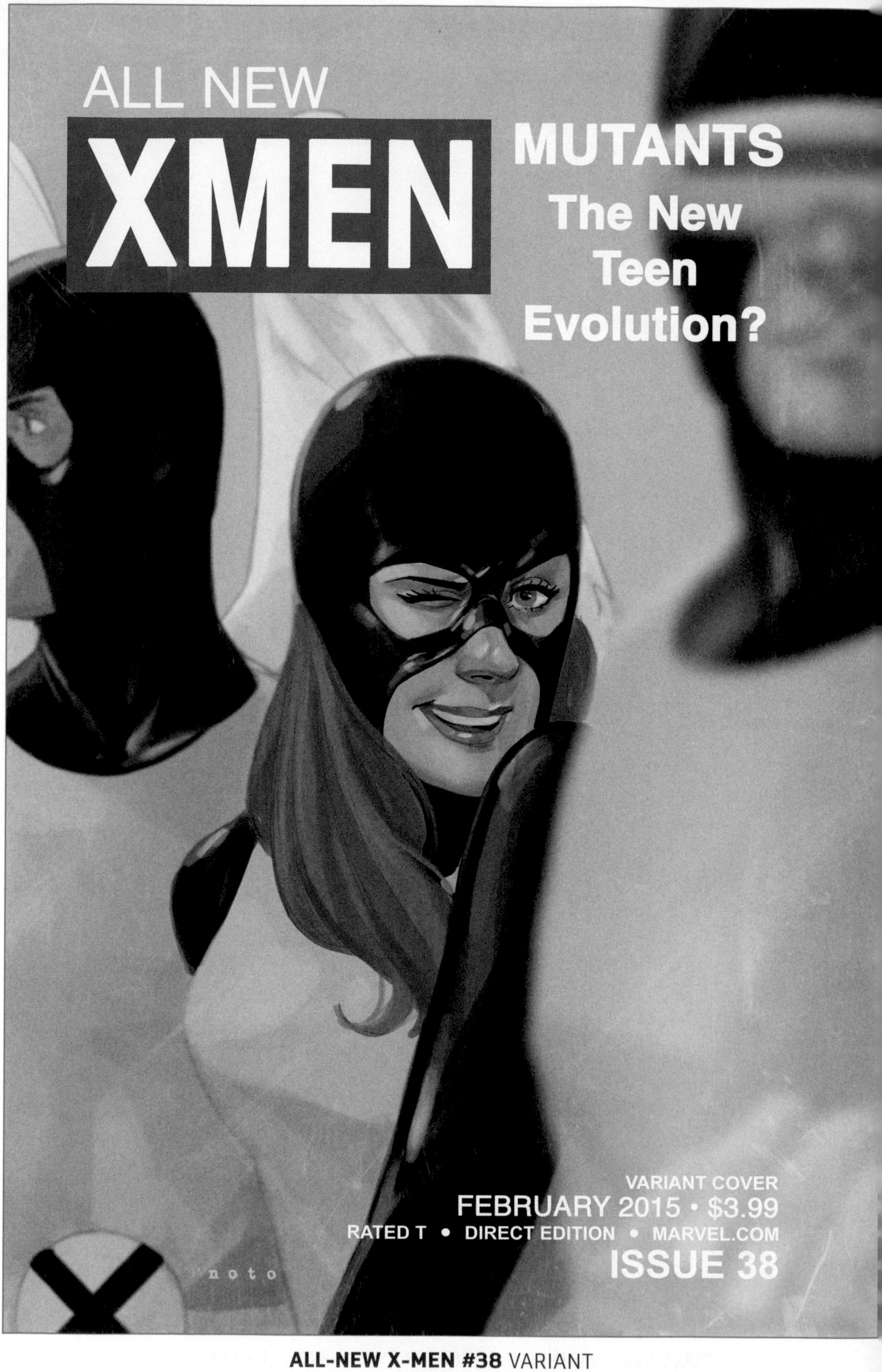
ALL NEW
XMEN
MUTANTS
The New
Teen
Evolution?
VARIANT COVER
FEBRUARY 2015 • $3.99
RATED T • DIRECT EDITION • MARVEL.COM
ISSUE 38
noto

ALL-NEW X-MEN #38 VARIANT
BY PHIL NOTO

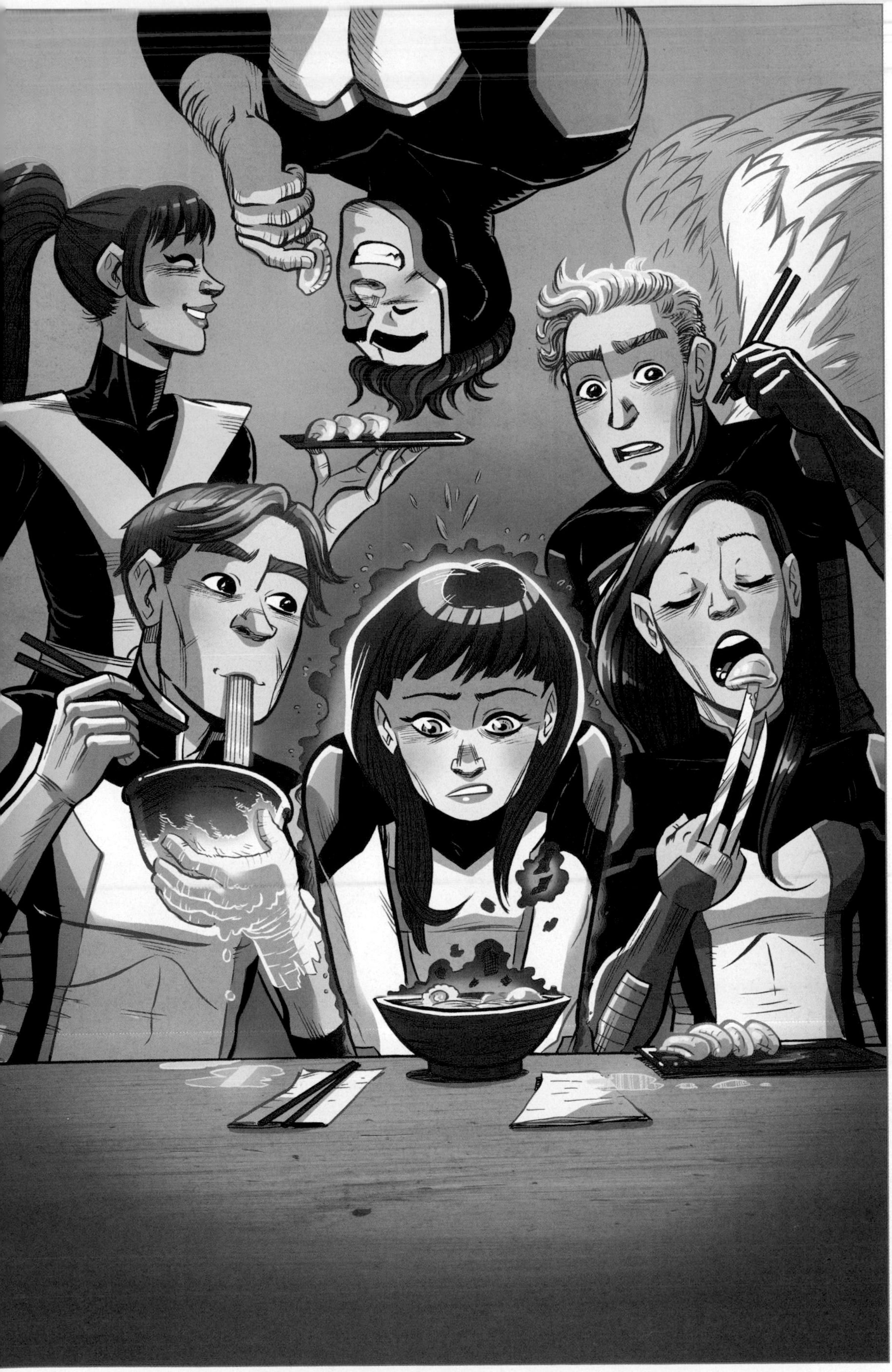

ALL-NEW X-MEN #39 WOMEN OF MARVEL VARIANT
BY FAITH ERIN HICKS & PAULINA GANUCHEAU

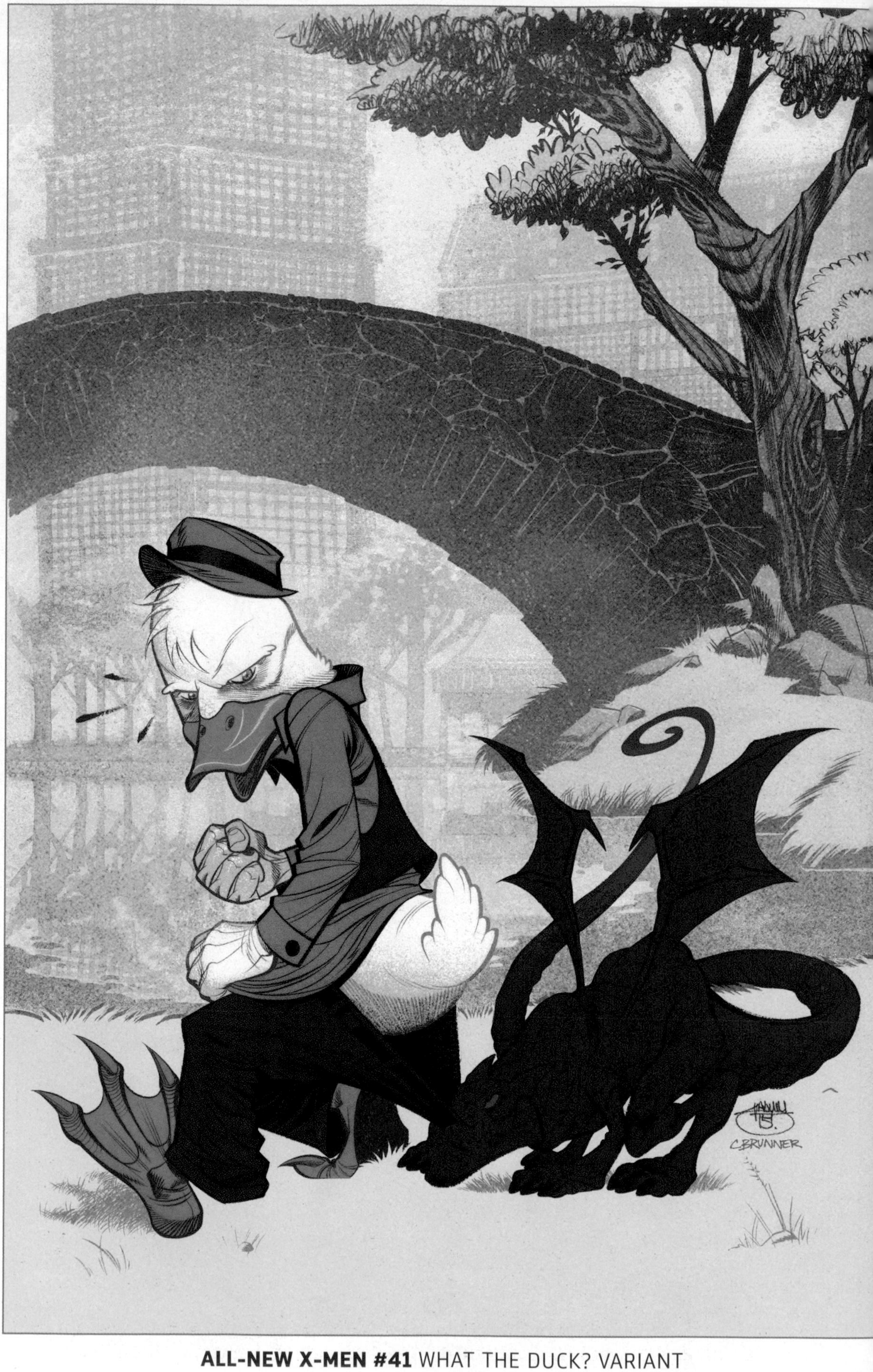
C.BRUNNER

ALL-NEW X-MEN #41 WHAT THE DUCK? VARIANT

BY SHAWN CRYSTAL & CHRISTOPHER BRUNNER

▼ #38, PAGE 4 ART BY **ANDREA SORRENTINO**

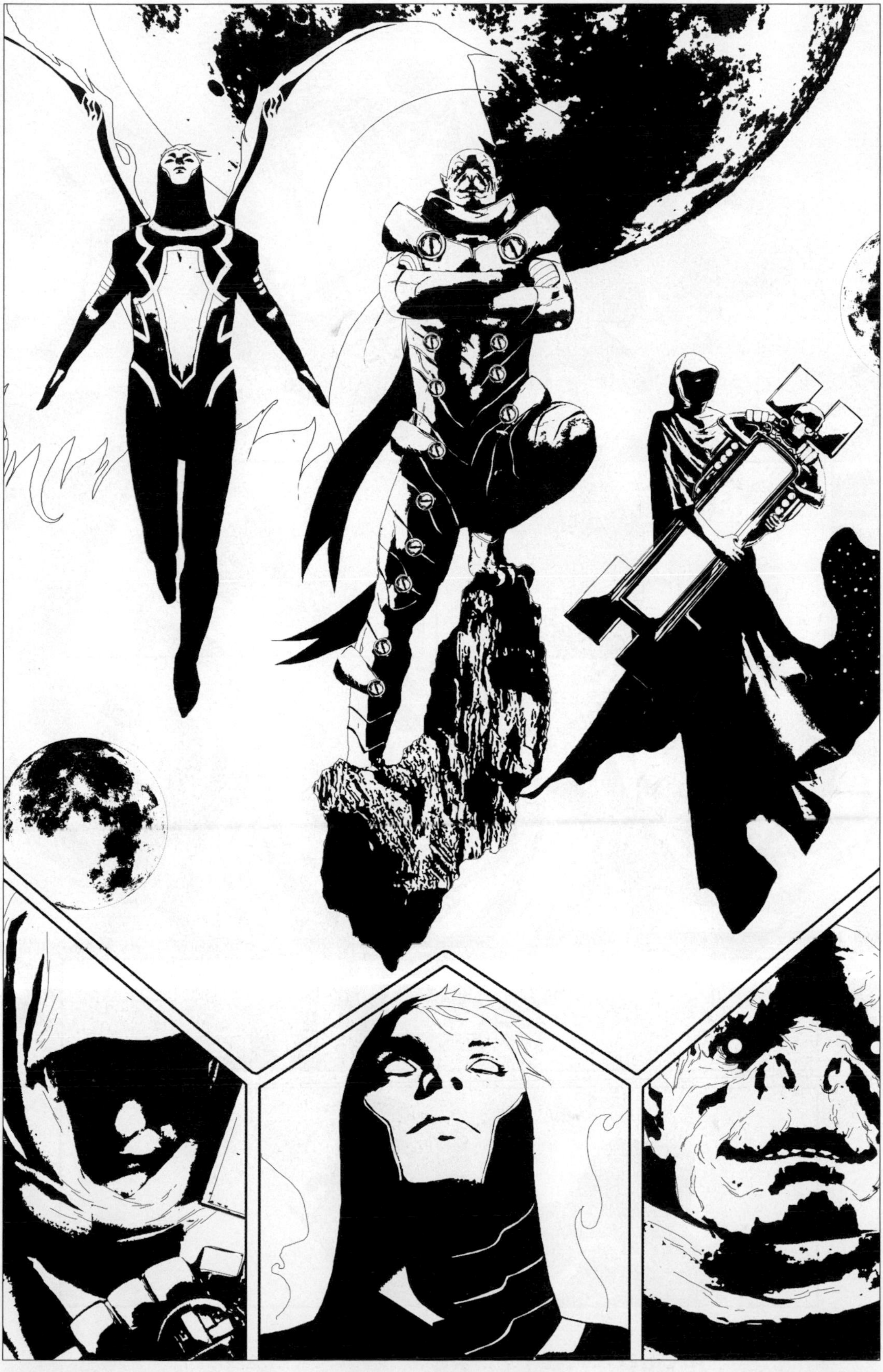

#38, PAGE 6 ART BY **ANDREA SORRENTINO** ▼

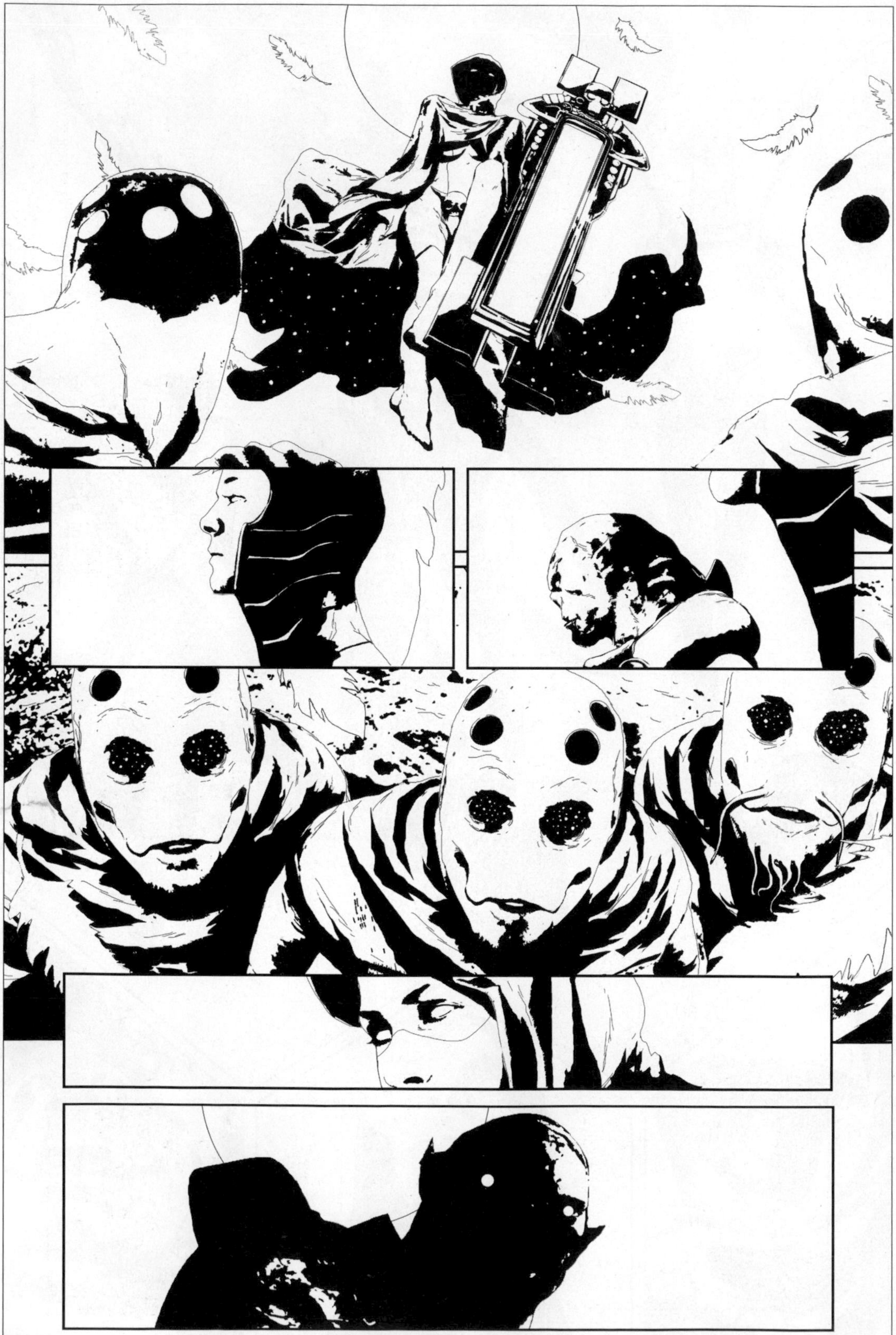

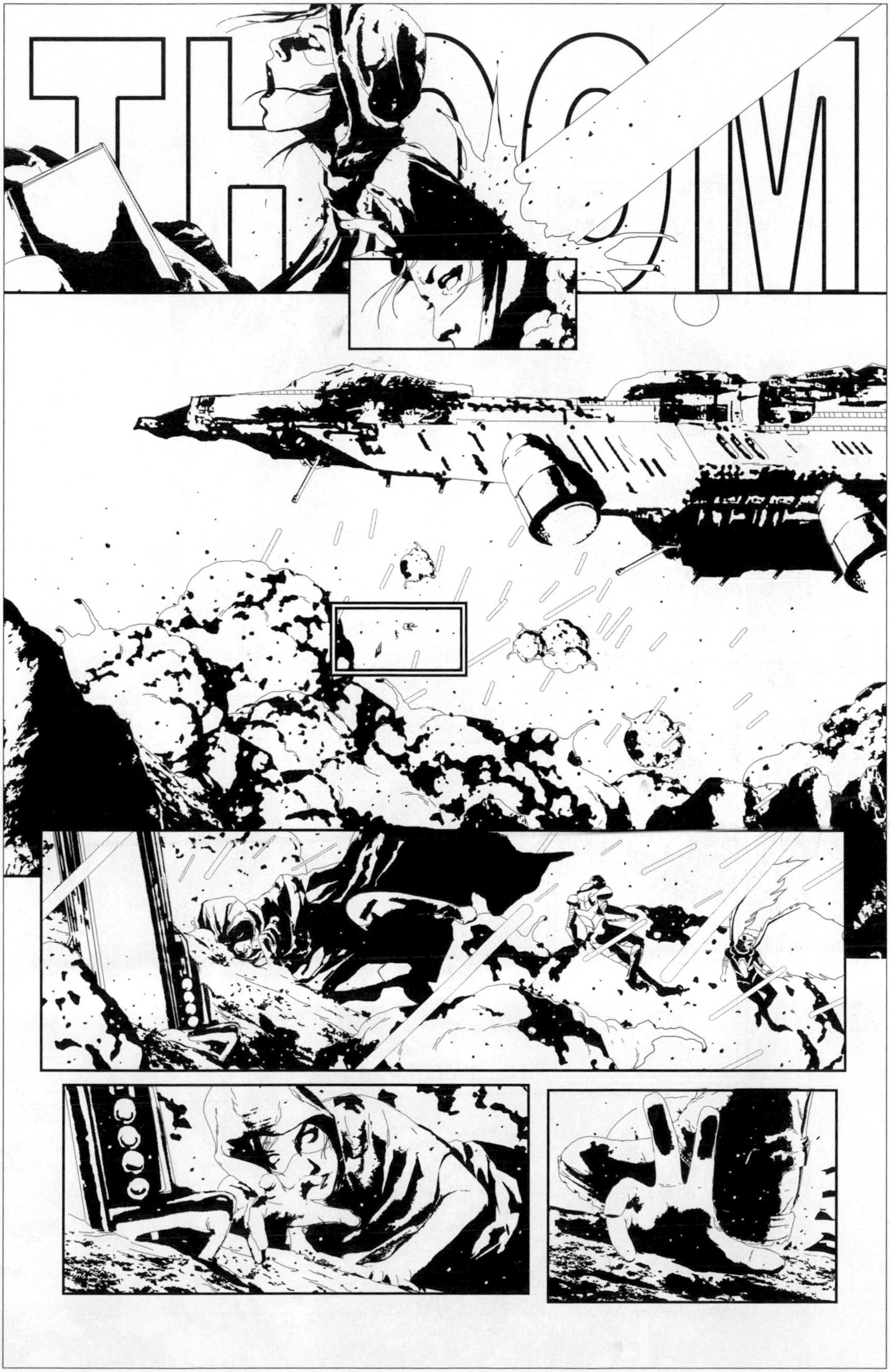
THOOM

#38, PAGES 8-9 ART BY **ANDREA SORRENTINO** ▼

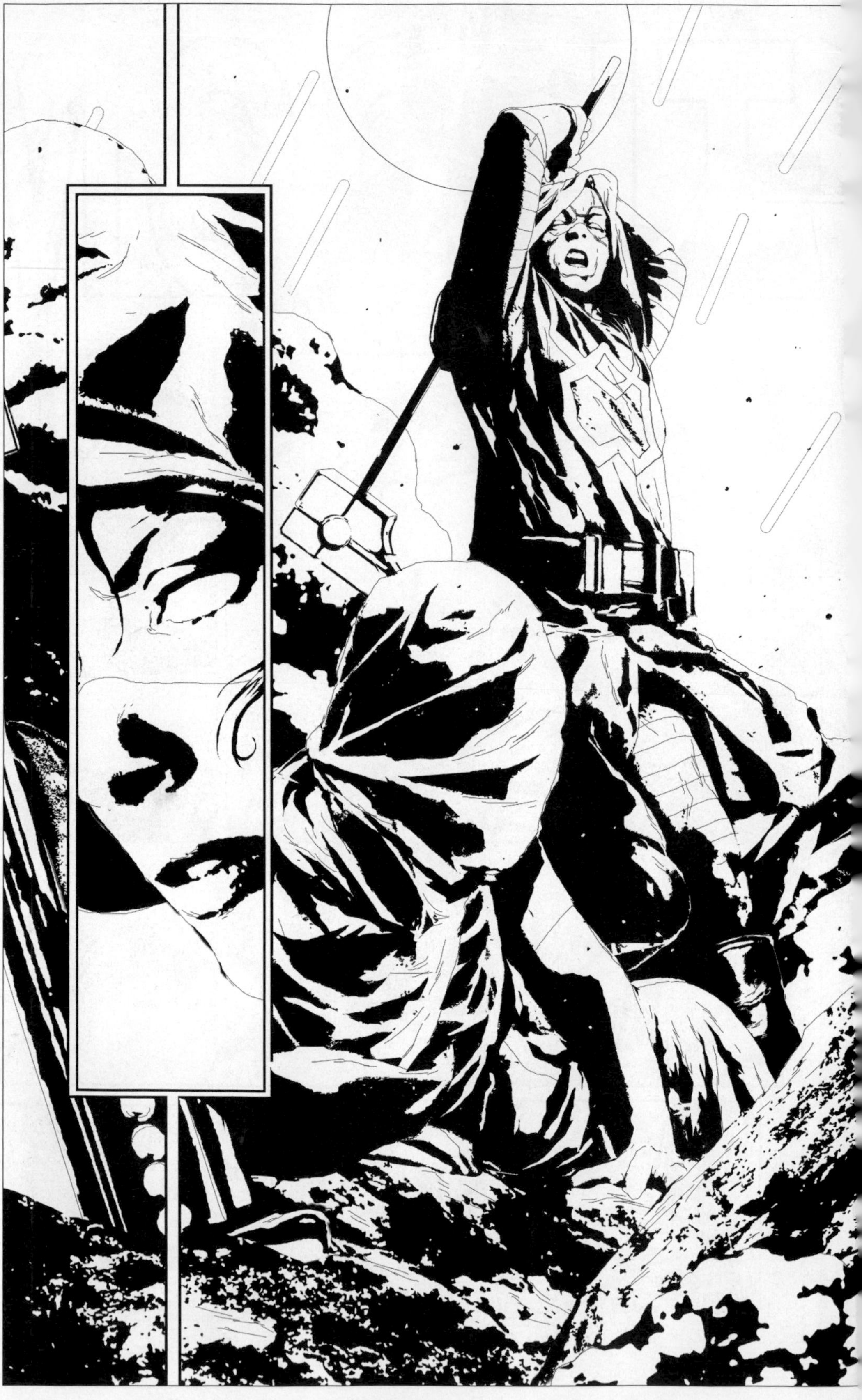

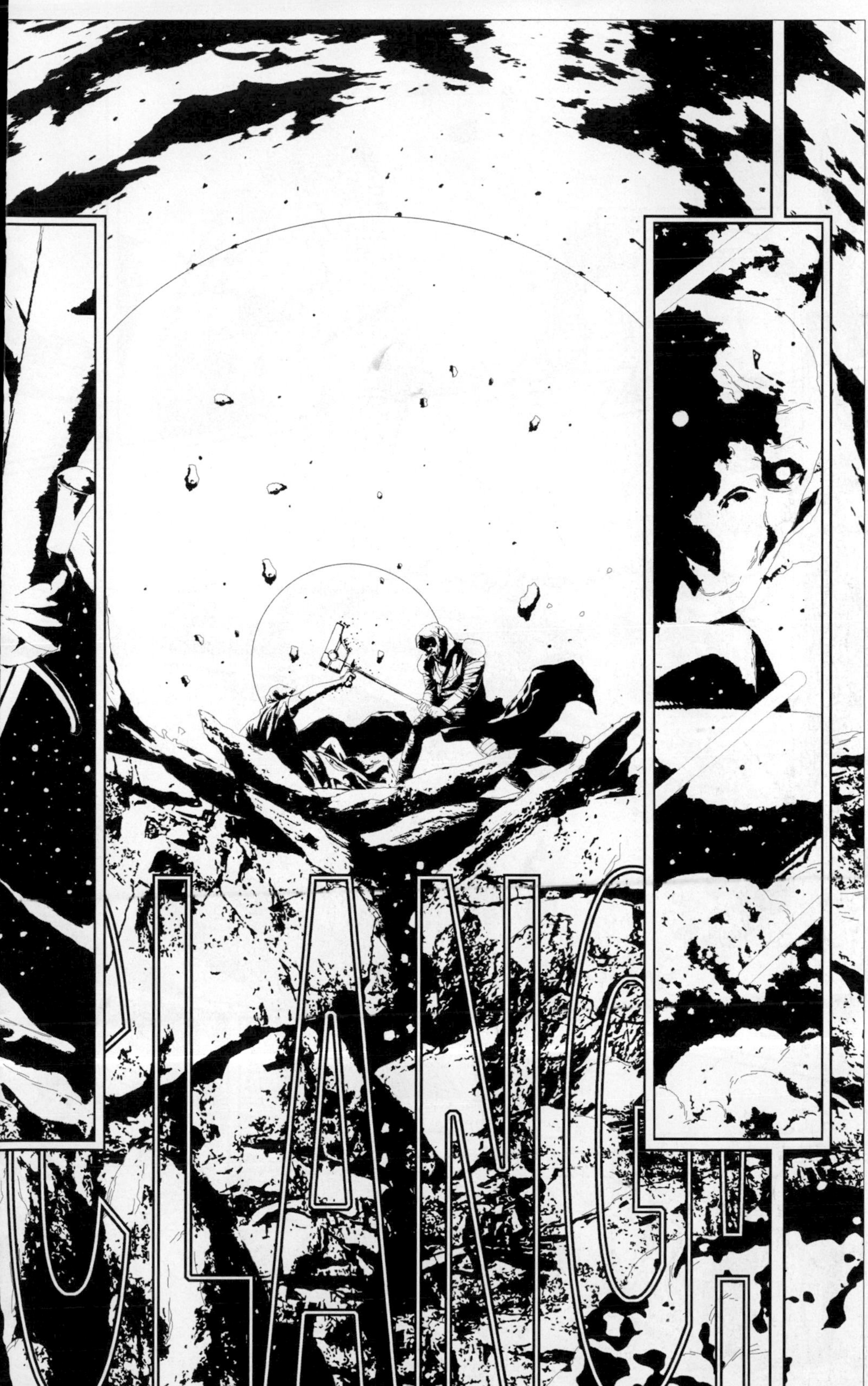
CLANG!

#38, PAGES 16-17 ART BY **ANDREA SORRENTINO** ▼

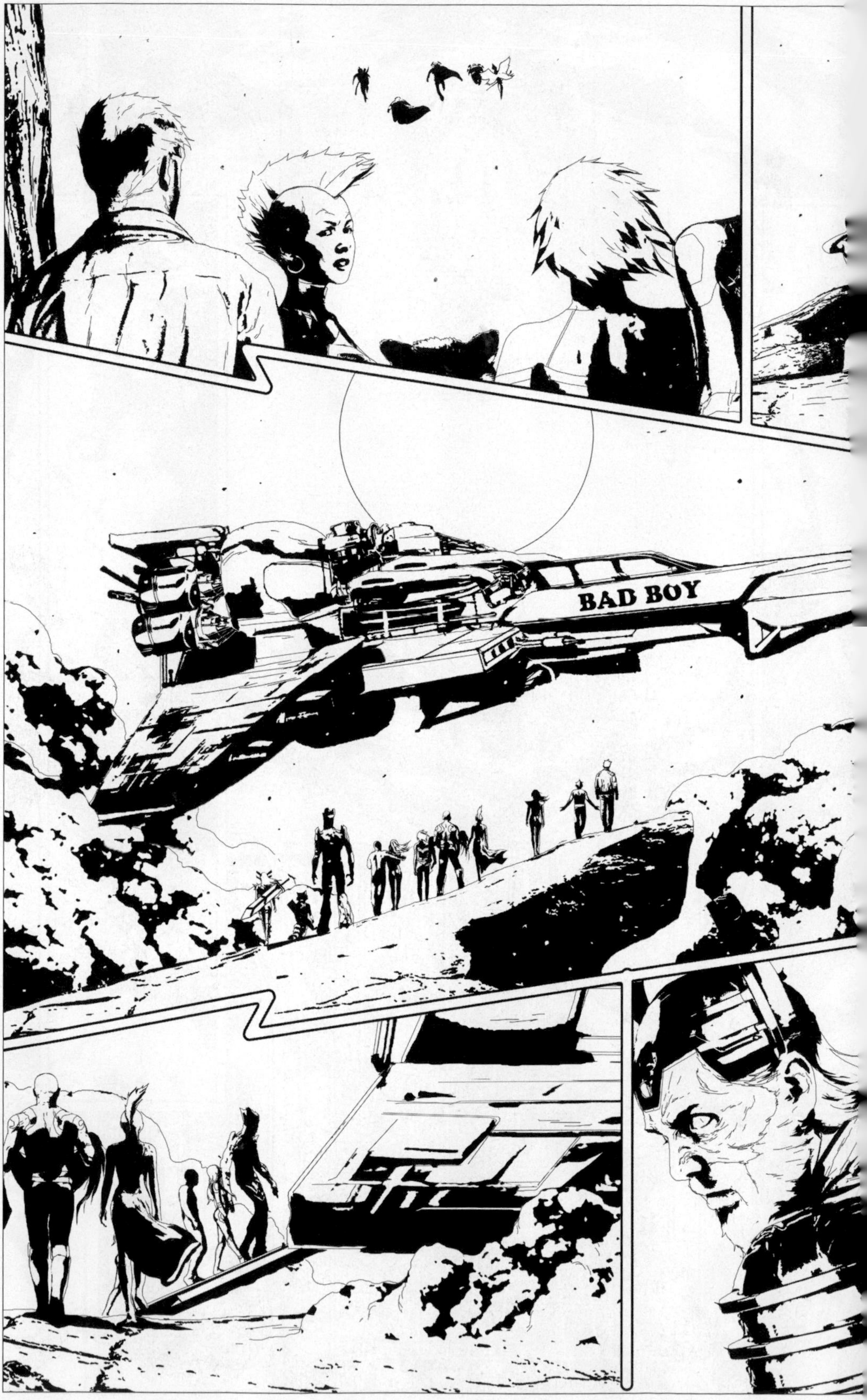
BAD BOY

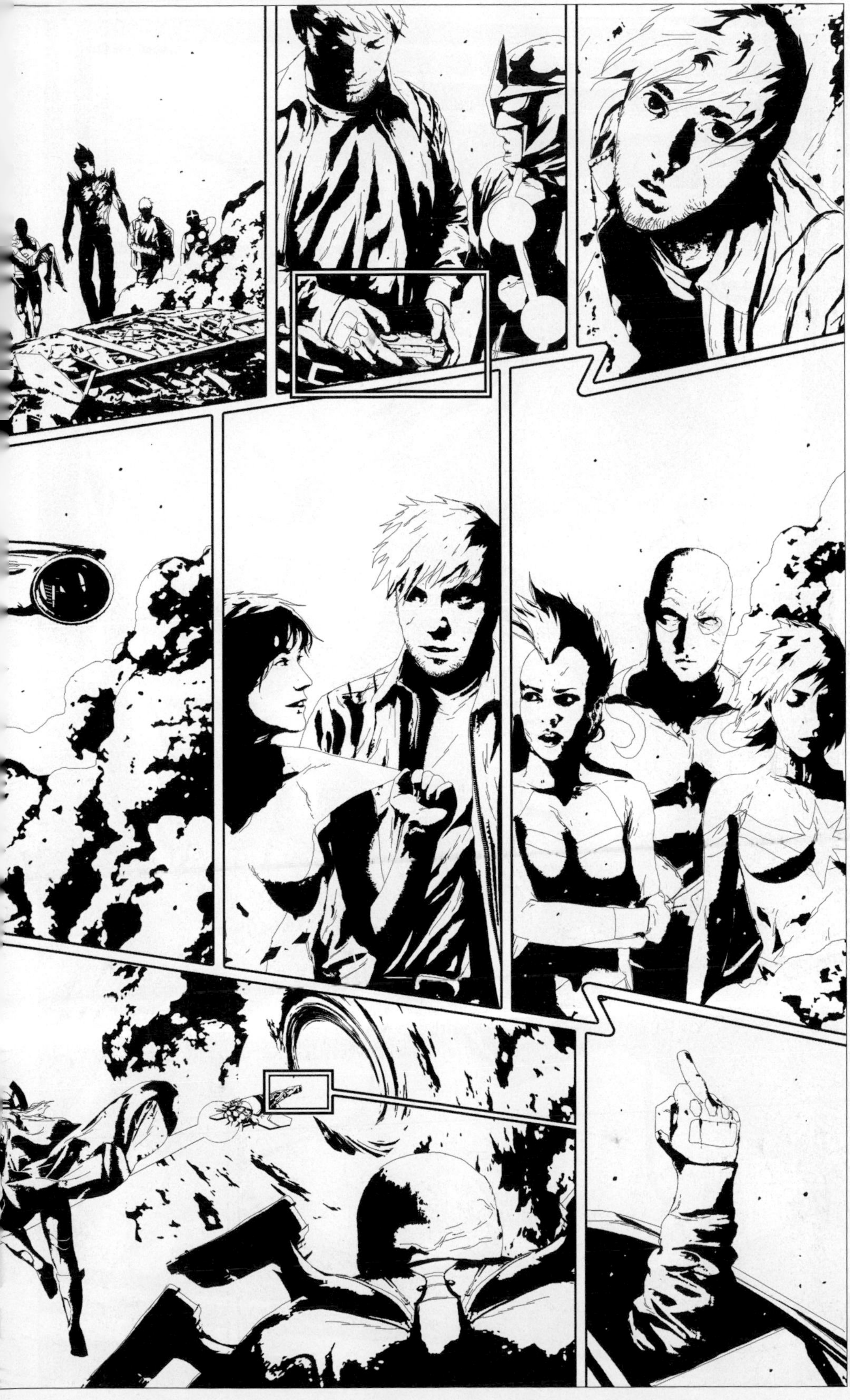

#38, PAGE 21 ART BY **ANDREA SORRENTINO** ▼

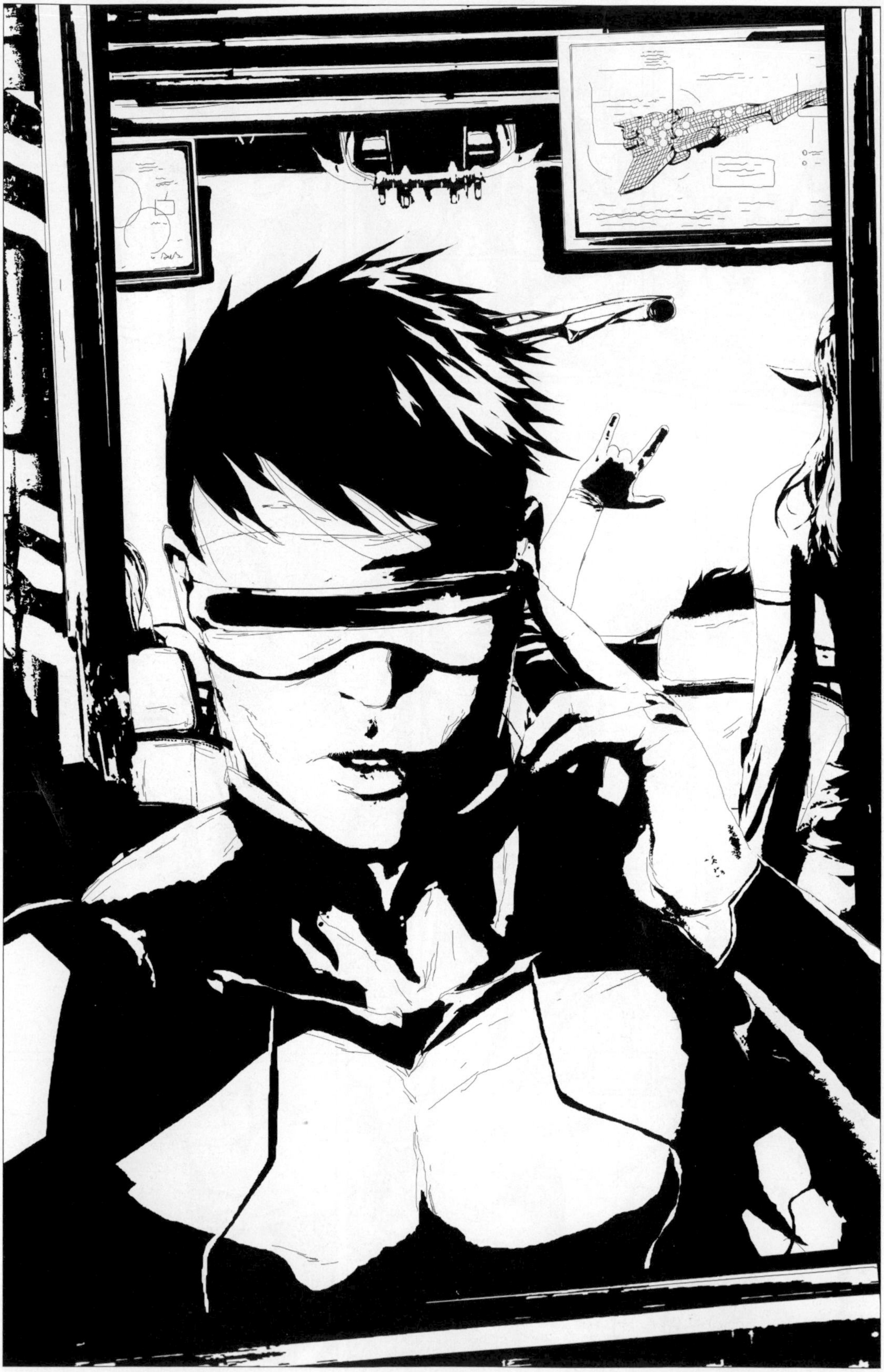

▼ #40, PAGE 4 ART BY **MAHMUD ASRAR**

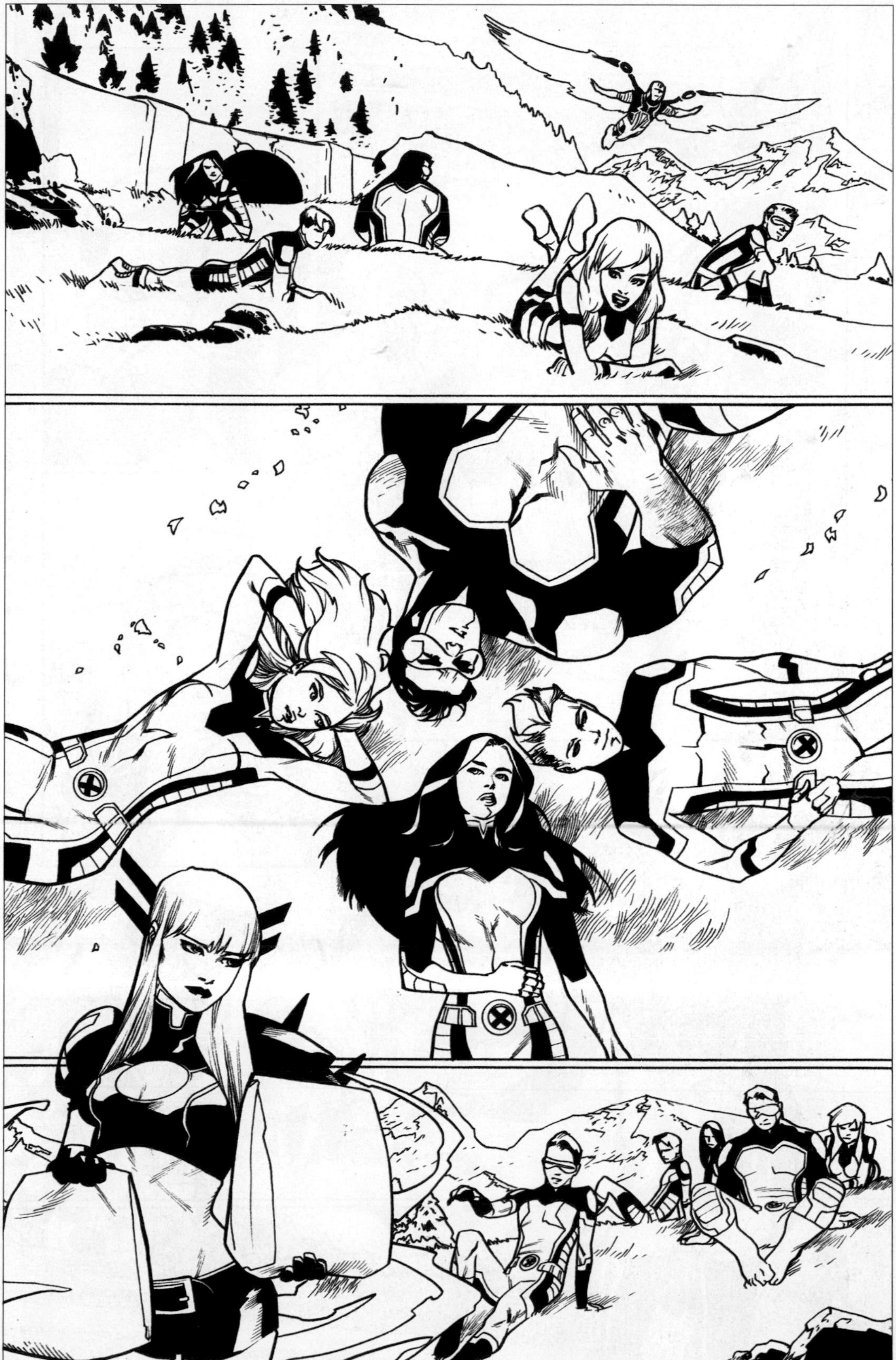

#40, PAGE 5 ART BY **MAHMUD ASRAR** ▼

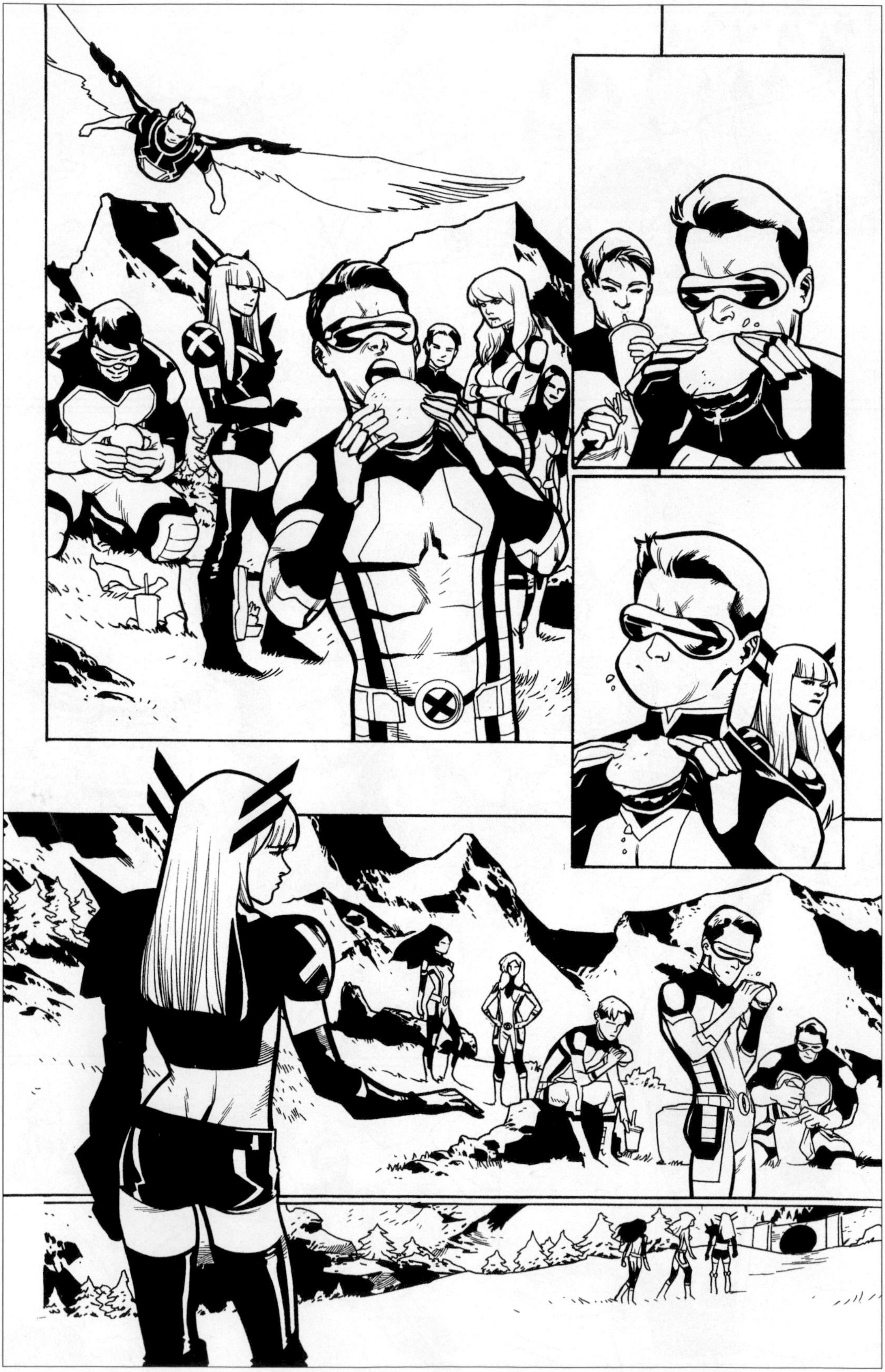

▼ #40, PAGE 6 ART BY **MAHMUD ASRAR**

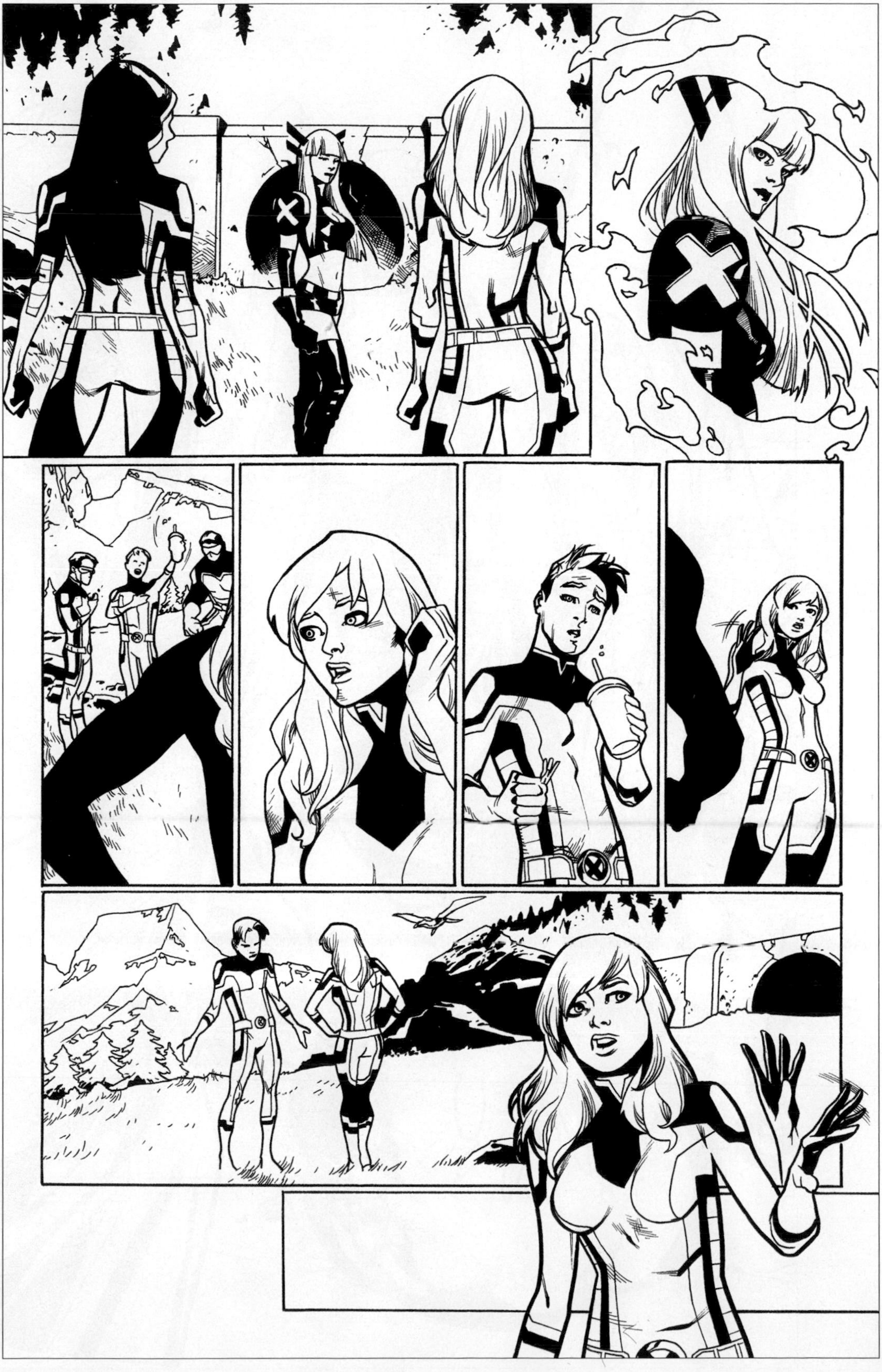

#40, PAGES 20-21 ART BY **MAHMUD ASRAR** ▼

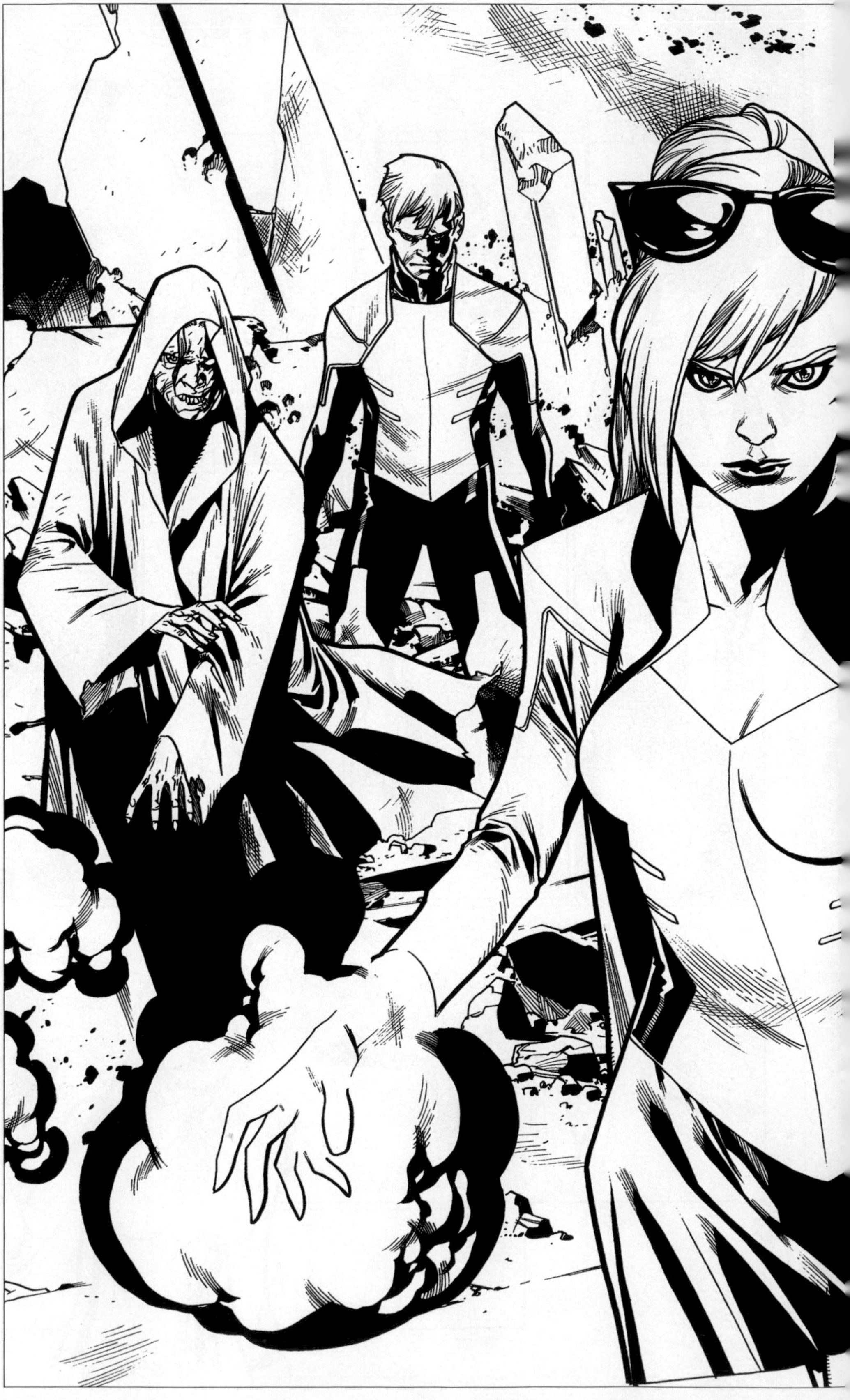

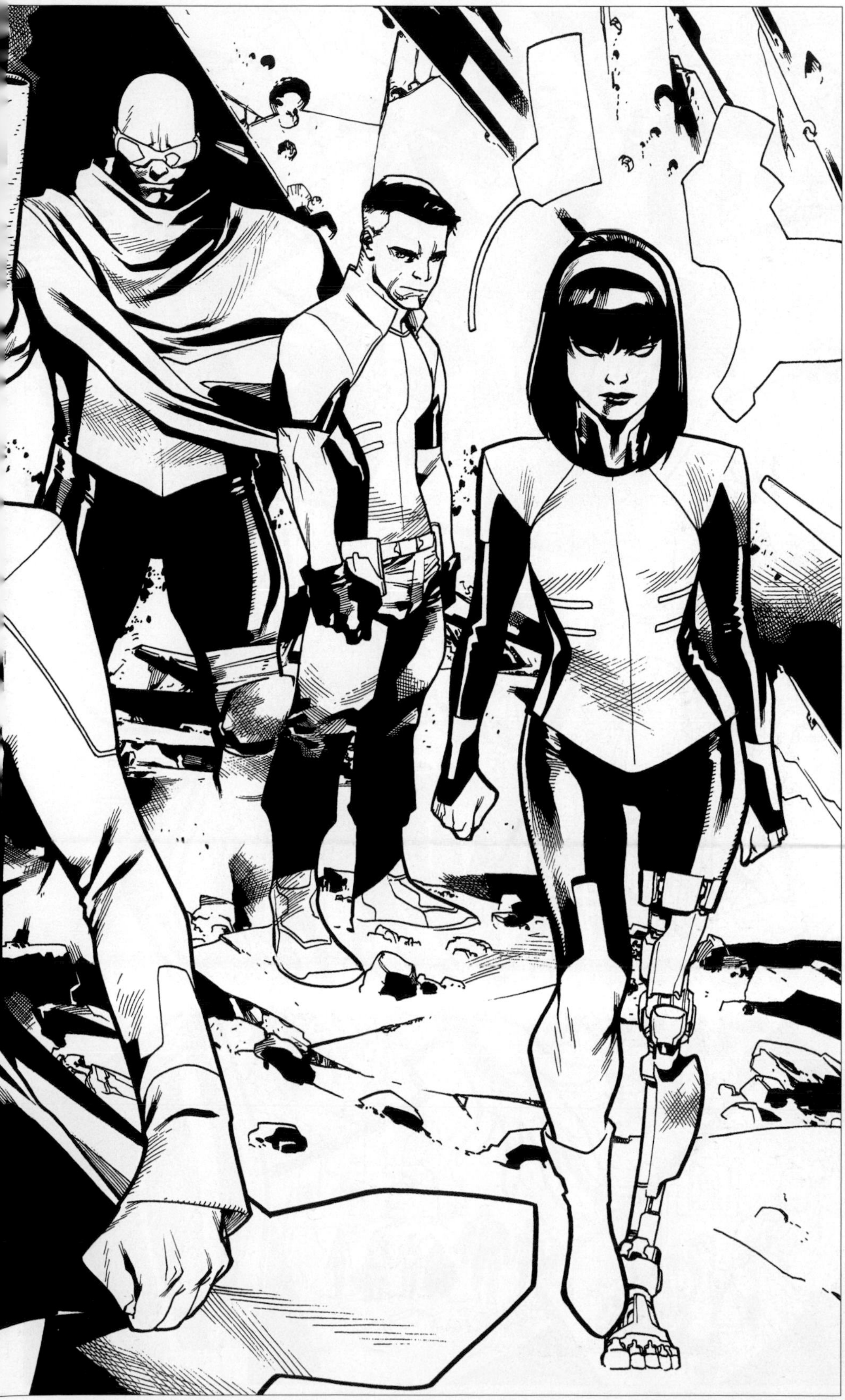

#41, PAGE 18 ART BY **MAHMUD ASRAR** ▼

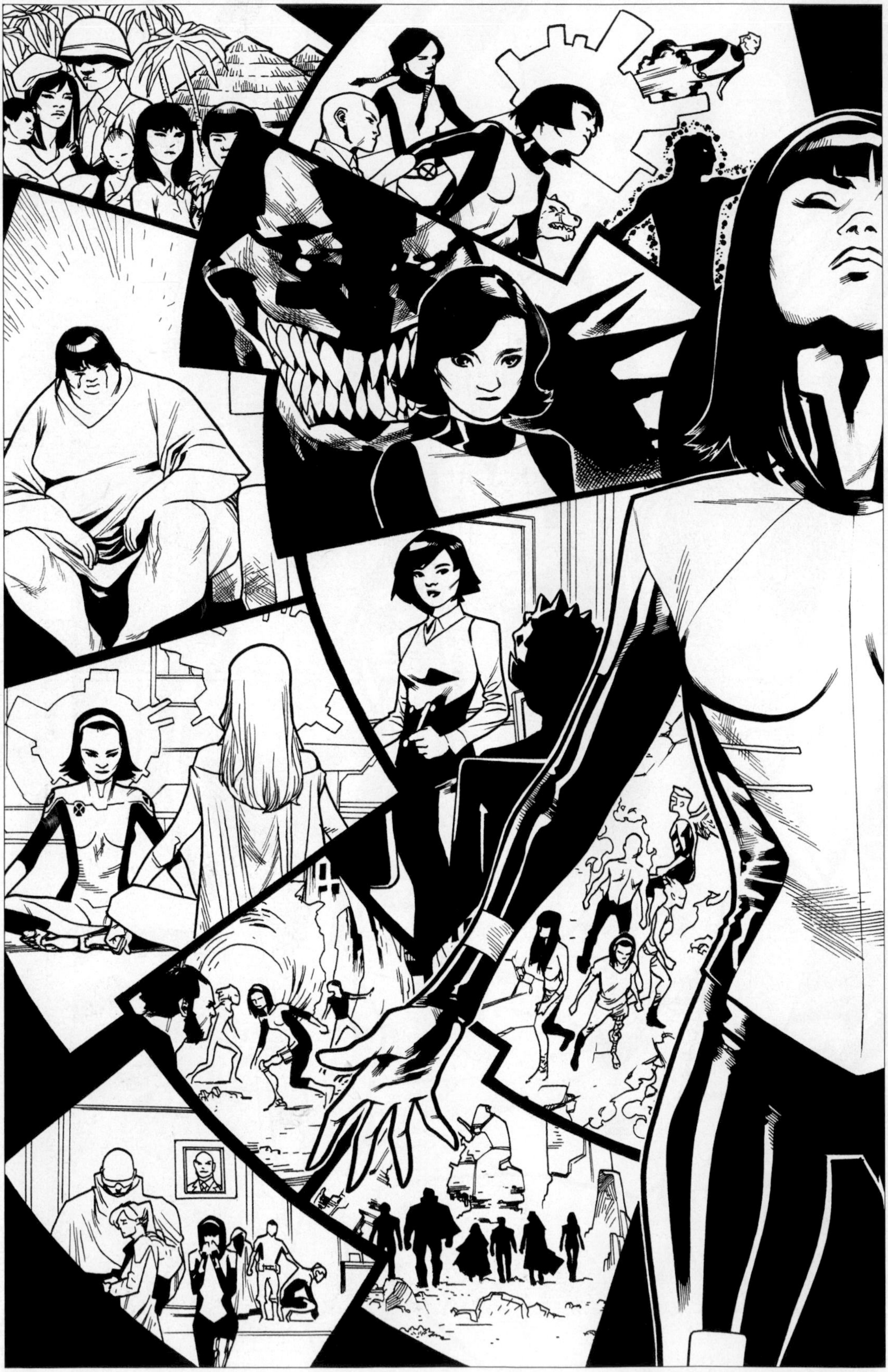

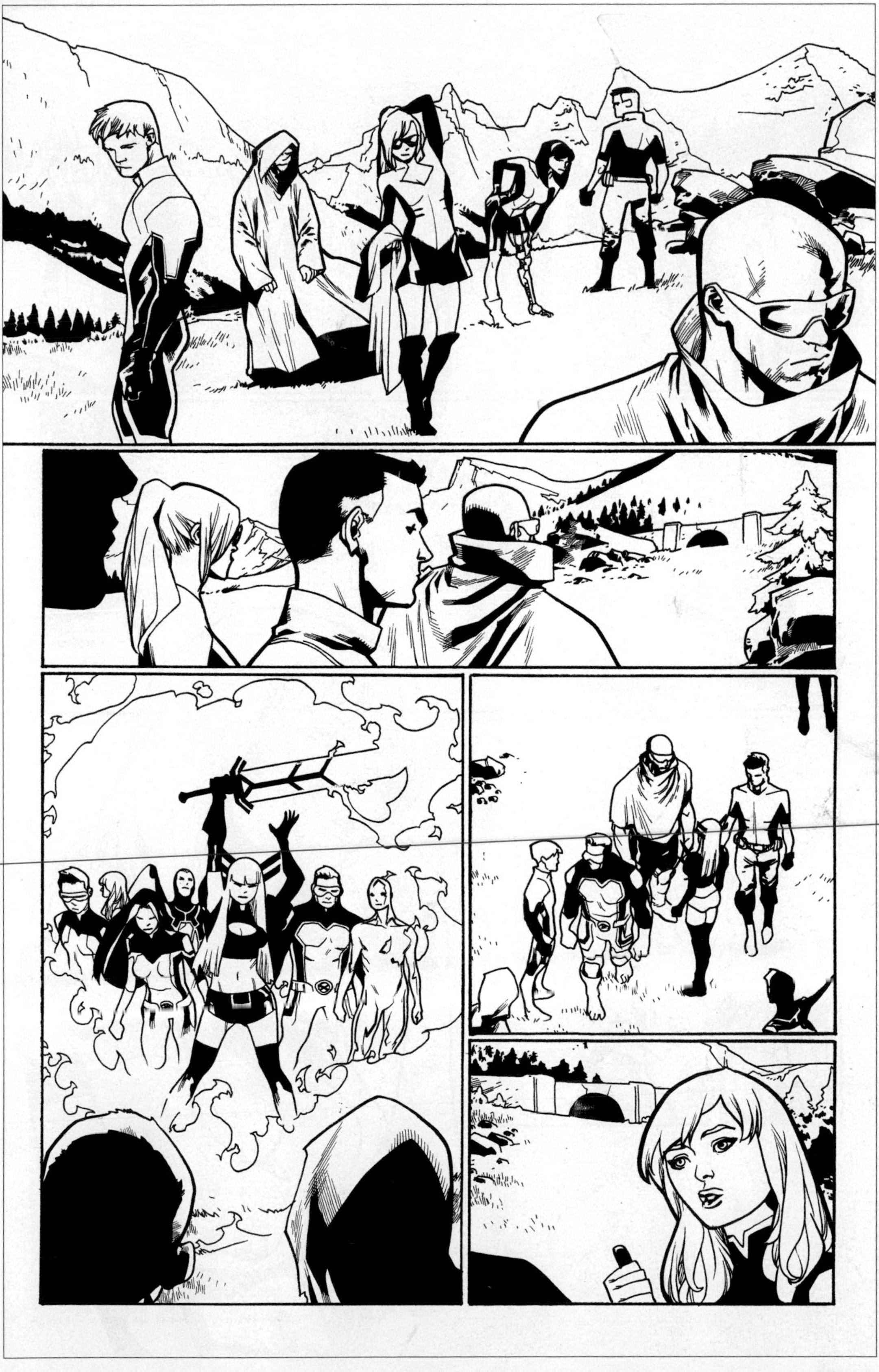

#41, PAGE 21 ART BY **MAHMUD ASRAR** ▼

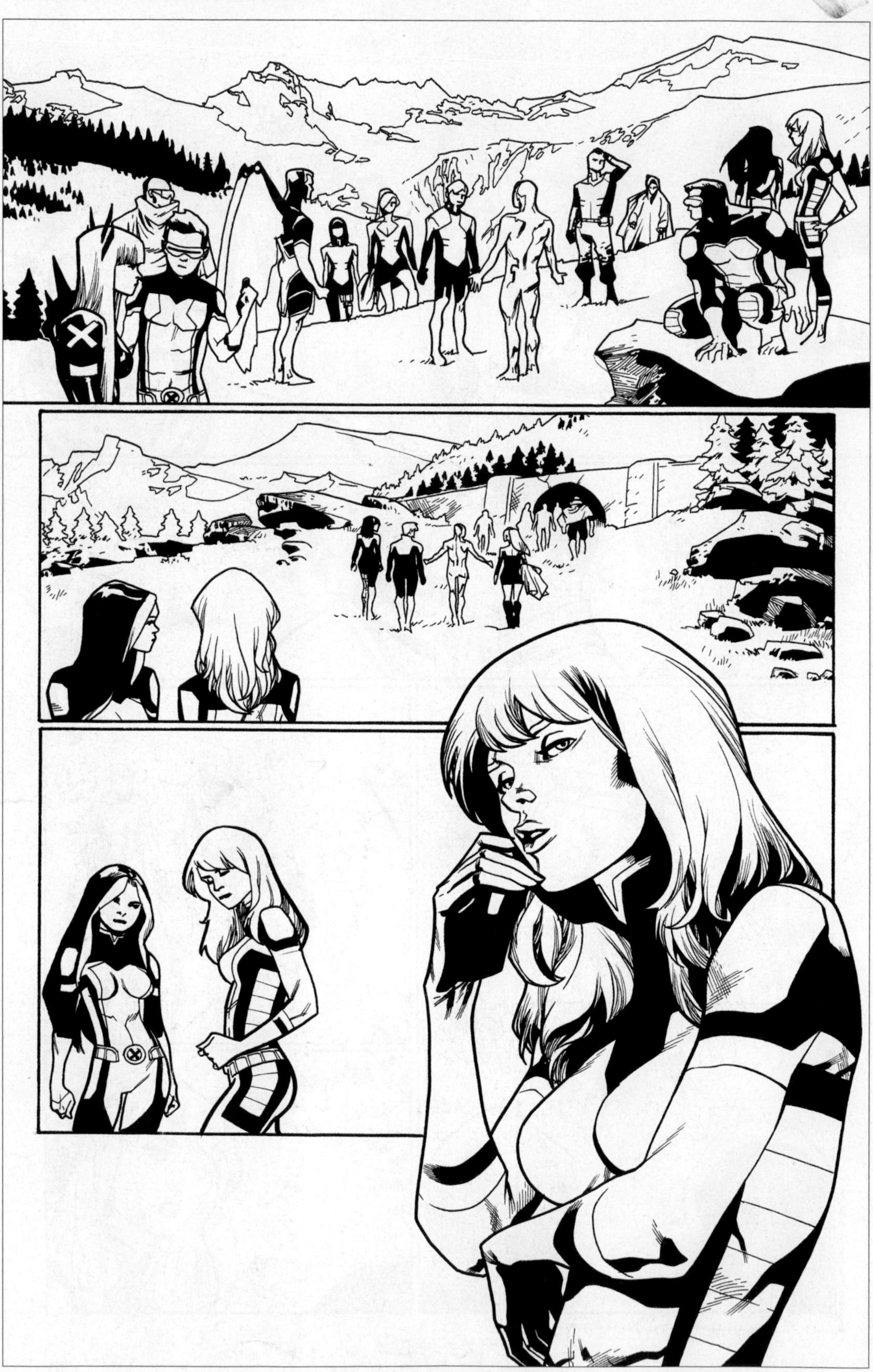

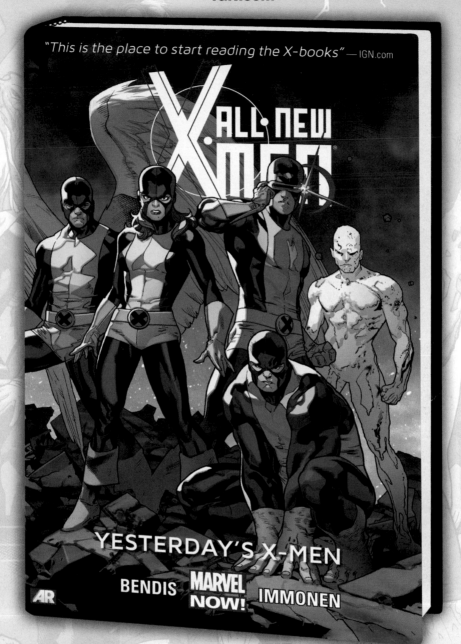

Issue #37
Madripoor tourism video ....Page 1, Panel 1

Issue #39
Recap of Cyclops in space .... Page 3, Panel 3

Issue #40
History of Utopia...Page 1, Panel 1

Issue #41
Who are the Utopians? ....Page 7, Panel 1